THE ART OF
TONAL ANALYSIS

THE ART OF TONAL ANALYSIS

Twelve Lessons in Schenkerian Theory

By Carl Schachter

Edited by

Joseph N. Straus

OXFORD
UNIVERSITY PRESS

OXFORD

UNIVERSITY PRESS

Oxford University Press is a department of the University of
Oxford. It furthers the University's objective of excellence in research,
scholarship, and education by publishing worldwide.
Oxford is a registered trademark of Oxford University Press
in the UK and certain other countries.

Published in the United States of America by
Oxford University Press
198 Madison Avenue, New York, NY 10016, United States of America

Library of Congress Cataloging-in-Publication Data
Schachter, Carl, author.
The art of tonal analysis: twelve lessons in Schenkerian theory / by Carl Schachter; edited by Joseph N. Straus.
pages cm
Includes bibliographical references and index.
ISBN 978–0–19–022739–5 (HC) 978-0-19-090917-5 (PB)   1. Musical analysis. I. Straus, Joseph Nathan, editor.
II. Title. MT90.S27 2016
780—dc23
2015016976

Contents

Editor's Preface

Carl Schachter is an extraordinary musician and musical thinker, and the world's leading practitioner of Schenkerian theory and analysis. He has written extensively on the masterworks of the tonal common practice and on the analytical delights and challenges that they present. Although his articles and books have been broadly influential, and are seen by many as models of musical insight and lucid prose, perhaps his greatest impact has been felt in the classroom. At the Mannes College of Music, the Juilliard School of Music, Queens College and the Graduate Center of the City University of New York, and at special pedagogical events around the world, he has taught generations of musical performers, composers, historians, and theorists in a career that began at Mannes in 1956 and continues to the present day.

In fall 2012, Schachter taught a special doctoral seminar at the CUNY Graduate Center. With more than thirty enrolled students and auditors from all the different musical disciplines packed into our seminar room, he talked about the music and the musical issues that have concerned him most deeply. This book consists of edited transcripts of those lectures. We have smoothed out some rough edges, deleted some digressions, added some guideposts and transitions, but apart from these relatively modest editorial interventions, this book is a faithful record of the classes.

The text is accompanied by three sorts of musical examples. First, there are annotated scores. These represent the editor's attempt to convey visually material that Schachter presented and demonstrated from the piano. Second, there are short analytical reductions transcribed from the classroom blackboard. Third, there are more extended analytical reductions (Schenkerian graphs or sketches). Some of these have appeared in print before, but most appear here for the first time.

In the course of his lectures, Schachter refers to a variety of secondary literature. Instead of interrupting the flow of the presentation with footnotes, references in the text are indicated with author/date citations in brackets, and the relevant source can be found among the Works Cited.

We are grateful to the stellar editorial team at Oxford University Press, starting with Suzanne Ryan, who enthusiastically supported this project from the beginning. At an early stage, we benefitted from the incisive comments of three anonymous reviewers solicited by OUP. In the preparation of the musical examples, we had the invaluable assistance of four brilliant doctoral students at the CUNY Graduate Center: Megan Lavengood, Christina Lee, Simon Prosser, and Inés Thiebaut. Their work was supported in part by a subvention from the Society for Music Theory, for which we are grateful.

Musical analysis is in many ways an ephemeral art, somewhat like musical performance in its immediacy and spontaneity. It is perhaps better suited to the classroom than to the pages of the professional or general literature. In that spirit, we hope that the twelve lessons in this book will give a vivid account of Schachter as a teacher, demonstrating for a wide audience his art of tonal analysis.

Joseph Straus
New York, January 2015

THE ART OF
TONAL ANALYSIS

Linear Progressions and Neighbor Notes

In this first class, we will focus on two basic concepts: linear progressions and neighbor notes. The works we discuss will include two works by J. S.Bach (the chorale, "O Gott du frommer Gott," and French Suite 1, Allemande, 1st reprise) and one by Schubert ("Du bist die Ruh").

LET'S START WITH ONE OF SCHENKER'S BASIC CONCEPTS: THE *LINEAR PROGRES-sion.* A linear progression is a stepwise motion in one direction between two tones that are related to each other harmonically. That is to say, at a prior level the two tones form a vertical interval. Very frequently they are members of the same chord; sometimes they belong to two closely related chords, such as IV and II⁶. The linear progression creates a profound connection between line (or melody) and harmony. That, I think, is what makes this concept one of Schenker's great achievements. He himself seemed to believe that the linear progression was one of the most important components of his whole theoretical apparatus, and he felt that performers in particular needed to be conscious of linear progressions, and to give expression to them in their performances, in one way or another.

Let's take the opening of Schubert's Ab-major "Impromptu" as an example [Example 1.1]. The motion Ab-Bb-C in the first four measures of the melody gives a kind of aroma, you might say, of the Ab-major chord, diffusing it over the melodic line. At the same time, in the bass, you similarly get the motion Ab-Bb-C. Starting in measure 9, the rising linear progression (Ab-Bb-C) is answered by the falling one (C-Bb-Ab) in that part of the piece. And while linear progressions most commonly descend, there are very many rising linear progressions as well, as in the Ab-Bb-C motions here.

At the end of the section (mm. 42–46), we have a chromatically inflected bass that traverses the interval of a descending fourth (Ab-Eb), and that fourth of course belongs to our tonic chord (Ab major). Questions sometimes arise about linear progressions of a descending fourth in the bass, such as the motion from Ab down to Eb in measures 13–16 of the Schubert. Doesn't moving down a fourth in the lowest part create a dissonance? No, it does not. We learn in two-part counterpoint that the fourth is only dissonant, if at all, as a *vertical* interval; as a horizontal, melodic interval, it is always consonant. Therefore a bass line like Ab-Eb-Ab is fully consonant no matter whether the V is above or below the I. I know that I've said that the first and last tones of the linear progression form a vertical interval *at a prior level*. But at that prior level there is as yet no linear progression.

EXAMPLE 1.1 *Schubert, Impromptu in A♭ major, Op. 142, No. 4, mm. 1–47, annotated score.*

At the beginning of the piece, the linear progressions unfold within the framework of the four-measure *hypermeasures*, and they do not straddle two hypermeasures. At the end of this section, you can hear how the first phrase (mm. 39–42) ends on the tonic in its fourth measure, just as in the opening. But when the next phrase begins (m. 43), the downward passing motion is already under way, so that the descending linear progression through a fourth actually originates in the last note of the previous phrase, and then continues into the last phrase. A pianist who plays this as though measure 43 is a beginning out of nothing would, I think, do injustice to the music. This is an issue that is very prevalent throughout tonal music, namely, that sometimes you have tonal structures that conform to the rhythmic divisions of the music, but other times the tonal structures overlap those divisions and create a kind of, I won't say conflict, but contrast, between the way one hears the different aspects of the music. But setting that issue aside for a moment, the basic idea of a linear progression involves expressing harmony through a melodic line.

The first note and/or the last note of a linear progression will be the ones that will normally connect to larger motions. Let's say we get G-F-E-D-C as a descending linear progression at the beginning of a piece in C major [Example 1.2].

EXAMPLE 1.2 *Hypothetical linear progressions.*

You might say that G, the initial tone of the linear progression, is highlighted, and is thus available to make connections with other things later in the music. Let's say that the next diminution (the next melodic idea) might be an arpeggio going G-B-D-F. The F at the top of the arpeggio could connect to that initial G, and then possibly continue to a hypothetical E-D-C at the end, so that we actually get an overarching motion G-F-E-D-C spanning some chunk of our hypothetical piece. Schenker uses the term "retained tone" for tones like our G, whose most important connection is to something further on in the music.

We should talk a little bit about Schenker's German term for linear progression which was *der Zug* (plural *Züge*). *Zug* in German is a little bit like the word "run" in English, in that it might have 100 different meanings, not all of which necessarily share common features. Many of the meanings of *Zug* are related to *ziehen*, which is a verb meaning "to pull" or "to draw along." The famous ending of Goethe's *Faust* is "*Das Ewig-Weibliche zieht uns hinan*"— "the eternal feminine draws us onward." So Schenker's *Zug* is something that is pulling toward some kind of goal. That it is goal-directed is implicit in the word itself, and that's something that "linear progression" doesn't convey very well in English. A "progression," to be sure, is something that progresses, that moves toward something, but somehow the English gets a bit bogged down in all of those syllables, whereas the German has just those three letters and one syllable. A lot of Schenker's vocabulary translates very poorly to English, and often the best device is to get something that is not a literal translation, but based in a slightly different way of making meaning. For my own part, when I talk and write about these things, I often just appropriate the German term *Zug*, as I do for other hard-to-translate terms like *Urlinie*, although Salzer's term "directed motion" would work perfectly well in some contexts.

Students have many sorts of difficulties in identifying linear progressions, and one of them is that not every stepwise motion is necessarily going to be truly a linear progression. Let's look at a chorale by J. S. Bach to explore this issue [Example 1.3].

EXAMPLE 1.3 *Bach, Chorale No. 85 ("O Gott, du frommer Gott"), annotated score.*

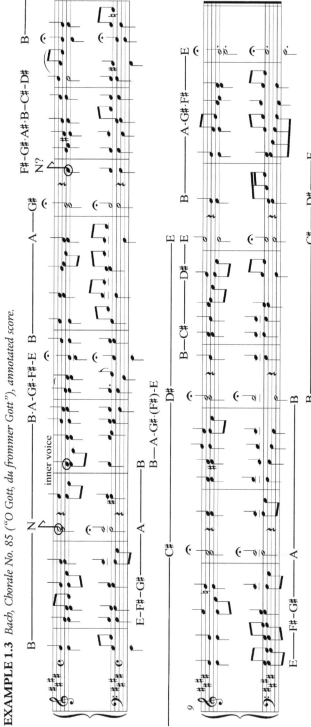

As is most often the case with Bach's chorales, the chorale tune itself is not by Bach. In this case, it's by one Ahasverus Fritzsch. I don't know much about him except that he wrote a very beautiful chorale melody here, and Bach set it several times so he must have liked it.

Looking at the chorale melody in the first 4 measures, we hear a linear progression from B down to E. It starts on the B at the beginning of the melody. (By the way, the first upbeats of the chorales very often have the initial structural tonic harmony; they're thus unusually important upbeats.) So we start with scale-degree $\hat{5}$ (B), but before the descent begins, we go up to the C♯ (m. 2). It is important to note that the linear progression is B-A-G♯-F♯-E, not C♯-B-A-G♯-F♯-E. In the latter case, the interval traversed, C♯-E, would not be part of an E-major chord, but both C♯ and E would be members of an A-major chord (or possibly a C♯-minor chord). The function of the C♯ within the melodic line is to be a neighbor note to B.

It is very often the case that you have an upper neighbor at the beginning of a descending linear progression, or a lower neighbor at the beginning of a rising one. In addition to having neighbor notes appended to the top or bottom of a linear progression, it's also possible to have other sorts of elaborations. For example, we might have a descending sixth, A-G♯-F♯-E-D-C♯ [Example 1.4].

EXAMPLE 1.4 *Interpreting a descending sixth.*

I'm not thinking of any specific piece right now, but in our imaginary piece it might very well be that the linear progression is essentially the fourth, A-G♯-F♯-E, and that what happens afterward (E-D-C♯) is a kind of lower-level tributary to the E. So, in deciding where a linear progression begins or ends, it's always necessary to look at the larger context.

In the Bach chorale, the linear progression is really quite easy to identify because the B comes back in measure 3, before the descent begins. The F♯ on the downbeat of measure 3 represents what in Schenkerian terminology would be considered an *inner-voice tone*. That's because it takes its point of departure from the inner-voice notes of the E-major chord, rather than from the top voice, which is B. So we see that a single melodic line might contain both an upper voice and an inner voice. The C♯ in measure 2 thus moves to the B in measure 3, not to the F♯. The B is actually implied already at the beginning of measure 3, above the F♯, but is delayed in appearance until the middle of the measure.

Now let's look at the bass voice. It begins with one of the most common linear progressions, namely, one that goes up from the tonic note to the third of the tonic harmony with a passing tone in between (E-F♯-G♯). But this time the progression does not stop on G♯; it continues to A, and then up to B. So what we have there is a linear progression of a rising fifth, from the tonic note to the dominant note, but it's given to us in stages. The first thing we hear is the rising third (E-F♯-G♯), and we might plausibly think that scale-degree $\hat{3}$ is the goal. But, after dipping down for just an instant, the bass continues moving upward. It would be quite possible to think of E to A as a linear progression that melodically anticipates the IV chord, the A-major chord, but then with the chromatic passing note A♯, the A is connected to the B, and we have a complete rising fifth. It's not at all uncommon for a linear progression to occur progressively in this way, in stages, where you think each tone you get to is a kind of goal, but then it turns out instead to be a steppingstone on the way to the next goal, and so forth. This possibility is a natural consequence of music's being an art that unfolds in time.

There's an amazing song by Brahms ("Meerfahrt," Op. 96, No. 4) that raises similar issues. The piano introduction starts on scale-degree $\hat{5}$ (E), which goes to F♯, sounding as though it's an upper neighbor [Example 1.5].

EXAMPLE 1.5 Brahms, "Meerfahrt," Op. 96, No. 4, mm. 1–12, annotated score.

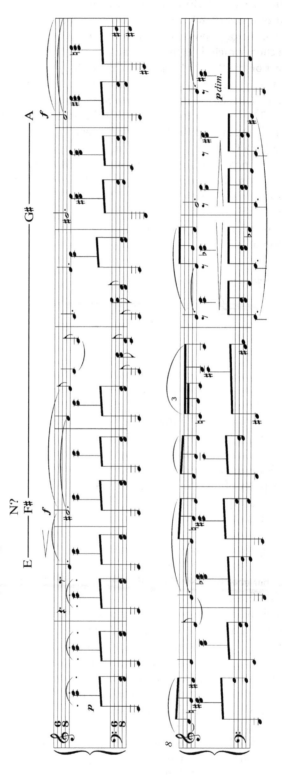

There is something quite disturbing sounding about that F♯, which seems almost to be going against nature. That's because F♯ is the rising form of scale-degree $\hat{6}$, which would normally continue to raised $\hat{7}$, and then possibly to the tonic note itself. But as an upper neighbor, the natural form of scale-degree $\hat{6}$ would have been ever so much more in conformity with the inherent tendencies of the tones involved.

Schenker makes the point in his *Counterpoint* book [Schenker 1987] that a neighbor-note figure can actually conceal a larger-scale passing motion. For example, let's imagine we're in C major and have a melody that goes G-A-G-B-C-D, beginning with scale-degrees $\hat{5}$-$\hat{6}$-$\hat{5}$-$\hat{7}$ [Example 1.6].

EXAMPLE 1.6 *Interpreting scale-degree $\hat{6}$: neighboring or passing?*

Scale-degree $\hat{6}$ might feel like a neighbor note, but it might also imply the possibility of a passing tone. Brahms explores just that sort of possibility in a most spectacular fashion. His melody goes from E to F♯ and right back to E. But at the same time, the F♯ leads up to G♯, the leading tone. Stopping on the leading tone would not be going against nature. Nevertheless, the leading tone, when it's that prominent, has a strong tendency to go to the tonic, and that is in fact what Brahms's melody does.

The melody starts with a strange motion up a major second and then back (E-F♯-E). Then comes the motion up a third (E-G♯)—not quite as strange, but still making demands on us. Then that leads into a surprising tonic, surprising because we certainly don't expect the major form of the tonic at that point. Frequently with linear progressions there is the possibility of initially thinking one has a progression of a third or a fourth, and finding out later that it is really a fifth or a sixth after all. Generally speaking, the significant linear progression is the largest one that can be assembled from the available tones.

Now let's return to the Bach chorale, and to the bass in the second phrase. The bass descends from B to E, but we don't have a stepwise connection, because the stepwise motion is broken up by the leap from G♯ to D♯. Nevertheless we could hear that D♯ as implying a kind of substitution for F♯, in which case the descent would be entirely step-wise: B-A-G♯-F♯-E. As we can see, it's not out of the question, sometimes, for a linear progression actually to have a leap, if that leap can be thought of as substituting for stepwise motion. In this case, it would have been quite possible for Bach to have used F♯ on the fourth beat of the measure, harmonizing it with a dominant seventh chord in $\frac{4}{3}$ position. But it's actually pretty boring that way. First, the $\frac{6}{5}$ inversion of the dominant seventh is a stronger position than the $\frac{4}{3}$. It stands out more, and D♯-E makes a nice reference back to A♯-B four beats earlier. Second, D♯-E gives a profile to the bass line that's totally lacking if you have the completely stepwise descent. Whether you call that altered motion down a fifth a "linear progression" or not doesn't matter so much. As long as you recognize its relationship to what would be a linear progression, the terminology doesn't seem terribly important to me.

The melody in the third phrase has a third-progression (*Terzzug*) from B down to G♯. In the fourth phrase, the melody has an ascending sixth-progression, from F♯ up to D♯. The F♯ in measure 6 raises an interesting question. You might think that it is just a neighbor note to G♯, and that we go right back again to our E-major chord. One could not say that's an incorrect analysis. But I think it's a less aesthetically satisfying analysis than thinking of the melody as providing the complete B-major triad. It makes a stronger dominant expression than if we felt that the tonic was being structurally retained until after the first beat of measure 7.

This is one of those cases where you might have two analyses, both of which are "correct" in that they don't involve any self-contradiction or any contradiction of the norms of melody and counterpoint and harmony. They're both internally consistent and according to the rules, but one of them might seem to do less justice to the individual character of the passage or piece. Also, as I mentioned, Bach's chorales very frequently start with an upbeat (the fourth beat of a measure) that bears a strong structural meaning. That happens not only at the very beginning of the chorale, but in the course of it, here in the upbeat to measure 7. There's something else about this melody that's quite beautiful: our neighbor-note C♯ has been the highest tone so far, but now (m. 8) we get one step beyond that to D♯.

Let's look now at the last four phrases of the chorale and think about a large-scale upper-voice linear progression. Look at the fermatas: B (m. 8), C♯ (m. 10), D♯ (m. 12), and E (m. 14). So we actually have a large-scale rising fourth: B-C♯-D♯-E. That is pretty much the fulfillment of a process that starts at the beginning of the piece, although we didn't know it at the time. It starts already with the initial B, the neighbor-note C♯ (m. 2), the return to B (m. 3), then up to D♯ (m. 8). This ascending motion above the B is really a sort of subplot to the story that the *Urlinie* tells. The main plot is actually how our B, which has been prolonged for a long time, finally reaches the lower E as its goal. But as a subplot, we also have that beautiful motion up to the high E.

Now I want to compare what happens in the second phrase and the last phrase. Both involve the linear progression B-A-G♯-F♯-E, but the effect is quite different. Starting in the middle of measure 3, the melody notes that belong to the tonic chord (B, G♯, and E) are all in fact supported with tonic harmony. The other notes—you might call them the dissonant notes (A and F♯)—are not given terribly much prominence. In the last phrase, however, the G♯ is reduced to a passing tone, and we have much more emphasis on the A and the F♯. The F♯, especially, is supported at the cadence both by a II chord and a V chord. As a result, there is an intensity in just the tonal materials of that next-to-the-last measure that very much sets this final descending fifth progression apart from the one we had before and makes it much more definitive.

Just one more nice detail. Look at the bass voice in the fifth phrase (mm. 9–10). It is a slightly embellished version of the bass in the first phrase, and leads up to A. In the sixth phrase (mm. 10–12), the A goes by step down to B (at the fermata). Note that we go down from A to B; the rising step A-B is inverted to a falling seventh.) As a result, and taking the fifth and sixth phrases together, we have another ascending linear progression E-F♯-G♯-A-B, beautifully composed by Bach to form part of a rising octave motion in the bass. From the fermata on B (m. 12), we go to C♯ (at the next fermata in m. 14), then immediately D♯ and E (mm. 14–15). So the B-C♯-D♯-E of the melody in the seventh phrase (mm. 13–14) also occurs in the bass. I'm not going to try to discuss an *Ursatz* or other concepts of deep stucture, but you can see how much insight you can get into a piece just using the concepts of the linear progression and the neighbor note.

Let's turn now to the beginning of the Allemande from the first French Suite of J. S. Bach, and we'll start with the bass in the first long phrase (through the third beat of m. 5) [Example 1.7].

EXAMPLE 1.7 *Bach, French Suite No. 1, Allemande, mm. 1–12, annotated score.*

We have a prolonged tonic at the beginning, and the D is transferred up an octave in measure 2. What then happens to the D? It moves to C (m. 2), B♭ and A (m. 3), G and F (m. 4), and finally to E and D (m. 5). We have here a beautiful example of a linear progression through an octave (*Octavzug*). The cadence in measure 5 sounds to me much more contrapuntal than harmonic. That is because it is part of this large design. I would hear the E as a more important bass note than the A, so that this would be a cadence using an inverted dominant chord (V$^4_3$).

At the same time, however, there is a very strong implication of I-IV-V-I harmonically, with the IV arriving in measure 4 (changing temporarily to a Neapolitan), and one can't deny the dominant quality of the harmony on the second beat of measure 5. But that dominant quality is not stressed very much in the voice leading. This way of beginning a piece—affirming a tonic more by counterpoint than harmony—is very common for Bach. He stays around the tonic at the beginning, often with a pedal point on the tonic and with some kind of I-V-I, I-II-V-I, or I-IV-VII-I present in the harmony above the pedal bass, following which the bass descends an octave. The first two Preludes of the first book of the *Well-Tempered Clavier* (*WTC*) begin in just this way.

The top voice is also very interesting. We start with the D, but then the G, instead of residing in the inner voices, jumps up and reaches over, leading us to scale-degree $\hat{3}$ in the upper octave. (It's again similar to the second Prelude from *WTC I*, which also starts on scale-degree $\hat{1}$, and then goes up to scale-degree $\hat{3}$ as the initial tone of the structural melodic line). Once we reach the F, the melodic line starts to descend in parallel tenths with the bass. Again, both the C-major and C-minor preludes from *WTC I* do very much the same thing.

Let's continue now up to the point where the harmony obviously reaches a very important goal with a tonic at the beginning of measure 9. If we trace the bass from the middle of measure 5 to the downbeat of measure 9, we see that it again descends through an octave: D-C-B♭-A-G-F-E-D. But with those giant leaps in the bass, the harmonic aspect of the cadence in measure 9 comes much more to the fore than it did in measure 5, when we had the first cadence. At the same time, it's quite clear that Bach is going over the same ground in a somewhat different way. Joel Lester has an idea about form in Bach, which he believes often comes in parallel sections [Lester 1999]. That is, the same idea is going to recur, but in a more elaborate or more complex form than its first appearance. And I would say that this bass, with its two octave descents, is a good example of that. The tonicization of B♭ in measure 6, which is somewhat prefigured in just the third note of the melody, is part of that.

Let's now look at the right-hand part in the same passage. We start on F in the middle of measure 5 and then, with the technique of *reaching-over* we get to E♭-D, connecting back to F. The D then goes to C (m. 7, first beat) and to B♭ (m. 7, third beat). Then, via reaching-over, we get G to F (m. 8), but notice a very important tone that might get lost if one doesn't do Schenker with this piece, namely, the high A in measure 8. That A continues the line from B♭, taking it down to G, and finally to F. As a result, with these *reachings-over* and *transfers of register*, we complete a second octave descent in the upper voice, again in parallel tenths with the second octave descent in the bass. At the conclusion of the passage, the bass descends a fourth, D-C-B♭-A, but I'll leave it to you to figure out the somewhat complicated upper voice that goes along with it.

Let's turn now to Schubert's well-known song, "Du bist die Ruh," and we'll start by going over the text, a poem by Friedrich Rückert. Rückert was a professor of Oriental languages, which in that time and place most probably meant Persian or Sanskrit. It did not, I think, mean Chinese or Korean or Japanese. The imagery of the Near East, of Persian poetry, is very noticeable in some of Rückert's poems. Schubert didn't set many of his poems but they're among his most beautiful, especially this one and "Daß sie hier gewesen." Let's read through the text, and I'll translate as we go [Example 1.8].

EXAMPLE 1.8 *Schubert, "Du bist die Ruh," annotated score.*

EXAMPLE 1.8 (*Continued*)

Du bist die Ruh–you are rest
die Friede mild—gentle peace
Die Sehnsucht du–you are longing (or desire)
und was sie stillt–and what fulfills it.

So he is saying to her (these are most probably the words of a man addressing the woman he loves), "You are rest, gentle peace, longing, desire, and fulfillment."

EXAMPLE 1.8 (*Continued*)

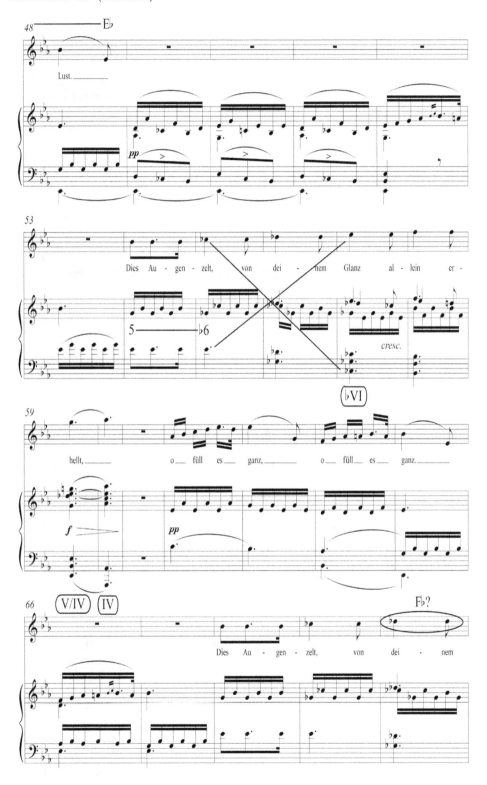

EXAMPLE 1.8 (*Continued*)

Ich weihe dir—I dedicate to you
voll Lust und Schmerz—full of pleasure and pain
zur Wohnung hier—as your dwelling here
mein Aug' und Herz—my eye and heart.

That's the first strophe of the song, which consists of two quatrains (four-line verses). The poem contains five of these four-line verses, and in a moment we'll see how Schubert deals with that.

Kehr' ein bei mir—move in to me
und schliesse du—and close
still hinter dir
die Pforten zu—the gates softly behind you.

When he says "move in to me," that has to be understood in connection with what he said at the end of the previous verse—"I dedicate to you my eye and heart as your dwelling place." He's asking her to move into his eye and heart, not necessarily to his apartment, although I suppose that could happen too!

I'll skip over the fourth quatrain. The music for the second strophe (the third and fourth quatrains) is almost completely the same as the first one, but the third one changes.

Dies Augenzelt
von deinem Glanz
allein erhellt,
O füll es ganz!

"*Augenzelt*" is where we possibly get into some Eastern imagery in the poem. That is, "*Zelt*" is a tent, or it could be something like a canopy, something stretching over one, and so an "*Augenzelt*" (an eye-tent or eye-canopy) would be a way of saying "whatever is in my vision," as though the limits of vision are in a way like the walls of a tent. So this canopy, this tent, this vision is illuminated only by your splendor ("*Glanz*" means splendor, radiance). "*O füll es ganz!*"—"Oh fill it completely"—in other words she's already giving him all the brightness of his life, but he wants her to fill his life completely.

You'll notice that Schubert repeats that verse. That's because, as I said before, the poem consists of five such verses. Schubert combines the first and second verses to make up the first musical strophe, and he combines the third and fourth verses to make up the second musical strophe. Now he again wants two verses to make up a third musical strophe, but Rückert has given him only one more. As a result, Schubert has to do something, namely, to repeat the fifth verse, to maintain a kind of balance. It would not do to have a final strophe only half as long as the preceding ones.

The Breitkopf edition of this song (part of the old, complete edition of Schubert's music) has a controversial note in measure 70. In this final strophe of the music, the second verse is pretty much exactly the same as the first. But in other editions, and in virtually every performance that I've ever heard, it's done with an F♭ in the melody in measure 70. The Breitkopf edition has D♭ in measure 70, just as in the analogous spot in measure 56. And the Breitkopf editor offers quite an interesting explanation in the critical commentary that they published together with that edition. He says that if you look at the song from the beginning, you'll see that the right hand of the piano part almost constantly doubles the melody (or at least its main tones). So part of the sound world of this piece is that kind of doubling in the piano part of the melody. The only time we don't have that doubling is when the melody moves more rapidly in sixteenth-notes; doubling those would not be practical with the kind of piano texture Schubert is using. The very first edition of this song, which was published in Schubert's lifetime, has the F♭, as do most subsequent editions. But the Breitkopf editor said that in this piece, with all of the doubling by the piano of the vocal line, if one does something as prominent and important as that F♭ in the vocal line, wouldn't we expect it to be doubled in the piano? And if the piano does not have the F♭, shouldn't we conclude that the vocal line shouldn't have it either? After all, it's very easy to have a misprint where a note a third away is taken for the intended note, so the Breitkopf editor concluded that the F♭ was a misprint, and that Schubert simply wanted the same vocal line in the second verse that he had in the first, including the D♭ in measure 70. On the other hand, of course, the world doesn't always go according to our expectations of what would be logical. The F♭ is quite beautiful and it's irresistible to singers, assuming that they even know that there is another version (which in most cases they probably don't). But I have to say the intelligence of the editor's note is very striking, and whether or not you agree with his notion, the train of thought that led him to it is quite special.

Now, returning to the beginning of the vocal line (mm. 8–11), let's consider whether or not there's a linear progression here. If we did have a linear progression, it would be through a fourth, B♭-C-D-E♭. The first E♭ in measure 10, would be an incomplete neighbor reaching over and resolving to the D [Example 1.9].

EXAMPLE 1.9 *Schubert, "Du bist die Ruh," mm. 8–11: linear progression?*

But there's another way to think about it, and let's look back to the piano introduction for some guidance. There the upper voice begins on B♭, and the C is its upper neighbor. Then, in measure 4, the E♭ enters, decorated by its lower-neighbor D, itself decorated by its own mini-neighbor C. So there are two neighbor-note figures, one decorating B♭ and the other decorating E♭.

When we are dealing with a Schubert song, we have to think of the connection of the music to the words. We have these two neighbor-note figures—B♭-C-B♭ and E♭-D-E♭—and I think they represent the two lovers. The singer is asking the girl to become part of him. The song is of someone blissfully in love certainly, but wanting it to go even further, wanting a complete merging of the two identities to one. But in the piano introduction, we have two separate identities and two separate musical figures in two distinct voices. In the first four bars of the vocal line, the two melodic figures, like the two lovers, have become one [Example 1.10].

EXAMPLE 1.10 *Schubert, "Du bist die Ruh," mm. 8–11: two neighbor notes.*

I've put the second B♭ in parentheses. The parentheses are not intended to suggest that the B♭ is only implied, because it is actually present, but not in the voice part, in the melodic line itself. In another piece, it might be very possible to have exactly the same sequence of notes, B♭-C-E♭-D-E♭, and interpret them as a linear progression of a rising fourth, with the first E♭ as a neighbor note. But in this Schubert song, the E♭ is not a neighbor note, it's a chordal tone. The D is the dependent tone there, not the E♭; the E♭ is the main tone. Schubert had an uncanny sensitivity to the possible ways in which words and music could relate to each other. In interpreting his music, you should think first of the words and approach it as if you were the singer.

Think about the rhythm of the words themselves, without regard to the music:

> *Du bist die Ruh,*
> *der Friede mild,*
> *die Sehnsucht du,*
> *und was sie stillt.*

Except for the very first word, *"du,"* the natural inflection is entirely iambic (unstressed syllable followed by stressed syllable). Schubert found a very wonderful way of dealing with this sort of word rhythm—usually iambic, but not always—and that is with a metrical accent on the first beat, but then a longer note on the second beat, which makes it possible for the singer to emphasize sometimes one of them and sometimes the other. So at the beginning, the singer can sing "*Du* bist die Ruh," not "Du *bist* die Ruh." And similarly at the beginning of the following verse: "*Ich* weihe dir," not "ich *weihe* dir." There's something especially lovely about the kind of connection Schubert establishes between "*du bist*" and "*ich weih-.*" He uses the same notes for both, but in retrograde motion: B♭-C for "*du bist*" and C-B♭ for "*ich weih-.*"

The poem, by the way, was first published, as far as I know, without any title. Schubert used just the first four words of the poem as his title. Rückert himself published a later version of the poem (I don't know whether Schubert knew that later version before he composed the song) in which the title was "*Kehr ein bei mir*" ("move in to me"). That of course is the element in the poem that Schubert is trying most to embody in his music.

Now let's work through the first stanza and discuss it harmonically. Considering the first vocal phrase (mm. 8–11), it's essentially I-V-I, with the V coming in at the end of measure 10. The C-minor chord in measure 9 results from 5-6 motion over the bass, E♭. The motion from the C-minor chord to the I⁶ chord is particularly beautiful, I think.

In measures 16–19, the bass goes stepwise down through a linear progression of a fourth: E♭-D-C-B♭. There's a question about where to place the beginning of the dominant harmony. You could say the dominant arrives in measure 17, as V⁶. Or you might consider that B♭ chord as essentially passing, with the true arrival on V taking place in measure 19. It's again one of those cases where you can't say one explanation is correct, and the other one is incorrect, but where there still might be reasons for preferring one to the other. Because measure 17 is so eventful, with the sixteenth-notes in the melodic line and the diminished-seventh chord in the harmony, I myself am very much in favor of feeling the V⁶ in measure 17 as passing, with the arrival on B♭ coming only at the end of the phrase (m. 19).

Let's look at the upper voice as it continues in measures 20–25. The basic shape of this melodic line involves a descent from B♭, which is established so strongly in the melody before this point. As a result, the C in measure 20 is a neighbor note before a descending-fifth progression: B♭-A♭-G-F-E♭. Much of that final descent to E♭ occurs over dominant harmony, which tends to confirm that the melodic C is a neighbor note.

In the little piano interlude in measures 26–29, modal mixture (C♭ versus C♮) is used very expressively. I think it is used to refer to the *Lust und Schmerz* (the pleasure and pain) of the poem, with the natural form of scale-degree 6̂ suggesting pleasure and the flat form suggesting pain. *Lust* and *Schmerz* are referred to throughout the poem in a very consistent way.

Modal mixture plays a big role also in the final strophe. Starting in measure 54, with the reference to *Augenzelt*, we find a sudden profusion of flats: C♭, G♭, etc. In the key of E♭ major, these notes involve a borrowing from the minor. So they have a very rich and very beautiful darkness, just as the poem is talking about illumination, radiance. So Schubert is actually darkening the harmonic color initially in order to then emerge from the darkness later. The G♮ (m. 54) becomes G♭ on the words "*deinem Glanz*", and then back to G at the end of the line ("*allein erhellt*"). It's like lowering the lights at the beginning and then turning them onto their full brightness.

From the point of view of the musical structure, the motion from E♭ major to C♭ major (mm. 54–55) involves a 5-♭6 motion over E♭. It is a transformation of the diatonic 5-6 that we had without any mixture at the beginning (mm. 8–9), now becoming 5-♭6 by using the lowered, minor form of scale-degree 6̂. Because he lowers the C♮ to C♭, Schubert also has to lower the G♮ to a G♭: chromatic 5-♭6 with a mixture of minor is the operative thing here. When we get to measure 57, the C♭-major harmony is correctly labeled as ♭VI, but don't forget that it arises out of the chromatic 5-♭6 in measures 54–55. In the first two strophes, the C♮ was usually a neighbor note to B♭. The melodic C♭ in the last strophe (m. 55) is also a neighbor note, but in a more elaborate way. C♭ moves up to E♭ as part of a voice-exchange with the bass, which goes from E♭ to C♭ (mm. 55–57). Once the C♭ has been transferred to the bass, via that voice exchange, it moves down to B♭. So it's still a neighboring motion: B♭-C♭-B♭, only the C♭'s resolution is now in the bass, thanks to the preceding voice exchange.

Here's a sketch that compares the first two strophes with the third one [Example 1.11].

EXAMPLE 1.11 *Schubert, "Du bist die Ruh," analytical sketch.*

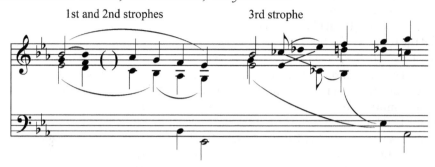

Notice how the transition from darkness to light is achieved through the mixture of major and minor and the transfer of the culminating A♭ to a higher octave. In many respects, the two phrases, different as they are, represent variations on the same basic musical idea.

Now I want to talk about the wonderful suspensions in measures 54–60. What's unusual in the voice leading is that we have a series of reachings-over. Each note in the vocal line gets retained in the piano as an alto voice while a new soprano note crosses above it. And each new alto note is made into a dissonant suspension that needs to resolve and does resolve. Something similar happens in the *Recordare* movement of the Mozart Requiem [Example 1.12].

EXAMPLE 1.12 *Mozart,* Requiem, *"Recordare," mm. 1–6.*

There again you get an upper voice retained as an alto. A new voice reaches over it, and turns it into a dissonant suspension that has to resolve. It does resolve, and then in its turn, it leaps up and reaches over to become the upper voice in the next measure.

Let's look finally at the end of the vocal line of the Schubert. The last quatrain occurs twice (measures 53–65 and 68–81), and brings in the goal E♭ (Î of the *Urlinie*) both times. The first time (m. 65), the vocal line reaches that E♭. But the second time (m. 79), the vocal line ends with the singer on B♭ and the E♭ doesn't come until the final chord in the piano part. Thus the *Urlinie* completes itself before the final cadence of the song occurs. The singer seems to end in a state of expectation for something that is to happen in the future, and the piano part is a kind of hint that that is going to take place. But it doesn't actually happen, at least not in the vocal line.

A singer can create a wonderful effect of lifting his or her face, not quite ending, but looking very much into the future. (I mentioned earlier that the poem's speaker is a man addressing the woman he loves. The song, however, is completely convincing sung by a woman, and I think it is probably sung more often by women than by men.) Instead of the normal decrescendo at the end, one might create a subtle crescendo. It is a wonderful ending. Schubert's ability to create musically ideas as abstract as two beings turning into one is really astonishing. Obviously he is able to do more concrete sorts of tone painting, like the sound of a brook or leaves in the wind, but his accomplishment in "Du bist die Ruh" is something quite amazing and wonderful.

J. S. Bach, Menuet in C minor from French Suite No. 2 and Chopin, Etude, Op. 10, No. 12

We'll begin by discussing the C-minor Menuet from J. S. Bach, French Suite No. 2. Then we'll study Schenker's reading in Five Graphic Analyses *of Chopin's Etude Op. 10, No. 12, concentrating on Chopin's use of linear progressions and neighbor notes as motives. We'll discuss the principle of interruption and the technique of chromaticized voice exchanges. We'll also examine Schenker's approach to form as growing out of voice leading.*

Let's continue to discuss linear progressions, starting with Menuet II from J. S. Bach, French Suite No. 2 in C minor [Example 2.1]. (You should be aware that this movement is not included in some editions of the suite).

We'll start with the first four-bar group, concentrating on the right-hand part. There's a brief third-progression from E♭ down to C in measures 1–2, followed by an even briefer fifth-progression from C down to F in measure 2. That progression from C to F is very fleeting, but it is harmonically supported by an F-minor chord, and it does fall under the definition of linear progression that we developed in the previous class: a stepwise progression between two tones that are related to each other harmonically. Schenker himself sometimes labels as *Züge* very fleeting linear motions.

The descending third in measures 1–2 (E♭-D-C) is answered by a rising third in measures 3–4 (B-C-D), a third-progression within a prolonged dominant harmony. By the way, it's very common in the music of Bach and many other composers, that within a prolongation of the dominant you might find what is apparently a tonic chord, as on the last beat of measure 3. I say "apparently," because that tonic chord is there to support a passing tone from one note of the dominant chord (B) to another (D)—C is a passing tone within the ascending third-progression, B-C-D. The operative harmony here is V, not I.

Now let's turn to the bass line in this passage. There's a descending fifth in measures 1–3: C-B♭-A♭-G-F. You might think of it as two thirds, C-B♭-A♭ and A♭-G-F, but I would take the whole fifth as an integrated melodic structure. As I noted last week, when one has the

EXAMPLE 2.1 *Bach, French Suite No. 2 in C minor, Menuet II, annotated score.*

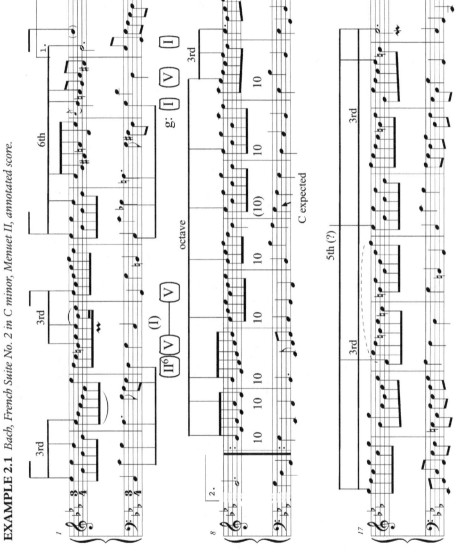

choice between a couple of smaller progressions and one larger one, the larger one usually (but not always) wins out. You might question the harmonic support for that fifth, because at the end of the progression, when the bass gets to F, we don't have an F-minor chord but a II⁶ chord. II⁶ excludes C, which was the first note of the progression, and it's usually the case that the supporting harmony includes both the first and last notes of a linear progression. But Schenker himself very often labels such things as linear progressions, and indeed the F-minor chord (IV, which would include C) and the diminished first-inversion chord (II⁶, which excludes C) are so close to each other in function that you could even think of this linear progression as entailing a 5-6 motion over the F, with C moving up to D. On that basis, I would call C-Bb-Ab-G-F a true fifth-progression [Example 2.2].

EXAMPLE 2.2 *Bach, Menuet, mm. 1–3, analytical sketch.*

Let's consider for a moment where the dominant harmony arrives at the end of this phrase. The definitive arrival of G in the bass would seem to be on the downbeat of measure 4, but we've already had an arrival on G on the second beat of measure 3. It's possible to have that cake and to eat it simultaneously, because we can show the G starting at that earlier point, but not starting in a way that fully expresses it until we get to the lower G. Notice again that rising third-progression B-C-D in the upper voice—the arrival of its final note (D) coincides with the definitive arrival of G on the downbeat of measure 4 [Example 2.3].

EXAMPLE 2.3 *Bach, Menuet, mm. 1–4, analytical sketch.*

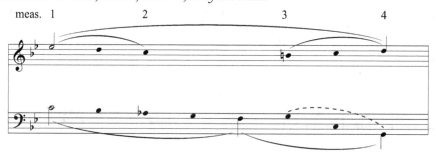

Let's push on now to the next phrase (mm. 5–8), looking first at the right-hand part. There is pretty clearly a descending sixth, from Eb (m. 5) all the way down to G (m. 8), and this raises an interesting issue. Schenker would very typically show, and that's because the composers would very typically write, a large-scale motion from Eb to D, arriving on D at the moment that the descending sixth concludes. If, following William Rothstein, we invoke an "imaginary continuo" for the passage, and if we think of this continuo as not just being a chord-by-chord progression but a sort of harmonic reduction on a larger scale, the note that would normally follow Eb would be D [Rothstein 1991]. Schenker would in his graphs sometimes put that note in parentheses as if to say, "this linear progression is a motion into the inner voice, and the initial top note doesn't get to the expected destination" [Example 2.4].

EXAMPLE 2.4 *Bach, Menuet, mm. 5–8, analytical sketch.*

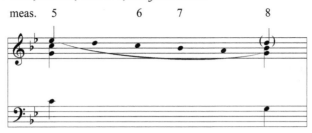

Something similar happens in the Sarabande from J. S. Bach's Partita No. 1 in B♭ major [Example 2.5]. In the first reprise, we have, stated quite explicitly in the right-hand part, a descending sixth, on a much larger scale and infinitely more complicated than what we have in the little Menuet. In the Sarabande (as in the Menuet), there is a large-scale motion from tonic to dominant harmony, supporting an upper voice that goes from scale-degree $\hat{3}$ to scale-degree $\hat{2}$ (the dominant harmony arrives at the beginning of the second reprise, in m. 13). But before that happens, or while that is happening, we have a motion down a sixth into an inner voice [Example 2.6].

Let's get back to the Menuet, and to the left-hand part in measures 5–8. First we get a descending fourth from C to G, and then the G itself is prolonged by I-V-I in G minor. Then, in the top voice after the double bar, we have an ascent through a complete octave from G to G and, tacked onto the end, a little descent, G-F-E♭. So we have an octave going all the way up, and a third coming down. By the way, the harmonic organization of this Menuet is reasonably common in music of the high Baroque and raises an interesting question. When you're in a minor key and the first reprise ends on the minor dominant, and then you start right off at the beginning of the second reprise with the relative major (or mediant), it's not necessarily clear which of those harmonies is the most important one in terms of the harmonic structure of the piece as a whole. In the case of our Menuet, however, E♭ major receives so much emphasis that it clearly has a higher rank than the G minor. But whatever the harmonic implications, this is definitely a beautiful example of a linear progression of an octave, from G to G.

Now let's look at the left-hand part in the same passage (mm. 9–16). Instead of looking directly at the bass, let's think about the sense in which it seems to follow the progress of the upper voice. It's quite frequent that you will have two simultaneous linear progressions that parallel each other, most often at the tenth, but also at the sixth or the third if the voices are close together. And quite typically one of them will seem to grow out of the underlying harmony and its points of articulation will tend to project a sound of that harmony, and the other one very often will not.

We can turn to the first Prelude from the first book of the *Well-Tempered Clavier* for an example [Example 2.7]. The bass in measures 1–19 is a descending octave scale that is bisected, you might say, in the middle by the dominant note. The right hand does a rather elaborate kind of motion, essentially (but not literally) a tenth above the bass. And where the bass stops on G (m. 11) the top voice stops on B. Now what would be projected by that melodic line in the absence of that bass would be E-B-E, which would not at all suggest the underlying tonality of C major. As a result, it makes more sense to imagine that the bass and its linear progression are the main thing, and the upper voice is simply following along.

EXAMPLE 2.5 *Bach, Partita No. 1 in B♭ major, Sarabande, mm. 1–16, annotated score.*

EXAMPLE 2.6 *Bach, Sarabande, mm. 1–13, analytical sketch.*

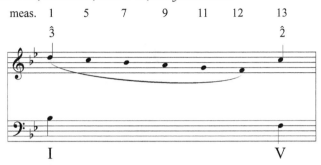

Returning to the Menuet, we can think of the bass in measures 9–16 as following the octave ascent in the upper voice in parallel tenths. But something happens in measure 13 that deviates from the pattern: the expected bass-note C is not present. As we have discussed previously, there are sometimes substitutions that can be made where something would be a stepwise progression but for some reason, let's hope a good reason, the composer decides to substitute some other note that is not part of the stepwise line. My feeling is that the compositional idea here is parallel tenths between the outer voices through an entire octave, but that in measure 13, Bach substitutes G for the expected C.

This relates to something similar at the beginning of the second Prelude from the first book of the *Well-Tempered Clavier* [Example 2.8]. Starting in measure 12, Bach breaks the pattern of parallel tenths between the outer voices, and I think he has a good reason for doing so. He wants to go into a higher register in the bass so that he doesn't get to the low ("cello") C too soon. That's where he would have gone if the pattern had continued, and he wants to save that note for the final tonic at the end of the piece. He avoids that problem by substituting C and D for F in measures 12–13, and then the motion in tenths resumes, but in a higher register.

Returning to the Menuet, we can think of the left hand as substituting G for C in measure 13. Bach could have easily continued the pattern if he had written C-D-E♭ in quarter notes in measure 13, but that sounds very weak.

Let's move on now to the final phrase of the Menuet (mm. 17–end), where we find what looks like a descending fifth-progression from G to C in the upper voice. In this descent, I would locate the F in measure 19: it's in the wrong register there, but is almost immediately linked to an F in the right register (m. 20). This sort of linkage is called *coupling*, and there is a veritable orgy of couplings in this piece. We just had the octave progression from G to G (mm. 9–15) so the F to F coupling in measures 19–20 is in very distinguished company.

Coupling is a Schenkerian term that comes from organ and harpsichord playing where you can couple two manuals. By pressing down one key you can get two sounds, most often an octave apart. In Schenker's analyses, coupling establishes a connection between two registers, which means, generally, perhaps always, that there has to be some kind of elaboration or composing out between the two coupled registers, and not just something like an octave leap G-G, or moving from G to F as an ascending seventh rather than a descending step. One can get along without the term *coupling*, but it was an important concept for Schenker. He often had a stepwise linear progression or an arpeggio connecting the coupled registers.

In the opening phrase of the slow movement from Beethoven's Ninth Symphony, arpeggios couple the two registers of the melody [Example 2.9].

EXAMPLE 2.7 *Bach, Prelude in C major, Well-Tempered Clavier,* Vol. 1, *mm. 1–19, score and analytical sketch.*

(a)

EXAMPLE 2.7 (*Continued*)

EXAMPLE 2.8 Bach, *Prelude in C minor, Well-Tempered Clavier, Vol. 1, mm. 1–18, score and analytical sketch.*

EXAMPLE 2.8 (*Continued*)

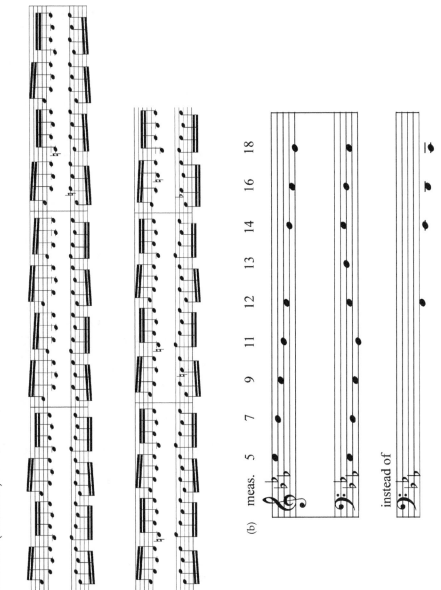

EXAMPLE 2.9 *Beethoven, Symphony No. 9, third movement, mm. 3–7, annotated score.*

First there is an arpeggio downward through an octave (with a neighbor note, A-B♭, and a passing tone, F-E♭-D), and then another arpeggio back up to the initial tone. That would be a coupling downward and then upward. I first became aware of the coupled octaves in this excerpt in a class taught by my teacher, Felix Salzer. He has included a graph of it as Example 222 in his book *Structural Hearing* [Salzer 1962], as well as a short but valuable discussion in Volume 1 (p. 128).

Now I want to digress for a moment and complain about the system of letters and numbers for designating registers created by the Acoustical Society of America. Our music—and I'm not just talking about tonal music now—has a normal registral area in the approximately two octaves above and below middle C, and going much above or below that area goes into more remote territory where registers begin to feel extreme. Therefore, the traditional system of register designations—which J. S. Bach used, for instance, in the beginning part of his Notebook for Wilhelm Friedemann Bach—is preferable. You start with middle C, which is designated "one line C," and it was very often written with one little line, like an exponent. Going up we have the "one line C," the "two line C," and the "three line C." Going down, "viola C" would be called "small C," "cello C" is "great C," and the octave below that would be "contra C." I like these designations because they are rooted in the human body and the human voice. Instead, the Acoustical Society of America calls middle C "C4," and attaches Arabic numbers to note names in all of the registers. Nowadays, if you want to write something in a standard music theory journal, you will have to use those numbers. And I'm not the only one who dislikes them; most people I talk to seem to agree with me, but nobody does anything about it.

I would like to close our discussion of this piece by returning to what we described as a descending fifth-progression in the melody in measures 17–24: G-F-E♭-D-C. It might make more sense to think of it as two third-progressions, G-F-E♭ and E♭-D-C. That's because of the way E♭ is brought in in measure 21. E♭ has been the main melodic note from the beginning of the piece. In measure 21, it returns not just in a rhythmically exposed place, but with what seems to be at least a partial nod to the opening music—measure 21 and the downbeat of measure 22 sound a lot like measure 1 and the downbeat of measure 2.

And that brings me back to something I wanted to say earlier about the first two phrases, measures 1–4 and 5–8. My feeling is that there's something deliberately, shall we say, incomplete (in a good way) about the whole first reprise (mm. 1–8). It's not going where you would expect it to go. After you hear measures 1–4, I think what you really expect is something very much like the last four measures of the piece, measures 21–24. That would give you a beautifully balanced antecedent and consequent, ending on the tonic (C minor). Instead, in measures 5–8, we get a consequent that goes to the minor dominant (G minor). In that sense, the return to the opening music in measure 21 completes an idea or fulfills an expectation that was left incomplete and unfulfilled in the first reprise. So it's the special role of the E♭ in measure 21, marking a return to the opening idea, that leads me to prefer to think of our apparent fifth-progression as really two thirds. The initial main melodic tone of the piece is the E♭. The G kind of takes over at the double bar, but then it descends via a third-progression to E♭ in measure 21. At that point, the E♭ itself descends via another third-progression to the final tonic. Reading a fifth-progression here (instead of the two third-progressions) would not violate any of the rules of counterpoint, but it would not be responsive to the specific design of the piece, in which the last four measures are heard as a much-delayed consequent to the antecedent of the first four measures.

Let's turn our attention now to a rather different piece, namely the Chopin "Revolutionary" Etude in C minor (Op. 10, No. 12). Despite its musical differences, we'll still be dealing with some of the same theoretical and analytical issues that we've already been talking about. I want to approach the piece by way of Schenker's analysis of it in *Five Graphic Music Analyses* [Schenker 1969]. Except for the *Eroica* analysis [Schenker 1997b], these are his most elaborate published analyses. One doesn't have to agree with every note in them by any means, but it is just marvelous what he has done. The German title is *Fünf Urlinie-Tafeln*, and these five "charts of the *Urlinie*" came about in the following way.

One of Schenker's most important pupils in Vienna was a man named Hans Weisse, and, for some reason, in 1931, Weisse, who was a very well-reputed and active musician in Vienna, decided he wanted to come to the United States with his family. At Mannes at that time, there was someone who knew about Schenker and knew about Weisse—a cellist from New York named Gerald Warburg, who was a trustee at Mannes. Warburg had studied with Weisse in Vienna and had gotten very interested in Schenker (although I don't think he ever met him). By coincidence, Mannes was looking for somebody to teach theory and composition at just that moment, and they hired Weisse. There had been musicians in the United States who knew something about Schenker and actually talked about Schenker in their classes, but there was nobody who went into the depth that Weisse did in those first few years. It would be fair to say that the transplantation of Schenker from Europe to America happened primarily though the activity of Hans Weisse. Sadly, Weisse died only about ten years after he came to this country.

Before he left Vienna, Weisse asked Schenker if he could have some exemplary graphs that he could use in his teaching in America. At the same time, he asked Schenker to take on four of the students he was leaving behind in Vienna (Felix Salzer, Greta Kraus, Trude Kral, and Manfred H. Willfort), and Schenker agreed. Schenker then, together with Weisse's four former students, worked on pieces for Weisse to use in his teaching at Mannes, partly in the hope that they would eventually be suitable for publication. There were supposed to be several sets of these pieces, but *Five Graphic Analyses* is the only one that was ever published.

Apparently the way it worked was that Schenker would assign a piece, the student would come back with a graph, and Schenker would tear it to pieces (I don't mean literally tear the paper to pieces, but he would tear the reading to pieces). He would say, "No, do that again next week and improve the following things." The student would come back the following week, and Schenker would say "Well that little bit is improved but the rest of it is terrible, do it again for next week," and so forth. Felix Salzer was the student responsible for the development section of the Haydn Sonata in the *Five Graphic Analyses*, and he told me that for weeks and weeks Schenker would say, "Do it again." Finally, Salzer told his fellow students that he didn't know what he would do if Schenker made him correct his graph again, because he felt that he had absolutely done everything Schenker wanted. He handed it to Schenker, who looked and looked and looked at it. After a long time, he turned it back to Salzer and said, "Next week do it in ink."

One of the challenges in analyzing Chopin's music is that the problem of establishing a definitive text is more difficult with Chopin than with any other of the great composers of tonal music. In fact, one might say it ceases to be a problem because it's simply an impossibility. He was somebody who was constantly working at his compositions long after they were published. He sometimes gave students copies of his music with minimal (but nevertheless often very telling) comments, additions, and subtractions. He lived at a time before there were reciprocal copyright agreements between different countries, so somebody who, say, went to France to buy the Twelve Etudes, Op. 10, could then simply go across the border to Germany and print them without paying any money to the publishers, and certainly not to Chopin. As a result, his music was published in France and Germany almost always within a very short period of time, and there were also British editions (which usually were the French editions with just a different title page). These editions may differ from each other, sometimes in considerable ways, but they all have to be considered authentic. In addition, the various published editions may differ from the autograph and, with some pieces, there may even be more than one autograph. So it's a very special task to edit Chopin's music.

I don't know that there is a single best edition of Chopin's music. The *Wiener Urtext Ausgabe* is interesting in that it prints more of the variants—the different kinds of things that Chopin wrote—than any of the other editions. And not just in footnotes at the bottom of the page (though they have some of those), and certainly not in endnotes after the music, but often in the score itself. That makes for difficult score reading, but these are not pieces that most people sight-read, so that really isn't a serious problem. It's probably the best edition around, although it makes terrible mistakes too sometimes, not specifically in the Etudes, but in general. For example, in the E-minor Prelude, Op. 28, No. 4, which is one of the most famous pieces of music ever written, the editors seem not to realize that Chopin's time signature is alla breve (cut time) and not common time.

Now, before we look at Schenker's analysis, let's begin by just thinking about the piece, especially about its overall form [Example 2.10]. Perhaps the first thing you might notice is that there is a recapitulation of the opening music, although exactly where it occurs presents an interesting question. The piece begins with an eight-measure introduction, then the tonic harmony arrives (m. 9), and then, at the end of measure 10, the main melodic line enters. When the opening music returns, roughly halfway through the piece, we once again get first the introduction (m. 41), then the arrival of tonic harmony (m. 49), and then the entry of the main melodic line. So when does the recapitulation begin? You could say it begins in measure 41, when the opening measures of the piece return, but that introduction is not on tonic harmony and is heard somehow as outside the frame that the composer puts into the piece.

Frame is a term of Edward Cone's, and it's a very important one [Cone 1968]. Cone talks about "external frames," like, for example, the silence before the beginning of the piece.

EXAMPLE 2.10 *Chopin, Etude in C minor, Op. 10, No. 12 ("Revolutionary"), annotated score.*

He also talks about "internal frames," which the composer builds directly into the piece itself. In the Chopin Etude, the return of the introduction in measure 41 acts as a sort of frame for the return of the tonic and then the main melody. In that way, the sense of return is distributed across a continuum, rather than being concentrated in one single place. Right at the start of the piece we get that sense of a triple beginning: an introduction; a resolution to tonic along with the ostinato pattern that dominates the main part of the piece; and then the main melodic line two measures later. So when the opening music returns, we find that we could start our recapitulation at any one of three places. That's a very special feeling that we get in this piece. (By the way, Chopin's D-major Prelude from Op. 28, although not quite as elaborate as this, has something a bit similar to this.) At the end of the piece, in what is maybe the most beautiful moment of the piece (although it would not have been possible without what had happened before), we get an eight-measure coda, which is without any question derived from the first eight bars. So there is a kind of frame at the end of the piece as well. In discussing the form of the piece in this way, we haven't put a precise name on it, but I think we've learned something about it which is of more importance than just saying that it's ternary or binary.

EXAMPLE 2.10 (*Continued*)

Now let's think about the form of the piece in a bit more detail, starting at the beginning. After the introduction, the first phrase (mm. 10–18) is an antecedent phrase that ends on a half cadence (m. 18), and wishes to resolve (which, eventually, at the end of the piece, it does). The phrase that begins with the pickup to measure 21 is the consequent, and it is a modulating consequent phrase that cadences on B♭ (m. 28). At that point, there is a change of material, as well as a change in the left-hand pattern, starting in G♯-minor in measure 29 (but not staying there very long). That seems to signal the beginning of what most people would call a "contrasting middle section." In that view, the piece is in three main parts—it's a ternary form. We have a first section that is a kind of period, with antecedent and consequent phrases. Then we have a middle section that is, in a sense, developmental in character (though it doesn't have the harmonic structure of the usual development section). Finally, we have a sort of recapitulation, starting with the introduction (m.41), a return of the main theme, slightly varied but still with an antecedent (mm. 50–58) and a consequent (mm. 60–77). The consequent phrase is extended and leads to the final resolution, both melodic and harmonic, in measure 77, followed by the eight-measure coda. All of that pretty clearly suggests a ternary form. And that's what a lot of people have said about this piece.

I should tell you right away that that's very much *not* Schenker's interpretation of the form of the Etude. Schenker had the idea that form emerges out of the levels of tonal

EXAMPLE 2.10 (*Continued*)

structure. This is not so much the case for the background level, although even the background has the germ of the possibility of form. Schenker points that out by saying that although the *Urlinie*—the 3̂-2̂-1̂, or 5̂-4̂-3̂-2̂-1̂, or even 8̂-7̂-6̂-5̂-4̂-3̂-2̂-1̂—is all in one direction and is thus totally unified so that it cannot be divided into parts, the bass does have a kind of division: it goes up from I to V and then down from V to I. The simple confrontation of those two fifth motions—one up and one down—gives the possibility of form, a possibility that is already present at the background level. In fact, one could even think in a rather specific way of the rise in intensity of the rising fifth and then the fall and relaxation of the falling fifth—these are elements that lead to a perception of form.

Schenker wanted to understand the form of a piece as growing out of its tonal contents, and not as being imposed from the outside as a kind of template, a so-called "jelly mold" (the term is Tovey's [Tovey 1949]) into which music is poured and solidifies. Schenker undoubtedly went too far in his dismissal of the idea that certain kinds of formal plans really are precompositional, that is, determinative of what happens in the composition. But he did shift the emphasis to issues that had rarely been touched upon before, and the sorts of things he says about form are extremely interesting. In practice, he actually relies a lot on the old-fashioned *Formenlehre*, and uses a lot of its terminology at the same time as he tells you how terrible it is.

EXAMPLE 2.10 (*Continued*)

Schenker's sense of the form growing out of the tonal structure is very strongly to the fore in his analysis of this Etude. To see how this works, let's look carefully at the first page of his analysis, which includes the *Ursatz* (along the top of the page) and three *Schichten* (or *levels*) arranged in order below it [Example 2.11].

It's worth mentioning that the German word *Schicht* really means *layer* more than *level*, but *layer* sounds terrible in English and *level* is the term we generally use, especially in scholarly work. Notice that Schenker doesn't call the *Ursatz* a *level*—the levels, for him, reside in the middleground, while the *Ursatz* is just itself. I confess I have no idea why he has made the bass notes of the *Ursatz* so tiny in this graph. There are many times in Schenker's analyses that it's very difficult to tell exactly what he means. It's one reason why his work had difficulty in catching on.

Still looking at the *Ursatz*, you see that the *Urlinie* (top voice) descends $\hat{3}$-$\hat{2}$-$\hat{1}$ near the end of the piece in measure 77, which is where we located the resolution to the final tonic in our formal survey. The dominant comes just before that in measure 73. As a result, we have $\hat{3}$ unresolved for the vast bulk of the piece, with $\hat{2}$ and $\hat{1}$ coming only at the very end. Schenker vertically aligns the *Ursatz* with the levels that occur underneath it. In the *Ursatz*, $\hat{2}$ arrives in measure 72, and that's also where it arrives in the first level of the middleground. But notice that the harmony at that point is II^6 rather than V. For Schenker, the only harmonies in the

EXAMPLE 2.10 (*Continued*)

Ursatz are I and V; II, IV, and other intermediate harmonies make their first appearance in the first level of the middleground. If you look down at the second level of the middleground in measure 72, you will see that instead of D♮, as in the *Ursatz* and the first level, we have D♭ (as in the music). That's because Schenker thinks of that Neapolitan note as an alteration, a transformation, of the diatonic note, D♮. So the D♮ of the *Ursatz* is there as a representative of D♭'s origin as a diatonic note. The D♭ in the music is heard in reference to the D♮ at the highest levels of the graph.

Turning back to the first level, you can see at the far left the label *2-Teilig*, which means "in two parts." This is Schenker trying to show you how the form originates: the totally unified and continuous *Ursatz* is divided into two parts at this level, very much like the way a fertilized ovum splits into two before an embryo can begin to develop. When we get to measure 41 in the first level, we have 2̂ with a dominant underneath it and the word *Teiler*. That marks the end of a section, and it's a particular kind of end, namely, what Schenker calls an *interruption*. The uninterrupted *Ursatz*, with its I-V-I in the bass and 3̂-2̂-1̂ in the top voice has thus been expanded, transformed, and divided at the first level of middleground first into 3̂-2̂ harmonized by I-V and then 3̂-2̂-1̂ harmonized by I-V-I.

Schenker came upon the notion of interruption rather late in his analytic career. That is to say, it's with the *Eroica* analysis [Schenker 1997b] and the *Five Graphic Analyses* [Schenker 1969] that he actually uses it for the first time. There is no explanation of it

EXAMPLE 2.10 *(Continued)*

in the *Eroica* analysis. He just says, "The first middleground layer shows the interruption $\hat{3}$-$\hat{2}$//$\hat{3}$-$\hat{2}$-$\hat{1}$.... See *Der freie Satz*." Well, *Free Composition* (*Der freie Satz*) [Schenker 1979] was not to come out for another five years, and Schenker was dead at the time it did, so I doubt he had thought out all aspects of interruption.

Interruptions can also occur at lower levels of the middleground, as we will see in a moment. But for an interruption at the first level, Schenker says in *Free Composition* that it works in such a manner that the *first* dominant and the *first* scale-degree $\hat{2}$ are the structural ones (those are not his terms, but it makes it simpler if we use them). In this piece, that would be at measure 41. Schenker says that the remainder of the piece is essentially going over the same ground a second time, and therefore the second dominant and the second scale-degree $\hat{2}$ (in m. 72) are on a lower level of structure.

That may seem like a controversial claim, and it is actually contradicted by this analysis. If Schenker were to have revised this analysis according to what he says in *Free Composition*, then in the *Ursatz*, the D and the dominant G underneath it would occur in the middle (m. 41) and not all the way at the end (m. 72). I can very easily see that for a piece like this one, with that enormous climax at the return in the second half of the piece, you might want to see the dominant harmony and scale-degree $\hat{2}$ in measure 72 as having the greater structural force. But I can also see it as Schenker suggests in *Free Composition*, namely that we should position

EXAMPLE 2.11 *Schenker's analysis of Chopin, "Revolutionary" Etude, from* Five Graphic Analyses.

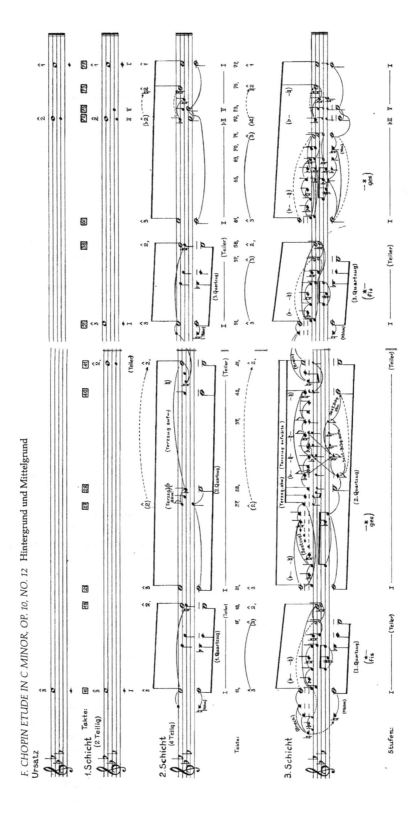

the structural dominant, the *Ursatz* dominant, at the end of the first half of the piece. My own preference is for taking each piece on its own terms and not necessarily finding an overall rubric that will fit everything. As far as the Etude is concerned, I lean toward Schenker's reading in *Five Graphic Analyses*, where the final cadential dominant is the big one, rather than the one in the middle of the piece. This is largely because the introductory character of the music at measure 41 makes it sound like a new beginning rather than an ending.

Now let's look at the second *Schicht*. This one is labeled *4-Teilig*, that is to say, it is in four parts, and what Schenker is trying to show is that each of the two parts of the first *Schicht* splits into two in the second. The first three of those four parts involve a linear progression in the bass, C-B♭-A♭-G, with the notes connected by a beam to show that they really belong together. Before the first of these fourth-progressions (*Quartzüge*), you see a harmony that Schenker has labeled *Nbhm* for *Nebennotenharmonie*, or neighbor-note harmony, with B going to C in the bass, and F going to E♭ in the upper voice. That's Schenker's summary of the eight-measure introduction. The harmony as a whole is a dominant-seventh chord in $\frac{6}{4}$ position, including not only the B and F shown in the graph, but also D and G (the A♭ is a neighbor note to the G). Now notice especially what Schenker leaves conspicuously absent from the designation of that chord: there is no Roman numeral, no label that says V. When the music of the introduction returns in measure 41, with its quite palpable G in the bass, marked *fortissimo*, Schenker's graph does show the G, but still gets away without a Roman numeral there because he calls it a *Teiler* (divider) instead.

One of the most important lessons Schenker has to teach is the importance of counterpoint and voice leading in tonal structure. Many things that were regarded as harmonic by previous theorists, Schenker took as contrapuntal. He doubtless goes a bit too far sometimes—in this piece (particularly where it sounds as though the timpani are coming in with the low G), there is quite definitely a dominant character to the harmony. But Schenker is also showing something important, because he is showing that the tension of each of the three dissonant notes leading into a resolution into the tonic is even more important than designating it as some kind of chord (with a Roman numeral).

Now a word about the concept of the *Teiler* (divider). We see it used in the first *Schicht* under scale-degree $\hat{2}$ in measure 41 and in three places in the second *Schicht* (mm. 18, 41, and 58). It specifically refers to the harmonic motion (though what happens in the top voice is also part of it). You could say that a *Teiler* is something that closes off a musical motion of some kind. At one point, Schenker was trying to make distinctions between "true" dominant chords and "dividers," and there is even an essay in *Meisterwerk* [Schenker 1996] that tries to explore that. But he is not, in my opinion, consistent in his own work on this topic—in some places he says *Teiler* and in others he says V, so it's not something I think one wants to agonize over. When we have an interruption, or something like an interruption, the use of the word divider is, I think, expressive and very good. There are places in *Meisterwerk* where Schenker just writes "I-Teiler-I" instead of "I-V-I," and I don't know that he gains very much from that. Just to clarify the terminology: *interruption* has to do with both the top voice *and* the bass; the *Teiler* has to do specifically with the bass. You can have a *Teiler* without an interruption—it does happen.

Staying with the second *Schicht* for a moment, I want to focus on the span of music from measures 21–41, which Schenker calls the "second fourth progression" (*2. Quartzug*), with C-B♭-A♭-G in the bass. What he is showing here is, I would say, the greatest flash of analytical insight in this whole analysis. At the bottom of the first page of the Foreground analysis [not shown here], Schenker writes a footnote saying that all conventional concepts of modulation will founder on this music: "It would be wrong, for instance, to speak of modulation to B-flat major, a-flat minor, f minor, etc. The voice leading of the middleground alone offers the correct solution to the problem!" Let's look closely and see if we think he is right.

The first bass note of the fourth-progression (C) is obvious—it's in measure 21—and the B♭ arrives with the cadence in measure 28, which is a rather strong cadence, with an augmented sixth leading into the ⁶₄ chord. Finding the A♭ is rather more complicated. Look first at measure 40. There, we have A♭ in the bass of an F-minor chord supporting the climactic F-minor melody. As measure 40 moves to measure 41, we have octave A♭'s moving to octave Gs, so the end of the big fourth-progression, A♭-G, is strongly present at the conclusion of this section. Measure 40 is where the A♭ ends, but not where it starts. Look in the third *Schicht* at the bottom of the page and you'll notice a dotted slur that comes from an earlier A♭. It's like the two G's in measures 3-4 of the Bach Menuet: a note comes in at the beginning of a prolongation, but it hasn't declared itself as being as important as it's going to be later. So we have a premonition of that later A♭ (m. 40) in the G♯ of the G♯-minor harmony that comes in in measure 29.

Follow the progression in the third *Schicht* and in the music. From the G♯-minor chord in measure 29 (which Schenker notates enharmonically as A♭-minor) the music moves in measure 33 to an A♭-seventh chord in ⁶₅ position (it would be a dominant of D♭-minor if it were really a dominant at all). Notice that these two chords are connected with a voice exchange: using Chopin's notation in sharps, the B in the top voice of measure 29 is exchanged with the B♯ in the bass of measure 33, and the G♯ in the bass of measure 29 is exchanged with the G♯ in the top voice of measure 33. There is thus a strong connection between the G♯-minor (or A♭-minor) triad (m. 29) and the dominant-seventh chord that it becomes (m. 33).

So, within the big fourth-progression, B♭ has already gone to A♭, and the A♭ is, in a way, kept alive through the motion into that ⁶₅ chord. Once we're on the A♭ ⁶₅ chord (m. 33), the bass rises by step in a series of ⁶₅ chords, leading finally to the F-minor chord in measure 37.

When you first think about this passage, it seems almost impossible to imagine that the G♯-minor chord at the beginning and the F-minor chord at the end have any meaningful relation to each other. But if we play a slightly reduced imaginary continuo, you hear that it's a quite rational chord progression, and really leads us into our F-minor very beautifully, through a fantastic progression of ⁶₅ chords [Example 2.12].

EXAMPLE 2.12 *Chopin, Etude, mm. 33–37, harmonic reduction.*

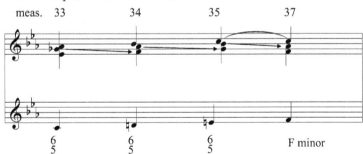

The G♭ of the A♭⁶₅ chord goes down to F of the B♭⁶₅ chord while the A♭ stays. From the E♭, there is an upward leap, bringing in a new consonant note, B♭. The same thing happens when the B♭⁶₅ chord moves to the C⁶₅ chord, which then resolves to F minor. And, as each ⁶₅ chord moves, there is a transferred resolution of the dissonant note.

Something similar happens in one of J. S. Bach's greatest chorale harmonizations, "Ach Gott und Herr" (Chorale 279) [Example 2.13].

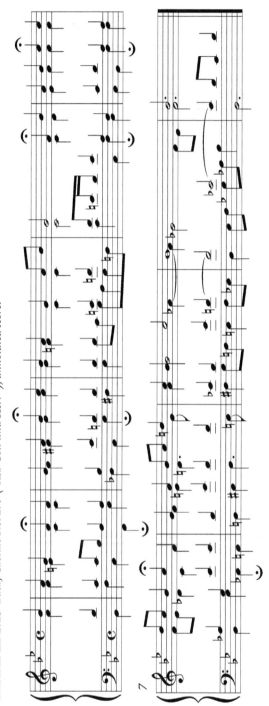

EXAMPLE 2.13 Bach, Chorale No. 279 ("*Ach Gott und Herr*"), *annotated score.*

The fifth phrase ends on A♭. Then we have F♮, G♮, and A♮—exactly the same progression as in the Chopin. The chorale is a prayer to be punished on earth so that one could be spared in heaven, and one should atone for one's sins on earth. And the text "let us atone here" is actually set to this sequence of ♮ chords.

Now back to the Chopin. I want to try to summarize what happens within Schenker's second *Quartzug* (mm. 21–41) [Example 2.14].

EXAMPLE 2.14 *Chopin, Etude, mm. 21-41, analytical sketch.*

The basic idea for the C-B♭-A♭-G fourth-progression is from the tonic, C-minor, passing through B♭-major and F♮ to the dominant, G-major. That is elaborated as C-minor, a cadence on B♭-major, then from A♭-minor and A♭♮ through that fantastic progression of ♮ chords to F minor, first in root position, then in ♮ position with A♭ in the bass, and finally to G major, the dominant. So that's where Schenker gets his second *Quartzug*.

What Schenker is really trying to say is that chopping the piece up into a ternary mold ignores what is compositionally the most fascinating aspect of this piece: how that idea of the descending fourth can be expressed in such a mind-altering way, and the amazing kind of compositional imagination that shows. And therefore one must find some way of regarding that C-B♭-A♭-G, both in its original presentation and its new guises, as form-creating. That's the basis on which Schenker makes binary divisions—of the one-part Ursatz into two parts in the first level, and of the two parts in the first level into four parts in the second level—and not a ternary division. He would probably acknowledge that there is an effect of contrast and a sense of beginning a new section when we get to G♯ minor in measure 29. At that point, the second of Schenker's four parts seems to sprout a new part of its own. In other words, there is a certain validity and truth in the A-B-A idea of this piece, but it can't be allowed to be your whole conception of the form. Your thinking about form has to have a quality of plasticity, not making rigid categories all the time, but responding to things like Chopin's fantastic elaboration of the fourth-progression, because that really is where the genius of the music shows.

Chopin, G♯-minor and E-major Preludes from Op. 28

We'll compare Schenker's reading of the form of Op. 10/12 with our own reading of the G♯-minor Prelude Op. 28/12. After concluding our discussion of the Chopin Prelude, we'll look at another highly chromatic Chopin Prelude, Op. 28/9. We'll be examining the possibility of large-scale arpeggiations as deep middleground top-voice structures.

W E'RE GOING TO SPEND MOST OF OUR TIME TODAY TALKING ABOUT TWO Preludes from Chopin's Op. 28: No. 12 in G♯ minor and No. 9 in E major. I want to start out with some general observations about the form of the G♯-minor Prelude, and especially its relationship to the form of the C-minor Etude (Op. 10), which we discussed last time. The form of the Etude might be seen as ternary, with an expository A-section, a contrasting B-section, and then a recapitulation of the A-section.

As we discussed last week, that is not at all how Schenker described the piece in the *Five Graphic Analyses* [Schenker 1969]. For Schenker, and from the perspective of large-scale voice leading, the determinant of the form of the piece is the repeated descending fourth-progression in the bass, from tonic to dominant. The second of those descending fourths encompasses what many people would see as the contrasting B-section in the Etude. In Schenker's view of the form of the Etude, the *Ursatz* is divided into two parts, and each of those parts is also divided into two, marked with interruptions.

Very much the same sort of thing could be said about the G♯-minor Prelude. On a first impression, you might say that its form is ternary, with an expository A-section (mm. 1–20), a contrasting B-section (mm. 21–40), and a recapitulation of the opening A-section (mm. 41–end). But a Schenkerian view of the piece would see instead an *Ursatz* divided into two parts (mm. 1–40 and mm. 41–end), with each of those parts itself divided into two (mm. 1–8, 9–40, 41–48, 49–end) with interruptions, just as in the Etude. The second of those four parts contains what many people would think of as the B-section of the piece. So, in both pieces, Schenker would take a binary view grounded in large-scale voice leading, rather than a ternary view grounded in the arrangement of the themes [Example 3.1].

Let's undertake a phrase-by-phrase perusal of the piece. The first phrase (mm. 1–8) consists of an octave ascent, D♯-D♯ (a foreground coupling that involves scale-degree $\hat{5}$),

EXAMPLE 3.1 *Chopin, Prelude in G♯ Minor, Op. 28, No. 12, annotated score.*

followed by a descent of a fourth, D♯-C♯-B-A♯. The second phrase of the Prelude, starting in measure 9, takes us toward E minor as a key, but that raises an important theoretical issue that I discussed in an article called "Analysis by Key" [Schachter 1999a]. The basic idea is that when music seems to move to another key, you shouldn't necessarily assume that the new, temporary tonic is the principal note, the one that participates in the long-range harmony and voice leading. In the Prelude, E minor (as a triad and as a key) has a very transient life and becomes part of something rather larger. I would prefer to say that our first step is not toward E minor per se, but is actually toward B major, which locally functions, or seems to function, as a dominant of E minor, but actually has more long-range implications than E minor does. So our first big step harmonically is toward B (m. 17), and let's take it step-by-step from there.

EXAMPLE 3.1 (*Continued*)

First we have B major (m. 17), then it changes to B minor (m. 20). And then in measure 21, we continue that B minor, but we move from it, descending by step from B to A (m. 24) to G (m. 28). G becomes the dominant of C (m. 29), which sounds like VI in E minor, and this is where our E minor seems to be, you might say, fulfilling the promise that we thought had been made previously. And, in an obvious sense, the music is now in E minor: we have C in the bass (m. 29) going to B with dominant-seventh harmony (last beat of m. 30 and m. 32). That takes us again to E minor in measures 31 and 33–34.

Working out the details of this passage is not altogether easy because it's not so very clear when we are at least temporarily fixed on E minor and when we seem to be more on the C-major chord with E minor felt as the mediant of C major. What happens next is very surprising and important. In measure 35, we have a dominant-seventh chord of E minor, with B in the bass. Let's disentangle the figurations in that measure. The main notes of the right hand are A (doubled) and F♯, and the G♯ and E♯ are neighbors. In the left hand, the

EXAMPLE 3.1 (*Continued*)

main notes are B, F♯, and D♯; the E♯ and C× are neighbors. Notice that the neighbors in the left hand occur right at the time when we have the main tones in the right hand, and vice versa, so we actually never get a pure B dominant seventh chord in the measure. As a result, it's very rich and fantastic sounding. And then notice what happens to the A♮ in measure 36. In order to move to A♯, it becomes G×. Chopin doesn't always notate these enharmonic changes—often he does, but not by any means always. But even if it were not notated as G×, even if he had kept it as A♮ the whole time, it would still have actually turned into a G×, because of where it's going, namely, to A♯ (m. 37). Harmonically, the dominant-seventh chord in E minor becomes the German augmented sixth chord leading to the dominant of D♯ minor (m. 37).

We can summarize what has happened, from the moment we arrived on that B-major chord in measure 17 until we get to the A♯ (in both bass and upper voice) in measure 37, by saying that the whole thing is a prolongation of B, and that the main agent of the prolongation of B is the neighbor note, C. In other words, although a lot of the passage can be thought of as being in E minor, the large-scale prolongation centers on B and its neighbor note, C.

Now that we have the large-scale bass in mind, let's focus on the upper and inner voices, starting back in measure 17. I would say that the top-voice tone of the B-major chord in measure 17 is B, although really one can only determine which is the top voice by looking in a larger context. If B is the main upper-voice tone, then the repeated G♯-F♯ happens in an inner voice. B then goes to A (m. 24) and G (m. 28) in parallel octaves with the bass.

Now let's think about the inner voices, starting with D♯ and F♯ in the B-major chord at measure 17 [Example 3.2]. We can think of them as moving up to E and G (within E minor), then to E♯-G♯ and F♯-A, as part of the V⁷ of E in measure 35. Then, as we just discussed, the A gets reinterpreted as G× when V⁷/E is reinterpreted as an augmented-sixth chord in D♯, and the inner voices push up to F×-A♯ within the large-scale dominant, D♯ major (m. 39).

EXAMPLE 3.2 *Chopin, Prelude in G♯ Minor, mm. 17–39, analytical sketch.*

Even at the last minute, when the inner voices reach F♯-A over the V⁷ chord, it could still go back to E minor. But instead, the A (reinterpreted as G×) pushes up to A♯. And it is an effect of incredible power when that dominant arrives with the A♯ on top.

Now let's back up and think about the large-scale top voice. We've already established that in the first four measures, we go up an octave from D♯ to D♯ (mm. 1–4) followed by a descending fourth-progression, D♯-C♯-B-A♯ (mm. 5–8). After that, we have a line that descends from D♯ through C♯ (m. 14) to B (m. 17). That's not so easy to hear, so let's look closely at what happens in measures 13–17. There's a top voice that goes D♯-F♯-E-D♯. You could read that as just an upward leap of a third, and then stepwise back down.

But there's another, better way. D♯-E is a basic motive in this piece, and with that in mind, we might think of the E as a neighbor note and the F♯ as a reaching-over of a chordal tone, and as a preparation for the neighbor note, E. While that is happening on top, right underneath it we have an alternation of B and C♯. The C♯, which I consider the main melodic note here, is a motion out of the inner voice on B. It's as though the main melodic line is a stream of water—it goes underground as a sort of spring for a bit, and then surfaces above ground again. That is, the *Urlinie* goes into the inner voice at that point, and then clearly shows itself on B starting at measure 17.

Let me digress for a moment to point out something that Schenker writes in *Free Composition* [Schenker 1979] about interruption from scale-degree 3̂ versus interruption from scale-degree 5̂. Schenker observes that when you have a line from 5̂ interrupted at 2̂ (5̂-4̂-3̂-2̂), it is possible to keep the scale-degree 5̂ as a retained tone above the descent to scale-degree 2̂, and that's because scale-degree 5̂ belongs both to tonic harmony (at the beginning of the descent) and to dominant harmony (at the end of the descent, when we get to 2̂ in the upper voice). On the other hand, when you have a line from 3̂ interrupted at 2̂ (3̂-2̂), you can't keep 3̂ above the dominant harmony at the end. That gives us a possible problem in interpreting an interrupted line from 5̂, because if we are keeping scale-degree 5̂ above the 5̂-4̂-3̂-2̂, we might say that scale-degree 5̂ is simply retained as the main structural tone, and that 5̂-4̂-3̂-2̂ is just a lower-level motion into the inner voice. The problem is that in that case there is no true interruption. Schenker himself doesn't really talk about that, but it can be an issue in analysis.

There's an analogous problem right in the passage we are discussing, even though interruption is not really involved. Starting in measure 13, the push of the line is downward: D♯-C♯-B. At the same time, even as the line descends, we've got D♯ hovering above it. I would in this case consider the retained D♯ a kind of *cover tone*, not really part of the basic voice leading.

Thinking about the larger harmonic trajectory, Chopin chooses a rather roundabout way of going to his big dominant climax. We're headed toward an A♯-chord as V of D♯ (m. 37), but we get there by way of A minor and C major, which are very distant regions. Let's see how the upper voice works to help clarify the larger motion. Starting in measure 21, we're on B in the upper voice—that's still the structural scale-degree 3̂ that we attained in measure 17. The line then descends B (m. 21), A (m. 24), G (m. 28)—we are saved from parallel octaves with the bass by interpolated dominants of the A and the G. The G is V of C and takes us to C in measure 29. At that point, the upper voice has two arpeggiations: G-C-E. At the end of each arpeggiation (last beat of mm. 30 and 32), the harmony changes underneath the E requiring it to go to D♯. The second time, a reaching-over takes the line up to F♯-G, creating a complete octave arpeggiation of C major: G-C-E-G.

Let's back up now and think of the upper line from the beginning of the piece. We begin with D♯ as the main melodic tone (*Kopfton*). D♯-C♯-B is the first stretch of the *Urlinie*. From B (mm. 17 and 21), there's a motion into the inner voice, B-A-G. From the inner-voice G, arpeggiations lift the line through G-C-E, and eventually to G (m. 33). That brings us within striking distance of the G𝄪 that we're going to need. G over an E-minor chord (m. 33) turns into G♯ (m. 35). The G♯ goes to an A (m. 36) that gets reinterpreted, as we have seen, as G𝄪, and then up to the A♯ (m. 37). That A♯ is scale-degree 2̂ of the *Urlinie*. Its arrival marks the end of the first half of the piece and the completion of 5̂-4̂-3̂-2̂, with the interruption of the *Urlinie* on scale-degree 2̂. If you take Schenker's later discussion of interruption, that would be the more structural of the two scale-degree 2̂s (compared to the second one right before the end of the piece). If we take his earlier formulation of interruption, as in his analysis of the "Revolutionary" Etude, this 2̂ would be actually a precursor to the main one, which would come at the end.

Now let's talk a bit about register, and about Schenker's concept of *obligatory regis-ter* (*obligate Lage*). That is the idea that the top voice and the bass have a kind of home register that they mostly occupy, but from which they depart (for a sense of variety) in order then to come back to. Compared to other pieces by Chopin, the G♯-minor Prelude moves within a rather narrow *ambitus*, especially the top voice. That's partly a result of those devilish repeated notes in the right-hand part that require you to stay regis-trally close to where you were. In that context, this motion up to the high A♯ (m. 37) is really something very spectacular. The upper voice starts on D♯¹ (m. 1) and moves up an octave to D♯² (m. 5) and then descends D♯-C♯-B-A♯ in that register. Then we start over again on the low D♯ (m. 9). I think you would agree that the upper D♯ seems to be the *obligate Lage*, with the first D♯ preparatory to it. Certainly, in playing it, one phrases toward that high D♯. Again, we go up the octave to D♯², followed by C♯ (m. 14) and B (m. 17) in the same register. So the *Urlinie* has descended 5̂-4̂-3̂ within the same register. But the *Urlinie*'s 2̂ (A♯) goes into a higher octave. Schenker's term for such a thing is *Höherlegung*, which we could translate as "placing higher." In English, it's usually called an upward transfer of register.

Most of what we've been talking about can be seen in my own graph of the piece [Example 3.3]. I did not have as much space at my disposal as Schenker did in *Five Graphic Analyses*, so I did not include the *Ursatz*; rather, I start with the first level of mid-dleground (at the upper left of the first page of the graph). Let's use the graph as the basis for talking about the second half of the piece, and especially about the cadential phrase where the *Urlinie* descends. If you thought of the piece as in ternary form, what I'm call-ing the second half of the piece would be the return of the A-section. Starting in measure 41, the upper voice goes up an octave and then down a fourth, just as in the opening. Then, starting in measure 49, it goes again up an octave arriving at the end of measure 52. We reach D♯ in our top voice, but only as the last eighth-note—the high D♯ does not have any complete harmonic support. The harmony changes in measure 53 to IV⁷, and Chopin obviously wants the chordal seventh in the tenor brought out—notice the accent sign over the left-hand part (which probably applies to the bass also). The change of harmony turns the D♯ into a suspension, requiring a resolution to C♯. And I think this C♯ is scale-degree 4̂ of the *Urlinie*. Now look what happens in the bass at this point (mm. 53–57). It goes C♯-D♯, then again C♯-D♯, and finally to E (m. 57). That's something Arthur Komar might have called a "bifurcation," that is, that something appears twice, but with only one meaning [Komar 1968]. If I eliminate the bifurcation, it's simply C♯-D♯-E, and the alto in the same measures goes E-D♯-C♯, creating a voice exchange. A voice exchange like this, especially with a passing ⁶₄ in the middle (m. 56), is a common way of prolonging a seventh chord.

In this passage, each of the measures starts with an appoggiatura or suspension: D♯-C♯ in measures 53 and 55 and C♯-B in measures 54 and 56. Then, in measure 57, a question arises, where we have B-A♯-A♯-B repeated in a kind of hemiola rhythm. Do we want to think of the B at the beginning as resolving to A♯ (as in the appoggiatura resolutions in the previous measures), or would it be better to think of the B as dominating for four measures, and not resolving to A♯ until measure 61? I find it more satisfying musically to hear the resolution to A♯ as coming in measure 61. It's a bit like the opening of Mozart's G-minor Symphony. Schenker's analysis of the piece shows the repeated E♭-Ds of the opening melody as a single large E♭-D, which he imagines as being realized through those repetitions. The *Urlinie* closes on scale-degree 1̂ (G♯) in measure 65, and then we have the coda.

I want to call your attention to a detail in my second-level graph, namely, my treatment of the G-major arrival in measure 28. I didn't actually write 5-6 over the B in the bass, but you can tell by my slur from B to G♯ in the bass that I interpret the G major as actually emanating from a

EXAMPLE 3.3 *Chopin, Prelude in G♯ Minor, complete analytical graph.*

EXAMPLE 3.3 (*Continued*)

chromaticized 5-to-6 motion: B-D♯-F♯ becomes B-D♮-G♮. F♯ moves to G♮ (that's the 5-6) and D♯ moves to D♮ at the same time (that's the chromaticized part). That passing movement establishes the connection between the B and G chords, with the B elaborated by the G [Example 3.4].

EXAMPLE 3.4 *Chopin, Prelude in G♯ Minor, mm. 21–28, harmonic reduction.*

I just want to mention two small details about the graph, and then we'll push on. First, you'll see several asterisks. When I did this graph, I was kind of obsessed with the G𝄪 of the augmented-sixth chord (m. 36), so every time there was a prominent G𝄪 or A♮, I made an asterisk. Second, you'll notice that I made heavy bar lines every four measures—these show the hypermeasures. That's all I'm going to say about this graph and about this piece. It's a wonderful piece, I think—a bit of a devil's dance.

Now I'd like to return to the "Revolutionary" Etude and to Schenker's analysis of it. Let's start in measure 41, where we reach the dividing dominant [Example 3.5]. The right-hand part here is not exactly the same as in the beginning, and I would like to try to find a reason for the changes. In the beginning, the highest voice arpeggiates B (m. 1), D (m. 3), F (m. 5), and Schenker shows that as the unfolding of a diminished fifth. Starting in measure 41, however, in the analogous spots we have D (m. 41), F (m. 43), and G (m. 45). Chopin could easily have written the preceding measure (m. 40) in such a way as to come out on B, and then he could have had B-D-F just as he had in the beginning. Why didn't he do that? One answer involves looking back to measure 37, to the beginning of that big melody in F minor. I think there is a very palpable connection between the high, *forte* A♭ on the downbeat of measure 37 and the high, *fortissimo* G on the downbeat of measure 45. That neighbor-note relationship, A♭-G (6̂-5̂ in C minor) spans across the return of the opening music and creates a very beautiful effect. Chopin could not have gotten that effect with a literal repeat of the opening music.

The persistent use in this piece of chromatic variants of scale-degree 6̂ as upper neighbors to 5̂ (G-A♭-G and G-A♮-G) has an almost programmatic quality. The piece is without question a tragic piece, and these neighbor notes have something to do with that. G-A♭-G is a well-known kind of lament figure, and the occasional inflection to A♮ seems to be an attempt to rise above that, but the moves take you always back to the same place, back to A♭-G.

I think that may be one reason the piece got the title of "Revolutionary." I don't think there's the slightest evidence for its having to do with the Revolution of 1830. The story one hears is that Chopin was devastated by the news from Warsaw, because the Russians crushed with great severity and brutality the attempts of the Polish people to revolt and to get their country back. Chopin supposedly lost—and probably did lose—a number of schoolmates. And the story is that he then sat down in a frenzy and wrote this Etude. That story is probably untrue, but you can understand how the programmatic quality of the music might have given rise to it. The introductory measures would seem to be a call to action, requiring a response of some kind. The B-D-F arpeggiation does resolve into the melody (C-D-E♭), but really every attempt of the tonic to rise is destined to fail.

EXAMPLE 3.5 *Chopin, "Revolutionary" Etude, mm. 1–6, 36–46, and 75–77, annotated score.*

EXAMPLE 3.5 (*Continued*)

Look, for example, at measure 75, which is where we get scale-degree $\hat{2}$ of the *Urlinie*. It occurs within *smorzando*, and the final scale-degree $\hat{1}$ (m. 77) is marked *sotto voce*. There is nothing life-affirming in that. Now compare the melody in measure 75 (C-B-D) to the melodic line that leads into the recapitulation of the opening music (mm. 40–41): C-B-C-D. These are basically the same melodic idea and help to relate the two big structural dominants in the piece. The first of those structural dominants (m. 41) is created by interruption, and sounds defiant and energetic. The second one (m. 75), which supports scale-degree $\hat{2}$ of the *Urlinie*, is evocative of say, *Coriolan* by Beethoven, or the funeral march from the *Eroica*. And when the final scale-degree $\hat{1}$ arrives (m. 77), it sounds very definitely as if somebody is dying. In the final four measures, however, there is a sense that the revolutionary fervor has returned, and that these dead shall not have died in vain. Some kind of program of this sort would seem to me not to do too terrible an injustice to the effect of this piece, and may also be the reason why the title "Revolutionary" has stuck. With the G♯-minor Prelude, I don't think we could make a program that makes much sense, but the Etude seems almost to call for one.

Let's turn now to the E-major Prelude [Example 3.6].

EXAMPLE 3.6 *Chopin, Prelude in E major, Op. 28, No. 9, annotated score.*

Some people analyze this piece with an *Urlinie* that rises a fourth: B-C♯-D♯-E. I think, however, that it is quite possible to hear instead a very subtle and wonderful descending *Urlinie*, but to do so one has to be quite un-literal in one's use of the theory.

The E-major Prelude is only twelve measures long. It's in three phrases of four measures each, and each of the three phrases has in the top voice a motion up a fourth from B to E. Let's take a preliminary look at the top voice, stealing a glance every so often in direction of the bass. In the first phrase (mm. 1–4), the upper voice goes B-C♯-D♯-E, arriving in measure 3, and then back down to B. The second phrase (mm. 5–8) is the most complex and difficult part of the piece from the point of view of harmony. Melodically, it rises from B through C and D arriving on E in measure 6 and staying there for four beats. Then it goes beyond E, up to F, G, and A♭ (m. 8), before descending again to B. In the third phrase (mm. 9–12), the melody ascends B-C-D-D♯-E. So the first phrase goes from B to E, the second phrase also goes from B to E and then beyond it up to G♯, and the last phrase goes from B to E again.

Let's try to make some more detailed sense out of this, starting with the first phrase. Our first move is to the A-major chord at the end of measure 1. I think of that as the upper third to the F♯-minor harmony on the next beat. Instead of going directly from I to II, Chopin inserts the A-major chord possibly to break up the looming parallel fifths and octaves. If you think of the bass motion as going from E to F♯, there's a 5-6 motion above the E, and then 5 again over the F♯. The same sort of thing happens sequentially in the last phrase, by the way, moving from E to F in the bass with 5-6-5 above (mm. 9–10) and then from F to G in the bass again with 5-6-5 above (mm. 10–11). So now we've gotten ourselves from I to II (first beat of m. 2), and we immediately get another 5-6 above the F♯. Then, when we get to V (third beat of m. 2) we get yet another 5-6 motion (F♯-G in the tenor).

On the downbeat of measure 3, the upper voice reaches its first climactic point, a kind of turning point, on E. The harmony at that point is a seventh chord on VI, with C♯ in the bass, but I think its contrapuntal function is of more immediate interest. You can think of it as an upper neighbor to the B on the third beat of measure 3, after which the bass rises B-C♯-D♯-E—that's an imitation of the rising fourth in the melody in measures 1–3. That is to say, from the low B, I think that contrapuntally conceived line is actually more to the point than the harmonic implications (which however, are certainly also there).

With regard to counterpoint in Chopin's music, you might be interested in the conversation that Chopin had not long before his death with the painter Eugène Delacroix. Delacroix was one of a handful of quite intimate friends of Chopin's. In his diary, he mentions how he had picked Chopin up in a carriage, and they had ridden out beyond the Arc de Triomphe and gone to a café. Chopin then began to speak about music. What makes logic in music, Chopin said, is counterpoint, getting notes to sound against each other. He said the problem with the way they teach nowadays is that they teach the chords before they teach the movement of voices that creates the chords. That's the problem, he said, with Berlioz. He applies the chords as a kind of veneer and fills in the gaps the best way he can. Chopin then said that you can get a sense of pure logic in music with fugue and he cited not Bach—though we know that he worshiped Bach—but Mozart. He said, in every one of Mozart's pieces, you feel the counterpoint. The fact that Chopin had this idea about counterpoint as being so foundational in music is, I think, very significant.

Returning to the first phrase, the problem in interpreting its bass line is that we have a plethora of B's. The first one in measure 1 is no big problem—it's part of the simple prolongational I-V-I of the opening tonic. The B on the second half of measure 2, however, can be confusing. It may be tempting to read it as a goal, and then to read the C♯ on the first beat of measure 3 as a part of a complete neighbor figure, going back to B on the third beat of measure 3. It would be much better, however, to regard the C♯ as the main thing, and B as a way of getting to C♯, which is the support for E, the climactic note in the top voice. The true goal B is the one on the third beat of measure 3. The B in measure 2 was on the way to C♯ in measure 3, which acts as a neighbor to the goal B in measure 3. Once we get to the B in measure 3, the bass ascends a fourth to E, in imitation of the upper voice, as I noted earlier. Within that ascent, there's a voice exchange with the upper voice, which is now descending: B-C♯-D♯ in the bass against D♯-C♯-B in the upper voice [Example 3.7].

EXAMPLE 3.7 *Chopin, Prelude in E major, mm. 1–4, analytical sketch.*

The second phrase of this Prelude (mm. 5–8) is the most fascinating one of all. Those of you who have studied harmony from Edward Aldwell's and my book [Aldwell and Schachter 1978] might remember that we give a long and rather elaborate explanation of this passage, which we describe in terms of large-scale chromatic motion based on voice exchanges and contrary motion. The first move we make is from E major (downbeat of m. 5) to C major (downbeat of m. 6) by way of G (third beat of m. 5—an applied dominant to the C-major chord). We've moved from I to VI, but the VI chord has a lowered sixth above the bass (C♮ instead of the diatonic C♯) and that requires that the third above the bass also be lowered (G♮ instead of the diatonic G♯). So it's a chromaticized 5-6 motion that gets us from E major to C major.

That's the point at which the voice exchanges begin—it's the C-major chord that sets things off, and the voice exchanges extend a series of closely related chords. In measure 6, we have a voice exchange between bass and top voice, a very normal kind of sixth-to-tenth voice exchange. We start with a C major ⁶₃ chord and we end up with a root position C chord, but now with the seventh added. The chord in the middle of that voice exchange (m. 6, second beat) is a passing ⁶₄ chord, and it brings in the B♭ that becomes the seventh of the C dominant-seventh chord on the subsequent beat. Next, on beat 4 of measure 6, the C seventh chord changes position: it's a strange voice exchange in which the bass C moves up to the alto and the alto B♭ moves down to the bass, on the last thirty-second note of the measure. It's not the usual sixth-to-tenth exchange, but in this case actually a seventh-to-second exchange.

The next chord, that striking A-major chord on the downbeat of measure 7, is a passing chord within the next voice exchange. The first voice exchange (first half of m. 6) brought in a chromatic note, B♭, which altered the harmony from a ⁶₃ chord to a seventh chord; the second voice exchange (second half of m. 6) stayed within that seventh chord; this third voice exchange brings in a C♯ and takes us from a dominant-seventh-type chord to a diminished-seventh chord (beat 2 of m. 7). Then there's one final voice exchange in which that diminished-seventh chord changes position: the G in the bass moves to the upper voice and the E in the upper voice moves to the bass. Within that final exchange we get another passing ⁶₄, which respells C♯ as D♭—we're looking ahead to the move to A♭ major in the next measure. As the E moves into the bass, it gets respelled as F♭, and that chord moves to the big cadential ⁶₄ in A♭ major on the first beat of measure 8.

Now let's briefly consider two passages from works by other composers that do different but related things. The first passage is from Beethoven's Second Symphony [Example 3.8].

Schenker cites this passage in *Free Composition*. We start on a dominant-seventh chord—actually it's our D-major tonic chord with an added C♮ (m. 326). Then the bass moves to D♯ (m. 327), which we hear as just a chromatic passing tone, but it actually alters the harmony

EXAMPLE 3.8 *Beethoven, Symphony No. 2, first movement, mm. 326–340, harmonic reduction.*

from dominant seventh to diminished seventh. Next comes a $^6_4$ chord (m. 328). The distinguishing feature of this, and of passages similar to it, is that the music leaps into the passing $^6_4$ chords in such a way—and also in such a rhythmic position—that we hear them much more readily at first as *cadential* $^6_4$ chords. In reality, the $^6_4$ chords are passing within the seventh chords, but it's the $^6_4$ chords that get the emphasis. If Beethoven had had the upward leaps (which are Schenkerian reachings-over) not on the $^6_4$ chords, but on the seventh chords, then the passing nature of the $^6_4$ chords would be obvious. But because the $^6_4$ chords are given so much emphasis, they threaten to disrupt the feeling of tonality. In fact, they seem to suggest new tonics of a very irrational sort. We might think we're in C minor (first beat of m. 330), E♭ minor (first beat of m. 332), and F♯ minor (first beat of m. 334), until things become clear when we get to the end of the passage. It's a magnificent passage!

There's maybe an even greater related passage in Schubert's song, "Der Wegweiser" (from *Winterreise*). The singer is a very unhappy man, trudging through a wintry landscape after he has been jilted by his girlfriend, who then marries somebody else. At first he sings, "Why do I avoid the roads where the other travelers go, and look for hidden passages through snowy mountain heights? I haven't committed any crime that I should shun people, but I feel this crazy longing which forces me into the wilderness." And then he says: "Signposts stand along the road, pointing to cities, and I travel beyond them, looking for peace, but never finding it. There's a road I have to go on, from which no traveler has ever returned." And that's the passage I want to talk about, the one that deals with a journey without return [Example 3.9].

EXAMPLE 3.9 *Schubert, "Der Wegweiser" (from* Winterreise*), mm. 55–67, annotated score.*

We have diminished-seventh chords connected with voice exchanges and with passing $^6_4$ chords in the middle. But the $^6_4$ chords get so much emphasis they come to sound almost like cadential $^6_4$ chords rather than passing $^6_4$ chords and we get the terrible feeling in this G-minor passage that we're going into B♭ minor (m. 61), C♯ minor (m. 63), and all sorts of strange places. There are other similar passages one could cite, including a wonderful one in the development section of Mozart's great G-major Piano Concerto, K. 453, first movement—it's one of the earliest that I know.

Now back to the Chopin and to its last phrase, which is actually the simplest of the three. The basic idea is triads moving parallel: E major (m. 9), F major (m. 10), and G minor (m. 11). But the triads on F and G are preceded by their upper thirds. The A-minor chord at the end of measure 9 is the upper third of F major, and breaks up the parallel fifths and octaves we would get in moving directly from E major to F major. From F major, we go to B♭, which is the upper third of G minor (m. 11). Then G minor turns into G major, and then we're done.

Now let's talk finally about the upper voice of this fantastic piece. I said before that some people want to hear this piece in relation to an ascending *Urlinie*: B-C♯-D♯-E. But I think it makes better sense to think of it as two arpeggiations, first from B to E (in the first phrase) and then from B to E and beyond it to G♯ in the second phrase. That climactic G♯ (spelled as A♭ in m. 8) is scale-degree $\hat{3}$ of the *Urlinie*. From there, I can imagine two alternative ways of describing the descent of the *Urlinie*, which differ in where they place the main dominant, and consequently also the melodic scale-degree $\hat{2}$ [Example 3.10].

EXAMPLE 3.10 *Chopin, Prelude in E major, two analytical sketches of the upper voice.*

Scale-degree $\hat{2}$ is not in the piece; in either reading it has to be supplied by the imagination of the listener. In the first reading, which is the one I prefer, the implied scale-degree $\hat{2}$ comes on the last beat of measure 8, effectively covering the melodic motion out of the inner voice (B-C-D-D♯-E) that takes place in the third phrase. In the second reading, the arrival of $\hat{2}$ is deferred until the last beat of the next-to-last measure. For myself, I prefer to have the scale-degree $\hat{2}$ near that climactic $^6_4$ chord, and not enmeshed in the middle, or near the end, of a sequence (as in mm. 9–11). But I don't say the other reading is wrong; it's definitely a possibility. And both of them are preferable to thinking that the idea of the piece

EXAMPLE 3.11 *Chopin, Prelude in E major, complete analytical graph.*

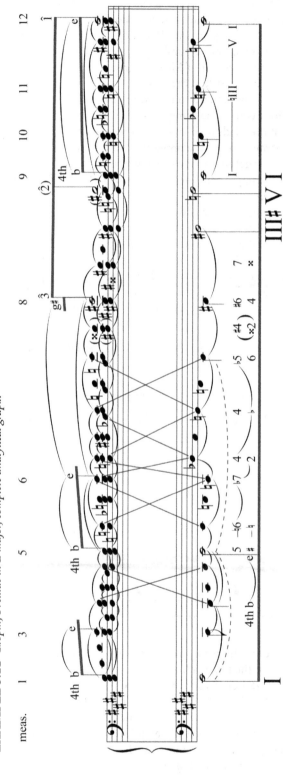

is an ascending line, B-C♯-D♯-E. You can see many of the things we have been talking about in my graph of the piece [Example 3.11].

Now I want to look with you at Chopin's autograph score [Example 3.12] in the hope of answering a basic question about performing this piece: how do you handle the dotted eighth- and sixteenth-note figure in the melody, which is so often heard against triplets in inner voices?

The first thing you might notice is the cross-out right before the time signature on the first line. The published time signature is C (common time), and I suspect that the time signature he crossed out was 12/8. If so, that might bear on this question of dotted eighths and sixteenths versus triplets. Now, you'll notice that most of the time, starting right in the first measure, if we have the dotted eighth- and sixteenth-notes, particularly if we have it in the right-hand part together with the triplets, Chopin not only aligns the sixteenth-note with the last triplet note, but also very often has a vertical line connecting them. In other words, Chopin apparently expects that the notated dotted eighth notes will have the duration of two triplet notes, and that the sixteenth-notes will occur simultaneously with the third triplet note.

This alignment of dotted eighths and sixteenths with triplets goes back into the eighteenth century, when it was very common to "tripletize" dotted figures when sounded against triplets. That practice wasn't universal, because there were no universal things in performance in those days. For example, there was a time when C. P. E. Bach and J. J. Quantz were both working at the court of Frederick the Great. C. P. E. Bach tells you unequivocally that if you have a dotted figure against a triplet, you should make the sixteenth-note coincide with the third triplet note [C.P.E. Bach 1948]. He thought it was very sloppy and ugly not to do that. On the other hand, Quantz says that in order not to confuse the listener and mislead him into thinking that you were playing triplets, when you have a dotted figure, you should make the short note as short as possible [Quantz 2001]. So here you have two people in exactly the same musical milieu, both of them great musicians, with diametrically opposed views.

There's one additional interesting wrinkle. In the E-major Prelude, Chopin writes not only dotted eighth- and sixteenth-notes, but also double-dotted eighth- and thirty-second-notes. Look, for example, at the first measure in the last system of the autograph. On the second beat of that measure, it seems obvious that Chopin originally wrote his usual tripletized dotted eighth and sixteenth. Then, he scratched out the sixteenth-note and moved the thirty-second-note to the right, where it is no longer aligned with the triplet. It seems very clear that he is distinguishing between the sixteenth-notes, which are aligned with the third triplet, and thirty-second notes, which come after the third triplet. At the same time, things are not totally consistent in this piece. Look, for example, at the *fortissimo* A♭ $^6_4$ chord—it's the first beat of the first measure on the third line of the autograph. The melody there is written in straight eighth-notes, and you can see that Chopin has actually crossed out the dot after the high A♭. So he's written duplets (which, by the way, were also sometimes played in unison with triplets—people didn't always maintain a strict, mathematically accurate two-against-three).

There's another document that bears on this discussion, namely, a copy of the Preludes in Jane Stirling's collection. Jane Stirling, a Scottish woman, was a piano pupil of Chopin's—not a very gifted one, I'm afraid, but very rich and very generous with Chopin. She studied this piece with Chopin and was using the first French edition which is written, like all the published editions, with the sixteenth-note printed after the third triplet.

EXAMPLE 3.12 Chopin, Prelude in E major, the composer's autograph manuscript.

EXAMPLE 3.13 *Chopin, Variation on the March from* I Puritani *by Bellini, composed for the* "Hexameron."

EXAMPLE 3.13 (*Continued*)

In Stirling's copy, you can see that Chopin once took a pencil and wrote a diagonal line between the third triplet and the sixteenth-note, as if to say "play those together."

Here's a relevant performance idea that I got from Ernst Oster for situations like this. He felt that something is missing if one simply plays the dotted eighth and sixteenth like a triplet, and what's missing is a sort of pointedness in the rhythm. Oster's idea was to apply a certain *rubato*, namely, to hold the first note of the triplet a little bit longer, but not obtrusively so. That leaves you with a little less time at the end of the beat, and so you have to rush a bit to compensate. That makes the rhythm more pointed.

Now I'd like to show you a curiosity that bears on this Prelude. The *Hexameron* was a collection of six pieces compiled by Liszt, all of them variations on a march from Bellini's opera *I Puritani*. There were six different composers involved: Liszt himself, Chopin, Czerny, Pixis (whoever he was), Herz, and Thalberg. This odd piece was written around the same time that Chopin was writing some of the Preludes, in the winter of 1837/38. Chopin's piece bears a striking resemblance to our Prelude No. 9 [Example 3.13].

Both pieces are in E major, marked *Largo*, use triplets in the accompanying figure and dotted eighths and sixteenths in the melody. You even get the occasional double-dotted eighth- and thirty-second-note. And notice that when the music gets to its loudest point (m. 10) we're in G♯ major, obviously related to the climactic A♭ major of the Prelude. Even the contour of the melody, which is by Bellini, bears some resemblance to Chopin's melody—notice that the Bellini starts out by arpeggiating B-E-G♯, a motion that I see as central to the structure of the Prelude. If there is some intertextuality between these two pieces, it flows from the *Hexameron* variation, which sticks close to Bellini's melody and was written first, toward the Prelude. This is not terribly important, but it does strike me as interesting and curious.

Schubert, Sonata in B♭ major, Scherzo

We'll work on the Scherzo of Schubert's B♭ Sonata. If time permits, we'll take a close look at another work by Schubert, the song "Frühlingstraum" from Winterreise.

I WANT TO START BY DRAWING YOUR ATTENTION TO SOME OF THE PECULIAR and fascinating aspects of the Schubert Scherzo, particularly from the point of view of its harmonic structure [Example 4.1]. The first thing you might notice is that the first reprise modulates to the subdominant (E♭ major in the key of B♭ major). That's not only unusual, in the obvious sense that composers don't do it very often, but also possibly problematic, especially when it happens early in a piece. There's the danger of "de-tonicizing the tonic," you might say, and making it sound like V of IV. That wouldn't be nearly as problematic in a minor key, because we usually don't think of a minor chord (like IV⁷) as a potential dominant. But it's also true that even in minor it's not that usual to modulate to the subdominant early in a piece (although the fourth Ballade of Chopin does exactly that). But in the Schubert Scherzo, the modulation from I to IV happens within the first sixteen measures, and takes place very rapidly near the end of the phrase—that's very unusual.

And it's not only the harmonic move that is unusual. Look at the upper voice at the end of the first reprise, right when we get the tonicization of E♭ (mm. 13–16). Basically you have a descending fifth-progression, B♭-A-G-F-E♭. Within that fifth-progression, the A♮ is extremely weird—any harmony teacher would put a huge red mark on it, because it so contradicts the idea of stabilizing the new key of E♭ major. That "Lydian" A♮ is a unique case, I think, and it throws into question the legitimacy of the tonicization of E♭.

Instead of tonicizing E♭ at the end of the first reprise, Schubert could have just stayed in the tonic, B♭. Or, even more commonly, the first reprise could have led to the dominant (F) instead of the subdominant (E♭). The diminished-seventh chord in measure 13 could have been expected to resolve to a G-minor chord as II in F, followed by V-I in F major [Example 4.2]. Does my recomposed ending of the first reprise resonate with any other part of the piece? Yes, it does. Measures 81–84 are an exact transposition of my recomposition of measures 13–16. In other words, the resolution of the diminished-seventh chord in measure 13 to E♭ instead of G minor (as II of F major) takes us somewhere we didn't expect to go. The expected (but rejected) turn to the dominant in measures 13–16 becomes the very music that ends the piece on the tonic in measures 81–84.

EXAMPLE 4.1 *Schubert, Sonata in B♭ major, Op. Post, D. 960, third movement (Scherzo), annotated score.*

Schenker, in his counterpoint book, has a very interesting discussion of how in working out species counterpoint exercises one wants to consider the various possible moves from any given point and evaluate them in relation to other moves that might be possible but that are not taken [Schenker 1987]. And he goes on to say that the same thing happens in listening to a composition—you evaluate what the composer did in relation to the range of possibilities and expectations. That's not the kind of insight that one usually associates with Schenker, who is usually thought of as understanding music only retrospectively, on the basis of decisions that have already been made. After all, the very presence of something in an analytical graph seems to exclude the possibility of other interpretations. But here Schenker advocates thinking about the turns that aren't taken.

This Scherzo is one of those pieces where I think something deliberately "incorrect"—not "incorrect" in the sense of violating some pedantic rule, but rather in terms of the language the composer is setting up—happens at the beginning, and the rest of

EXAMPLE 4.1 (*Continued*)

EXAMPLE 4.2 *Schubert, Scherzo, mm. 13–16, hypothetical recomposition.*

the piece is a kind of attempt, a very successful attempt I think, to "correct" the mistake, to get off the wrong road and get onto the right road and come to some kind of conclusion.

There are other pieces that go in this way, including Mozart's C-minor Fantasy, which Oswald Jonas discussed in a published article on the subject of improvisation [Jonas 1967].

EXAMPLE 4.3 *Mozart, Fantasy in C minor, K. 475, mm. 1–10, annotated score.*

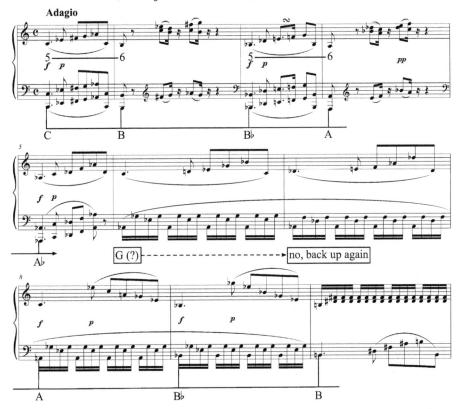

Jonas points out that the first gesture we have is from C in the bass, supporting a C-minor chord, to B, supporting an inverted-dominant chord [Example 4.3]. That's an example of what is called the "descending 5-6 technique." Then the same thing is repeated a step lower, in sequence: B♭ in the bass supporting B♭ minor to A in the bass supporting a major triad in first inversion. Now, when you start a bass line C-B-B♭-A you very much expect it to continue A♭-G, and to reach a dominant on that G. But if the sequence were to continue, we would end up not on the dominant of C minor but on an E♭-major chord with G in the bass. So when it gets to A♭ in the bass, the music seems to realize that it's done something wrong. It stops the sequential motion and goes back up again, as far as B, trying to get back to where it wants to go. It takes the remainder of the piece for it to find its way onto the proper path. Like the Schubert Scherzo, that would be a situation where the idea that we start with seems not to be a possible one—it seems like a wrong turn—and the music has to correct itself. We'll see another example of the same thing when we discuss the "Malinconia," the very chromatic introduction to the last movement of Beethoven's Quartet Op. 18, No. 6. That is another example of a composition correcting itself after it makes an apparent mistake.

Another strange moment in the Schubert Scherzo is the return of the opening music in measures 67–69, and I'll tell you a slightly autobiographical story as a way of getting into it. Many years ago, I had a student at Mannes who later went on to become a well-known composer. She was quite a good pianist as a young person, and she was offered the chance to be one of the people that the Metropolitan Museum sponsored in what was at that time a Young Artists series. Perhaps two weeks before her concert, she came to see me and play through her program. One of the things that troubled her in preparing the program was the reprise of this Scherzo. She correctly felt that it was impossibly wrong to emphasize the return of the opening melody by playing a big accent on the Bb in measure 69. Of course she would never have done anything that crude because, as she was aware, Schubert seemed to take such pains to integrate that moment of repetition into a larger unity. It would be an act almost of treason for a performer to do something like that. But she also felt that ignoring the return of the opening melody was not satisfactory either: partly because it was so unusual, she felt that something magical should happen right at that moment, but she didn't know what it should be. I actually didn't give her much help at the time, but her question started me thinking about the movement, and to think about it as a whole. And I realize that her trouble had to do not with just this particular spot in the movement but with the way the entire movement was put together.

The return of the opening music is approached in a very strange way. First we have A major (m. 56), seemingly far from our tonic key, Bb major. Then, starting in measure 61, we have what seems to be an incomplete dominant $\frac{4}{3}$ in A major. By moving the E up to F♯ (m. 64) we get a diminished triad in root position (very unusual), and it lasts for three measures. In measure 67, the *tremolando* accompaniment figure, which we had at the beginning and quite a way into the piece, returns. Then, in measure 68, the tonic chord comes back, but not yet the theme. Then finally the theme itself returns in measure 69. So, one by one we have all of these signposts telling us that this is going to be the recap, and exactly where in the process we want to label it isn't that important. I would myself label it harmonically in measure 68 and melodically in measure 69.

To understand this recap, and to get back to my student's question about how to think of it and play it, I think you need to take into account the large-scale shape of the piece. It may surprise you to learn that I take much of the movement as a rising line from Bb at the beginning of the piece up to D, right here at the recap. In other words, we have an unusually long *Anstieg*, or initial ascent. I hear the first eight measures as enclosed within the Bb in measure 1 and the higher Bb at measure 8. And Bb comes in again at measure 14 as we start the composing out of the Eb chord, with that descending fifth-progression that moves down to Eb as a motion into the inner voice (m. 16). The Bb is then carried over into the upper part immediately after the double bar (m. 17). The Bb then goes up to C in measure 19. This C wends its way down into the inner voice, as part of the melody in the tenor (mm. 21–25). To represent this graphically, especially if you're doing a very reduced graph, there is no harm in changing the register and putting a tenor line like this in a higher register to show the larger continuities. Otherwise you can leave the line in its actual register and use a diagonal line or an arrow to show that the upper voice is going into the low register. Or you could use longer upward stems to show that an inner voice is really the main melody.

Anyway, our upper voice has so far moved from Bb to C. In measure 25, the previous music is transposed down a fifth, and our Bb-C is imitated by Eb-F, first in the upper voice and then in the tenor—that gets us to measure 33. The Ab there leads us up to Db in measure 38, and this Db represents the next step in the upper voice: from Bb, to C, and now to D♭. Locally, we get to the D♭ through arpeggiation: F (mm. 27–33), through A♭ (mm. 35–37), and up to D♭ in measure 38. So we get out of that lower region and the inner voice area by arpeggiating the D♭ chord from the F, which is essentially, in the larger structure, an inner-voice tone. And it's the D♭, of course, that has a long-range connection with the C back in measure 19. Then we get another arpeggiation from F (m. 41 and m. 44) through A♭ (m. 47) up again to D♭ (m. 50), except that now the D♭ is written as a C♯.

So, if we think of it from the beginning, we've gone from B♭ in the first 16 measures to C in measure 19 to D♭ in measure 38 and again to D♭, spelled as C♯, in measure 50. The C♯ continues in measures 56 and then finally to D in measure 60. The D is retained in the upper voice until measure 68: that's where the B♭-major chord comes in and that's where I would place the scale-degree 3̂ of the fundamental line. So from measure 1 in this piece until measure 68, is an *Anstieg* or initial ascent: 1̂-2̂-3̂ or 1̂-2̂-♯2̂ (or ♭3̂)-3̂. You can see this, and a lot of other things, in my sketch of the piece [Example 4.4].

People sometimes find long-range ascents like this difficult to accept, because they've all been taught to look for 5̂ or 3̂ at the beginning of the piece. But, in fact, Schubert very often has these large-scale rising motions (arpeggiations or linear progressions) leading to a very high register, and very often to a structural note of some sort (but by no means always). It may be related to his being, at heart, a song composer, even in some of his instrumental music, even in as "instrumental" a piece as this. (Let's not forget that in vocal music high notes are very important, and play a role that is quite different from instrumental music—unless it's by a composer like Chopin, who writes so vocally for the piano, and who also is rather like Schubert in his love for these ascending motions.)

Anyway, this broader perspective about the piece led to my belated solution, two years after my student's recital, to the problem she posed about how to play the return of the opening melody in measure 69. My idea was to go into the downbeat of that measure as though it is not anything particularly important. Then, having played the downbeat, one realizes, "Oh my God, I'm home already!" So I think taking a little time after that B♭ on the first beat and then speeding up right after it leading into the next measure will create the desired effect.

The motivic aspect of this piece is also quite extraordinary. From the point of view of rhythm there are only two motives, represented by the first two measures in the melody: one motive has three quarter-notes and the other is one quarter- and four eighth-notes. They both go through all sorts of permutations and permutations of permutations, but let's mostly follow the first motive [Example 4.5].

It comes sometimes as three repeated notes (as in m. 4) and sometimes as a slurred octave leap, either ascending (as in m. 5) or descending (as in m. 6). You can see a further permutation of it in measure 8, with the return of the neighbor-note figure. The accompaniment pattern starting in measure 33 is actually derived from measure 1, which first becomes three repeated notes (m. 4) and then the octave leaps upward and downward (mm. 5-6). In measure 33, we have a kind of "upside-down waltz," in that the left hand, instead of the usual down-up-up goes up-down-down. It's definitely done with humorous effect. As we approach the recap, the upside-down waltz continues, but with smaller intervals, eventually becoming the tremolo figure that presages the return of the opening melody. So the arrival of the big D♮ in measure 68 is actually related to this extraordinary kind of economy in the use of the rhythmic motives in the piece.

There's a sort of tension between the form of the piece, which is basically a ternary A-B-A, and the large-scale voice leading I've shown. If Schubert had studied with Schenker,

EXAMPLE 4.4 *Schubert, Scherzo, analytical graph.*

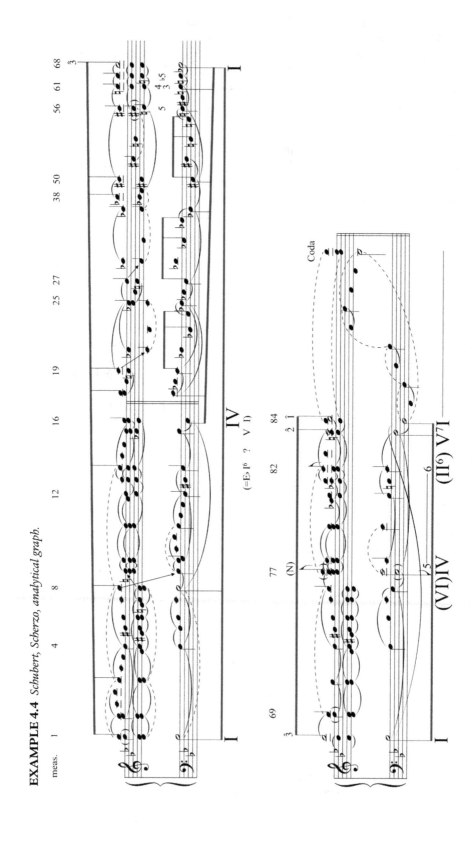

EXAMPLE 4.5 *Schubert, Scherzo, a rhythmic motive.*

he might have said to Schenker, "I want to do something very unusual in the Scherzo of this sonata. What I want to do is to have an *Anstieg* in the top voice, one that takes most of the movement to complete, but at the same time I want to have an A-B-A form." The problem this poses is that, by the very definition of A-B-A form, you can't have an *Anstieg* that goes all the way to the reprise, because if the piece begins on 1̂ then the reprise has to start over again on 1̂, but the *Anstieg* would lead to 3̂ at the same moment. Schubert is trying to do two things that are totally incompatible with each other, and Schenker would have warned him away from it. But Schubert found a way in this, and that's by having, on the one hand, this very gradual motion from the B♭ to the C to the D♭ and the D, and then at the same time he manages to make the arrival on that high D (m. 68) be a kind of harbinger of the return of the A-section, by bringing that three-note motive into its original neighbor-note form but a third higher (D-C♯-D instead of B♭-A-B♭). It's an extraordinary sort of thing.

We haven't talked about the bass at all, and I think we should. Let's look at some details of harmony and voice leading right at the beginning of the movement. We start on a rather high-register tonic, but very clearly the tonic. The bass moves down to A (m. 4), a lower neighbor to B♭ and the bass note of an incomplete V$^6_5$ chord. From there we go through a passing $^6_4$ chord (m. 6) to another position of the dominant seventh (V$^4_3$, with C in the bass, an upper neighbor to B♭), and then back to B♭ (m. 8). The chord with the F♯ in measure 5 is just an inflection of F in measure 6, leading us into the passing $^6_4$.

Notice that the rhythmic divisions and the harmonic groupings don't fit together with the division of this eight-measure phrase into 4 + 4. We have three measures on B♭, the A comes in the fourth measure, and then the F♯ (an inflection of the F) comes in the right hand in the fifth measure—that's a five-measure group. The entrance of the octave variant of the three-note motive in measure 5 sounds as though it's pointing out the midpoint of the eight measures and dividing them into 4 + 4, but measure 5 is still within the prolongation of the dominant that started in measure 4. So the harmonic prolongations and the groupings of the measures do not coincide with each other.

There's a rhythmic dimension to this also. Taking measures 4–8 alone, I think one would naturally scan the hypermeasures as a strong beat 1 (m. 4), a weak beat 2 (m. 5), a strong beat 3 (m. 6), and a weak beat 4 (m. 7), leading to a downbeat on measure 8. But the way Schubert sets this up, as two four-measure phrases, he makes you scan it as beat 4 (m. 4), beat 1 (m. 5), beat 2 (m. 6), beat 3 (m. 7), and beat 4 (m. 8).

And there are other, similar kinds of discrepancies elsewhere in this first reprise. The emphasis placed on the incomplete diminished-seventh chord in measure 5 is out of keeping with its function as a low-level chromatic passing tone within a harmony (V$^6_5$) that is itself an embellishing harmony to begin with. Skipping ahead to measure 14, we might think that the E♭$^6_3$ chord in that measure is going to be a passing $^6_4$ chord, just as the E♭$^6_4$ chord in measure 6 was a passing $^6_4$ chord. But when we hear that V-I of E♭ major (mm. 15–16), we feel in retrospect a kind of contradiction between the apparently passing function of the E♭ and its more central function as a temporary E♭ tonic in the larger scheme of things.

Now let's push on past the double bar. Starting in measure 17, we get a simple four-bar phrase (mm. 17–20). But the next four-bar phrase (mm. 21–24), the one with the tenor melody, doesn't complete itself until the following measure (m. 25). Tovey has a very nice way of describing such things. In reference to a passage like measures 17–25, he would say it's an eight-bar phrase "closing into the next measure" [Tovey 1931]. We hear the eight bars as an integral unit, but we can't say that the musical phrase stops at the end of the eighth bar (m. 24); rather it goes into the ninth bar (m. 25), where, at the same time, a new phrase is beginning. Some people might call that an elision, but I'd call it an overlap. *Elision* means that something is left out; *overlap* simply means that one thing is continuing while another thing has started. Elisions are very often overlaps, but overlaps don't have to be elisions.

To clarify the distinction, let's look at the beginning of Beethoven's Piano Sonata, Op. 110, first movement [Example 4.6].

EXAMPLE 4.6 *Beethoven, Piano Sonata, Op. 110, first movement, mm. 1–12, annotated score.*

The piece starts with a four-bar idea that overlaps with the beginning of the next idea, very much as the Schubert does. Measure 4, with the fermata, is on the fourth beat of the hypermeasure. The next measure (m. 5) is both the end of the preceding phrase and the beginning of the next. The phrase that starts there, in measure 5, wants to be an eight-bar idea, but bar 8 becomes bar 1 of the next phrase (beginning in m. 12). Beethoven could have composed a horrible eighth bar to conclude the phrase, but chose instead to "reinterpret"—that's Schenker's term—the eighth bar as a first bar. The hypothetical measure 12 that he didn't write is a missing bar (an elided bar) in that phrase. In the first phrase of the movement (mm. 1–4), however, there is no missing bar, and thus no elision. At the same time, in both phrases you can say there's an overlap, with the end of one phrase serving also as the beginning of the next. Getting back to the Schubert, I'd say that what happens in measure 25 is simply an overlap, not an elision. And there are many different kinds of overlap, beyond the ones we are talking about here.

Now let's look at the bass line and harmony in the same passage (mm. 17–25). I'd prefer to think that we don't really arrive on A♭ in the bass until measure 25—the apparent arrival in measure 21 is really in the middle of something. The bass line starts out by going E♭ (m. 17), D♭ (m. 18), C (mm. 19–20). Then, skipping over the A♭ in measure 21, it retraces its steps: D♭ (m. 23) and E♭ (m. 24), leading to the real arrival on A♭ in measure 25. You can see the same thing even more clearly in the next phrase: A♭-G♭-F (mm. 25–28), and then, skipping over the D♭ (which in this case is placed out of the bass octave), back up through G♭ (m. 30) to A♭ (mm. 33–34), leading to the cadence on D♭, which is the real arrival. We can imagine the first D♭ chord (m. 29) as resulting from a chromaticized 5-♭6 (C-D♭) over the F in measure 28.

That sort of voice leading is actually not altogether uncommon. Look at the second phrase of the slow movement of Beethoven's Piano Sonata, Op. 26, for example [Example 4.7]. Let's start with the E♭-minor harmony in measure 6. Its more significant continuation is the F♭ that follows in measure 7, and then through that F♭ up to G♭ and then the cadence on C♭. The bass motion from E♭ to F♭ is expressed as three descending thirds: E♭-C♭, C♭-A♭, and A♭-F♭. Looking back to the Schubert Scherzo, in playing measures 17–35, it is better to think of connecting C in measure 20 to D♭ in measure 22 than to play the A♭ in measure 21 as an arrival. Similarly, it is better to connect the F in measure 28 to the G♭ in measure 30 than to play the intervening D♭ in measure 29 as a point of arrival. That creates much more integration within the phrase, I think.

Now let's talk about enharmonics [Example 4.8]. We've already discussed the harmonic motion in the first part of the piece: B♭ (m. 1) to E♭ (m. 16) to A♭ (m. 25) to D♭ (m. 33). In measure 50, the D♭ is renotated as C♯ and what you might have expected—the $^6_4$ chord of G♭ minor—becomes instead F♯ minor (perhaps Schubert didn't feel like writing double flats at this point). But there is nothing in the music to make us hear this as an enharmonic change, and perhaps we're still hearing it in flats, as G♭ minor. If that's the case, then the arrival in A major (m. 56) is truthfully B♭♭, and its third degree (C♯) is really D♭. If that's the case, then the chord in measure 60, which we previously described as V$^4_3$ of A is really C♭-E♭♭-F♭, and thus V$^6_3$ of B♭♭. The music is aiming toward D in the melody (as scale-degree $\hat{3}$ in B♭ major) so at some point we need to get our E♭♭ to become a D. I would myself argue for resolving the enharmonic at the point where the B♭ chord comes in (m. 68)—until that moment it's still E♭♭. This enharmonic is actually a systemic. That is, it is not just a matter of notation but it is a matter of actual musical substance. But I don't want to suggest that it's a terribly important point in performance to show where an E♭♭ becomes a D.

Let me now try to sum up the relationship between the top voice and the bass in the long *Anstieg* to measure 68 [Example 4.9]. We start out with B♭ over B♭ (m. 1) and that goes to E♭ in the bass with B♭ in the soprano at the double bar (m. 17). The upper voice continues up through C to D♭, harmonized by D♭ (m. 38). The D♭ is rewritten as C♯ (m. 50),

EXAMPLE 4.7 *Beethoven, Piano Sonata, Op. 26, second movement, mm. 1–8, annotated score.*

Marcia Funebre

Eb ——→ Cb ——→ Ab → Fb

Eb —————— Fb —— Gb

EXAMPLE 4.8 *Schubert, Scherzo, mm. 16–68, two analytical sketches.*

a) Original notation:

b) Enharmonics resolved:

EXAMPLE 4.9 *Schubert, Scherzo, mm. 1–68, analytical sketch.*

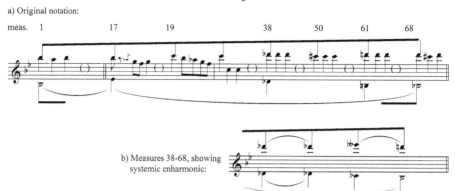

a) Original notation:

b) Measures 38-68, showing
   systemic enharmonic:

and then we get that strange incomplete $^6_3$ chord in measure 61, which might be E♭ over C♭, and from there to the B♭ major in measure 68. To simplify, we have a bass line that goes B♭-E♭-D♭-C♭-B♭. In this arrangement, it sounds as though the B♭ in measure 68 might very well go to E♭. That relates very much to the harmonic motion from B♭ to E♭ in the first reprise, which we've already talked about a good deal. It's also, I think, why the last statement of the opening idea (mm. 77–84) sounds so triumphant. It brings E♭ into the larger context of the piece precisely by *not* going there. If this music were the same as in the first reprise, we'd have gone to E♭, as we did in measures 13–16. Instead, the music is rewritten to take us triumphantly to the tonic.

Now I'd like to say something about the phrase rhythm of the piece, which gives us mostly four-bar phrases. One feature of the piece is that there are often interpolations of two measures in between the four-bar phrases. If you look at Schubert's compositional draft, now available in facsimile, you'll see that he usually has just the four-bar phrases, without interpolations. So we have a metrical grid that's mostly continuous and uninterrupted in the draft, but with interpolations in the final version.

Sometimes, the interpolations have an upbeat character, while sometimes they seem like a preliminary downbeat before the real downbeat [Example 4.10]. Look, for example, at the interpolation in measures 33–34. I think one hears measures 33–34 as hypermeasures 1 and 2 of what you think is going to be a new four-bar phrase. They're not simply an echo of something that came before; rather, they sound like a new beginning. Then, at measure 35, there's another hypermeasure 1, and a new four-bar phrase begins. The interpolation in measures 39–40 has a different character. It's heard as a continuation rather than a new beginning. As for the next interpolation, at measures 45–46, you could think of it either as a continuation (it does continue the previous harmony) or as a new beginning. However, the parallelism in the phrasing of the interpolation in measures 33–34 and this one, in measures 45–46, suggests that it, too, should be thought of as a new beginning, that is, as hypermeasures 1 and 2. By the same logic, the interpolation in measures 51–52 is just a continuation, as in measures 39–40. By the way, the *decrescendi* in measures 39–40 and 51–52 reinforce our sense that these are continuations. In measure 57, we get an interpolation of only one measure (clearly a continuation, not a new beginning), and after that, there are no more of these interpolated measures. So we go from two, to one, to none as we approach the recap. In determining whether those interpolated measures are "upbeats" to the next, or continuation of the preceding, or possibly new downbeats, it's obvious that only the context will tell us.

EXAMPLE 4.10 *Schubert, Scherzo, mm. 1–68, hypermeter.*

One more observation about these four-bar groups and the interpolations: in some cases, it's the fourth measure of the group that receives an accent—look at the *fp* marking in measures 38 and 50. In their book, *The Rhythmic Structure of Music*, Cooper and Meyer make a distinction between a strong beat and a stressed weak beat, and that is a very valid distinction [Cooper and Meyer 1963]. So, a *fortepiano* on the fourth measure of a four-measure group doesn't have to be the initiation of a new group—it can simply be a stressed fourth bar.

Now I'd like to turn to Schubert's "Frühlingstraum" [Example 4.11]. I'm particularly interested in the role that neighbor notes play in shaping this song. Indeed, one of the reasons neighbor notes play such an important role in musical structure is because they can assume so many contrasting shapes and colors. But before we get into the music, let me tell you how the text goes:

> *Ich träumte von bunten Blumen,*—I dreamt of colorful flowers
> *so wie sie wohl blühen im Mai;*—as they bloom in May;
> *Ich träumte von grünen Wiesen*—I dreamt of green meadows
> *Von lustigem Vogelgeschrei* —of the joyous cry of birds.

EXAMPLE 4.11 *Schubert, "Frühlingstraum" from* Winterreise, *mm. 1–43, annotated score.*

EXAMPLE 4.11 (*Continued*)

So the poem begins with a nice dream of flowers, and meadows, and birds in the springtime. And then a sudden change:

> *Und als die Hähne krähten,*—and as the roosters crowed
> *da ward mein Auge wach*—then my eye awakened
> *Da war es kalt und finster*—there it was cold and dark
> *Es schrien die Raben von Dach*—the ravens were screaming from the roof.

And then (m. 27 in the score where it says *Langsam*):

> *Doch an den Fensterscheiben,*—But on the windowpanes
> *wer malte die Blätter da?"*—who painted the leaves?
> *Ihr lacht wohl über den Träumer*—You're probably laughing at the dreamer
> *der Blumen in Winter sah*—who saw flowers in the winter.

EXAMPLE 4.11 (*Continued*)

I haven't given you the music beyond that point, but the text continues,

> *Ich träumte von Lieb' um Liebe*—I dreamt of love for love's sake.
> *von einem schönen Maid*—of a beautiful girl
> *von Herzen und von Küssen*—of embracing and kissing
> *von Wonn' und Seligkeit*—of pleasure and happiness.

> *Und als die Hähne kräten*—and as the roosters crowed
> *Da ward mein Herze wach*—then my heart awakened
> *Nun sitz ich hier alleine*—now I sit here alone
> *Und denke dem Traume nach.*—and think about the dream.

And then the final subsection, in $\frac{2}{4}$ time (m. 71):

Die Augen schließ' ich wieder,—I close my eyes again
noch schlägt das Herz so warm.—but my heart is beating so warmly.
Wann grünt ihr Blätter am Fenster?—you leaves on the window, when will you turn green?
Wann halt' ich mein Liebchen im Arm?—when will I hold my dear one in my arms?

That final line is repeated, and the brutal minor triad at the end tells you when that desired outcome is likely to be.

The first melodic gesture, in the piano introduction (m. 1) and when the voice enters (m. 5) is E-F♯-E in a dotted rhythm—that's a neighbor-note idea. It's not given any special emphasis, and actually in the continuation of this first section, you're not that conscious of hearing neighbor notes, though they are somehow there. Look at what we might call the alto voice in measures 5–7 (that is, the middle notes of the groups of three notes in the piano part): we have an E in measure 5, we have an F♯ in measure 6, we have F♯ going to E in measure 7, and the E continuing in measure 8, just as a standard inner-voice thing. At that point, we have the beginning of a motion from the inner-voice tone E through F♯ and G♯ to A, with the G♯ substituting for scale-degree $\hat{2}$. There's an implied B at that point in the upper voice, as part of a $\hat{3}$-$\hat{2}$-$\hat{1}$ descent.

Now let's digress for a moment to contemplate some of the interesting idiosyncrasies of scale-degree $\hat{6}$ as a melodic tone. Viktor Zuckerkandl writes that as soon as an ascending major scale reaches scale-degree $\hat{5}$, you find yourself on what he calls a "knife edge" between being aware of the pull of the lower tonic a fifth lower and, at the same time, the upper tonic, $\hat{8}$, pulling us upward [Zuckerkandl 1971]. And $\hat{6}$, he says, has this dual possibility of going back to $\hat{5}$, or, from $\hat{5}$ going on up to $\hat{7}$ and $\hat{8}$. And that dual nature of $\hat{6}$ is one of its distinctive features. There are times when it's hard to know whether one should think of scale-degree 6 as a neighbor note to $\hat{5}$ or as part of a rising motion $\hat{6}$-$\hat{7}$-$\hat{8}$, or $\hat{5}$-$\hat{6}$-$\hat{7}$-$\hat{8}$.

Let's take J. S. Bach's (actually Christian Petzold's) G-major Minuet from the *Notebook for Anna Magdalena Bach* as an example [Example 4.12].

EXAMPLE 4.12 *Bach (or Christian Petzold?), Minuet in G major, from the* Notebook for Anna Magdalena Bach, *mm. 1–8.*

I've had students who analyze the E (scale-degree $\hat{6}$) in measure 3 as a passing note on the way up to G. But I think it makes better sense to hear it as a neighbor that returns to an implied D (scale-degree $\hat{5}$) in measure 4—the context somehow cries out for a scale-degree $\hat{5}$ and I tell my students that it's not actually present in the music, but it's part of the imaginary continuo.

Similarly in the fifth and sixth measures of Mozart's Rondo in D major, K. 485, we could say that the B (scale-degree $\hat{6}$) ascends through $\hat{7}$ to $\hat{8}$: B-C♯-D [Example 4.13]. But I hear more strongly that we really have not ascended, at least not yet. In the accompaniment, we get $\hat{6}$-$\hat{5}$, and that $\hat{6}$-$\hat{5}$ neighbor-note motion is a very powerful melodic progression. The context will have to determine if $\hat{6}$ climbs up to $\hat{8}$ or returns to $\hat{5}$ as a neighbor note.

EXAMPLE 4.13 *Mozart, Rondo in D major, K. 485, mm. 1–9.*

Now let's go back to "Frühlingstraum," starting with the piano introduction. We start on E, embellished locally by its upper neighbor, F♯, and then we leap up to C♯, a note that I would take as the *Kopfton* of the *Urlinie*. From that initial E, it's very hard not to hear the right-hand part ascending through F♯ and G♯ to A (mm. 3–4). But at the same time, if you look in measure 3 at the left-hand part, you see there is also an F♯ returning to E as a neighbor note. This is a place where we will want to think of that F♯ as having a kind of "dual fate," thinking of it almost as implying a unison of two voices on F♯: one of them goes up F♯-G♯-A, while the other goes back down to E. Looking ahead at measures 9–12, we find the F♯-E again in the right hand of the piano part. All of these are very "underground" neighbor-note motions. Even though the singer does have this motive, it's not emphasized terribly much, but it certainly is a presence.

Now let's talk about the top voice structure. We have our main *Urlinie* tone in measure 5, the C♯, which is prolonged through the beginning of measure 8. At the end of measure 9, we have D going right back to C♯ in measure 10, followed by F♯-G♯-A (mm. 11–12). That sense of F♯ going up to A is stronger for me than the neighbor note implication, but notice that the piano part does have the F♯ as a neighbor.

If we were to take the first fourteen measures as a sort of self-contained small composition, and if we were to think that it has its own *Urlinie*, we would be looking for a descent from scale-degree 3̂ in measure 10. There's an implied 2̂ over the G♯ in measure 11 and again in measure 13, and we also get to A twice, in measures 12 and 14. We don't literally have scale-degree 2̂ in the top voice; instead the G♯ substitutes for it. The idea of going 4̂-7̂-1̂ is a rather frequent substitution for 2̂-1̂, particularly frequent in Schubert's music, as a matter of fact. So we have two descents from C♯ to A, but the second one (mm. 13–14) is stronger than the first. That's partly because above that second descent, there is a secondary line, E-D-C♯, which has the effect of reinforcing the main line.

I want to focus now on the *Schnell* section, measures 15–26. The triplet octave figures and their accompanying dissonant chords in measures 16, 18, and 20 pretty obviously represent the roosters crowing and the ravens screaming from the rooftops. These dissonant chords are related to French augmented-sixth chords, but not used in the most typical way. Instead of moving to the dominant, they embellish the tonic. Their function is primarily contrapuntal—they consist of neighboring notes. So whether you call them augmented-sixth chords, which of course they do relate to in a way, or whether you call them simply altered-seventh chords, which is probably better in this situation because of their static nature, they are common-tone chromatic chords with a neighboring function, very much related to the well-known openings of Brahms's Third Symphony and Schubert's C-major Quintet.

Schenker would probably not be willing to grant them chordal status at all. Rather, he would consider them sonorities that result from the contrapuntal motion of the voices, and he would say the only real harmony you have in measures 15–16 is in fact E minor. The G in the bass in measure 15 moves to its neighbor F♯, an octave higher in measure 16, and then back to G (you could show that with a dotted slur between the low G and the upper G). It's thus a complete neighbor, G-F♯-G, but one that has the character of an incomplete neighbor because of the way the dissonant complex over the F♯ tears the emotional fabric of the thing.

In Schubert, there are many dominant-type seventh chords as well as diminished-seventh chords that function essentially as neighbor notes. You'll note that, in the poem, there are three types of bird: the merry ones enjoying springtime; the annoying roosters, plunging the poet into the hostile real world; and the sinister ravens screaming from the roof, representing the beautiful past, the miserable present, and the frightening future. The three images are linked in the poem because all have to do with birds. They are linked in the song because they all involve neighbor notes.

The upper voice in the *Schnell* section begins on B. If we were to proceed through the music in a sort of ant-like way, one little step after another, we might say that the B in measure 15 comes from the A of the preceding cadence in measure 14. But Schenker's idea would be that the first section of this song is based on the linear progression, C♯-B-A. Until we reach the end of the *Ursatz*, which is not going to happen until near the end of the whole song, the A is not really established as a main tone. It is still, as you might say, under the shadow of the C♯. So there may be a stepwise connection from A (m. 14) to B (m. 15), but it is not a significant one in terms of the shape of the melody as a whole. Rather, the B that begins the *Schnell* section comes from the C♯ at the beginning of the vocal line.

The vocal line features a rising linear progression through a fourth: B (m. 15)-C♯ (m. 17)-D (m. 18)-E (m. 21). In the opening section, we had a big C♯-B-A in the upper voice. At the end of the first section, the C♯ is still hovering over us as a retained tone. When we get to the B, as we do at the beginning of the *Schnell* section, that B comes from the C♯ at the beginning of the first section. The B is prolonged by the linear progression up to E, and then moves down to A. So we can imagine the whole first section as prolonging C♯ over the tonic, which goes to B over the dominant at the beginning of the *Schnell* section, and then down to A with the tonic again, only now in its minor form (m. 22). What we get then, in measures 22–26, are quite explicit and nasty sounding neighbor notes (mostly A-B♭-A and E-F-E).

It's quite wonderful to see how Schubert works out the details. In measure 16, where the triplet sixteenth-notes in the piano part imitate first the crowing rooster and then the shrieking of the ravens on the roof, we have a chord essentially made up of neighbor notes that resolves into the E-minor ⁶₃ chord. That chord of neighbor notes, if you can even call it a chord, contains F♯, A♯, C♮, and E. Now look back to measure 15. There's a more diatonic version of the same chord there—F♯-A-E in the piano plus C♮ in the voice. If the A in that chord were an A♯, we'd have the same chord as in measure 16. Both of these chords consist of neighbor notes to the E-minor ⁶₃ chord. Something analogous happens in measures 18–20, first with neighbor chords to D minor (m. 18) and then to G minor (mm. 19–20). Thinking of the bass line in this passage, I would trace it from G within the E-minor ⁶₃ (m. 15) to F within the D-minor ⁶₃ (m. 18) and from there to the E in the cadential ⁶₄ chord in measure 21 (V in A minor). The intervening G minor (measures 19–20) I hear as part of the prolongation of the D minor chord.

After the tonic arrival on the downbeat of measure 22, the gestures in the rest of the section are very cadential or coda-like. The pedal point, for example, is a typical sign of a coda—which could mean, in analyzing the song, that we think of the actual structural ending of the song *before* the *Langsam*, which is another kind of coda. On what you might say are psychological grounds, I don't like that interpretation, but it's a possible one.

I think we are actually meant to hear some kind of miracle in the music that follows. In measure 26, we have that very brutal arpeggio going up A-C-E-A, followed immediately in the *Langsam* section by A-C♯-E in the bass, imitated by A-C♯-E in the right-hand part. And the singer here is speaking of the ice formations in his window that create the illusion of flowers—even with all the terrible things going on in this man's life, he is still capable of appreciating beautiful sights and is at least temporarily beguiled by them.

And amid all of this, the neighbor-note idea grows. For instance, in measures 29 and 30, we have a double neighbor around the D (D-C♯-E-D in the right hand of the piano and the voice) with the left hand of the piano a sixth lower (F♯-E-G-F♯). Then, that D in the melody goes to C♯ in measure 30, prolonged into measure 32. Then we have B in measure 33 in the vocal line, going to A in measure 34, and then again B-A (mm. 35–36). We have neighbor notes in profusion here, intensifying in measures 37–38 with the neighboring motion F-E, just as the singer asks a question of us, just as he speaks directly to the listeners to the song. I don't think there is another place in *Winterreise* where he speaks directly to the listener. It is incredibly moving, the end of this, where the main thing one hears is the F♮ to E, which is ultimately derived from the E-F♯-E of that first dotted figure at the very beginning of the song. And, at the end, the F-E expands to dominate the whole thing: the F arpeggiates up through A and D to the high F (m. 39) and the resolution of the *Ursatz* is actually dwarfed by the neighbor-note idea.

Handel, Suite No. 8
for Harpsichord, Courante

*We'll work on the Courante from Handel's Suite No. 8 for Harpsichord, paying par-
ticular attention to motivic features and to the segmentation of the harmonic structure.*

DESPITE ITS FRENCH TITLE (COURANTE), THIS PIECE IS A CORRENTE (THE
Italian type of Courante), in a quick $\frac{3}{4}$ time. Let's begin our discussion of it by looking for linear progressions in its opening measures [Example 5.1].

At first glance, you might opt for an ascending fifth-progression in the upper voice: F
(m. 1)-G (m. 2)-A♭ (m. 3)-B♭ (m. 4)-C (m. 5), with each note lasting for one measure. A much
better alternative, I think, would be to take a third-progression, F-G-A♭, and imagine the A♭-
B♭-C (mm. 3–5) as a counterpoint in tenths above a second F-G-A♭ that comes in through
imitation in the left-hand part (mm. 3–5). What speaks in favor of the third-progression
F-G-A♭ rather than the fifth progression F-G-A♭-B♭-C is that we have a rich diminution,
in the manner of a fugue subject, of the basic F-G-A♭ idea within measures 1–2, going to
the downbeat of measure 3, but the A♭-B♭-C is completely bare. Furthermore, the bass
(mm. 3–4) and top voice (mm. 5–6) imitate the figure of measures 1–2 almost in the manner of a fugue exposition. The goal A♭ is a focal point in all three statements of this "subject." Of course this would be a so-called "octave fugue" where the subject is imitated at the
octave rather than the usual fifth.

There's a nice detail of the voice leading in measures 3–5. The bass ascends F-G-A♭,
as we just discussed, and the upper voice does the same thing, F-G-A♭ (look at the highest notes in each measure). But these seeming parallel octaves are broken up through
the technique of *reaching-over*. Both the F (m. 3) and the G (m. 4) of the top voice move
down by step, producing suspended sevenths against the lower voice; the octaves are
broken up by the sixths to which these sevenths resolve. It's a perfectly beautiful voice
leading [Example 5.2].

Now I want to draw your attention to another detail of voice leading, this one in measures 1–3, which is rich in implications for the motivic life of this piece. In measure 1, there's
a small ascending third, from F to A♭. In measure 2, we might think we have another ascending third, from G to B♭. Or, we might have a fourth, from G to C [Example 5.3].

EXAMPLE 5.1 *Handel, Suite No. 8 in F Minor for Harpsichord, Courante, annotated score.*

It would be perfectly logical and perhaps more usual to take the B♭ as the main note in measure 2, because it is the seventh of the dominant-seventh chord. You may think it curious,
but I am very much for taking the C, not the B♭, as the main note, which means that the B♭
is a passing note. One of my reasons has to do with the prevalence of the rising fourth as a
motive throughout the piece, something we'll talk about more later. But you can get a little
hint of it right here: the first two notes of the melody, C-F, are a rising fourth, which is then
imitated by the rising fourth, G-C, in measure 2.

There are related things elsewhere in the Handel harpsichord suites. In the Air from
the Fifth Suite (the so-called "Harmonious Blacksmith"), the third has to be followed by
a fourth because there's no A following the F♯ that you could take to create a second third
[Example 5.4].

EXAMPLE 5.1 (*Continued*)

EXAMPLE 5.2 *Handel, Courante, mm. 3–5, voice-leading detail.*

EXAMPLE 5.3 *Handel, Courante, mm. 1–3, motives.*

EXAMPLE 5.4 *Handel, Suite No. 5 in E major for Harpsichord, Air ("Harmonious Blacksmith"), mm. 1–3, annotated score.*

In the beautiful Andante movement of the G-minor Suite, the opening melody has the same sort of thing: a rising third followed by a rising fourth [Example 5.5].

EXAMPLE 5.5 *Handel, Suite No. 7 in G minor for Harpsichord, Andante, mm. 1–3, annotated score.*

That seems to be a motive that is common to several movements of these eight suites.

Another interesting detail in the opening measures of our Courante has to do with $^6_4$ chords, some apparent and some real. In measure 3, even though C is the lowest note in the bass register, this is not really a $^6_4$ chord at all. The opening octave F in the bass in measure 1 remains in our memory, so everything in the left hand in measure 3 is an inner voice above that tonic note. There are many similar situations where the fifth is in the bass, but we still have the sense of tonic harmony. Oom-pah-pah basses and march basses often work that way—the fifth of the tonic may be momentarily the lowest note, but it's not really the bass note, and these are not really $^6_4$ chords. There are interesting situations where the same apparent chord gets treated in two different ways, either as a real tonic (and thus only an apparent $^6_4$) or as a real $^6_4$ (a cadential $^6_4$, representing the dominant).

The last movement of Schubert's D-major Piano Sonata, for example, has a typical march bass [Example 5.6]. In measures 1–4, the chords on the second and fourth beats stand for root position tonic chords—they're not $^6_4$ chords. But when we get to the cadence at the end of the phrase, IV (m. 8) is followed by a cadential $^6_4$ moving to $^7_3$ over the dominant (m. 9). Even though the notes in measure 9 are exactly the same as in the first few measures, the context tells us that the harmonic meaning is different: the fourth in the bass between A and D in measure 9 is in fact a dissonance, and part of a true cadential $^6_4$.

Now let's resume our discussion of linear progressions in the Handel Courante, starting in measure 7. In the bass, there's a descending fourth-progression from tonic to dominant: F-E♭-D♭-C (mm. 7–10). The upper voice is moving in parallel tenths with the bass, so we might be tempted to say there's also a linear progression in the

EXAMPLE 5.6 *Schubert, Piano Sonata in D major, D. 850, fourth movement (Rondo), mm. 1–10, annotated score.*

upper voice: A♭-G-F-E♮. But that's not in fact a linear progression because there is no harmony of any significance in this passage as a whole that contains both the A♭ and the E♮. So the E♮ should be thought of in a very broad sense as a neighbor note to F. It's better to say that there's first a descending third, A♭-G-F (within tonic harmony), answered by a rising third, E-F-G (within dominant harmony). That brings us close to the Schenkerian concept of *unfolding*. An unfolding occurs when a relatively complex melodic line represents the horizontalization of a brief two-part counterpoint. In the Handel, A♭-G-F-E-F-G reduces to A♭-F + E-G, which in turn represents two voices: top voice A♭-G and lower voice F-E. At the top of those unfolded thirds, there's a top voice that goes from A♭ (m. 7) to G (m. 10) and continuing to F in measure 11. That gives us a big descending third, A♭-G-F, in the upper voice from measure 7 to measure 11 [Example 5.7].

EXAMPLE 5.7 *Handel, Courante, mm. 7–11, analytical sketch.*

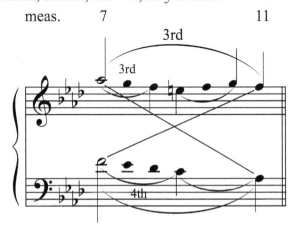

Now compare the tonic chords in measures 7 and 11. In measure 7, we have F in the bass and A♭ in the top voice. In measure 11, the roles are reversed: now A♭ is on the bottom and F is on the top. So the tonic harmony is prolonged through these measures, and the means of prolongation is a *voice exchange*. The voice exchange has the effect not only of prolonging the tonic but also of destabilizing it. And this is something that happens extremely frequently when we are modulating away from the tonic: we do something to make it less self-sufficient, less stable.

Handel destabilizes the tonic not only through the voice exchange, but also through the tones of figuration, especially the D♮ in measure 11. It is very often the little notes, the tones of figuration, that offer a clue as to key feeling, suggesting that we may be moving out of the orbit of the tonic key. Handel could have written measure 10 exactly as he did (with the D♮ as a passing tone between C and E), but if he had then used a D♭ in measure 11, it would very much have negated any feeling of departure from F minor.

There are many fascinating motivic things here. In measure 6 the melody outlines G-C-G. In measure 11, in a sort of composite of the soprano and alto voices, we get C-F-C. Compare both of these to the first three notes of the Courante in the right-hand part: C-F-C. These rising and falling fourths are important elements throughout the piece. In measure 12, our "fugue subject" is distributed between the alto and soprano: it starts in the alto with the usual rising and falling fourths, G-C-G, and then continues in the soprano. The continuation of the subject into measure 13 brings in another rising and falling fourth: D-G-D. By the way, dividing a motive between the voices is very Handelian. In general, Bach adheres more strictly to the norms of voice leading than Handel does, although there are places, especially in Book 2 of the *Well-Tempered Clavier* (the F-major Fugue, for example), where it can be a bit difficult to tell which voice something belongs to.

Let's work through the harmony and the bass line starting in measure 11, where our big voice exchange has brought us from I to I⁶ in F minor. The $^6_3$ chord in measure 11 is an example of a kind of chord beloved of all harmony books, namely a *pivot chord*: I⁶ in the tonic key becomes IV⁶ in the key of the dominant. Thinking now in C minor, the key of the dominant, the IV⁶ in measure 11 takes us to V (mm. 12–13) and then to I (m. 14). Just as in measure 3, the chord in measure 14 is not a $^6_4$ chord, it is the tonic in the key of the minor dominant. From the C in the bass in measure 14, we have an ascending fifth progression, C-D-E♭-F-G, and then the cadence in C minor that ends the first reprise.

Now let's work our way through the top voice in the same passage. In measures 7–11, the top voice descends A♭-G-F, as we discussed. From the F in measure 11, we have a small third-progression, F-E♭-D (mm. 11–13), but the main motion goes from the F in measure 11 to the E♭ in measure 14. There's an interesting possible alternative that I'll mention now and explore more fully later: instead of the F in measure 11 moving down to the E♭ in measure 14 we could imagine it moving up to the high G in measure 13. That is less plausible initially, but has some interesting large-scale possibilities, as we'll see.

So now we're in measure 14. Going along with our ascending fifth-progression in the bass, the upper voice might have followed a pretty simple pattern [Example 5.8]. But the genius in this passage is how Handel scrambles up the expected note-to-note succession. The normal thing to do would be C-B, D-C, E♭-D♮ F. But instead Handel creates a parallelism with a three-note motive: C-B-D then E♭-D-F.

This is a typical instance of reaching-over: you go down one step, then the reaching-over takes you one step higher than where you began, and then that new voice also goes down

EXAMPLE 5.8 *Handel, Courante, mm. 14–18, outer voices.*

a) Typical reaching over

b) Handel's variant

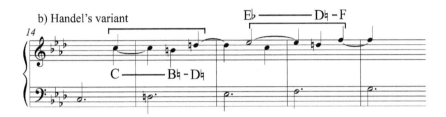

one step. There are many strictly polyphonic instantiations of that kind of thing, including the *Recordare* from the Mozart Requiem, which we discussed in a previous class.

In the Handel, the C in measure 14 goes to B in measure 15. Then a new voice enters on D (m. 15) and goes to C (m. 16). As it does so, another new voice reaches over to E♭ (m. 16) which goes to D (m. 17). The E♭ (m. 16) does not belong to the same voice as the D♮ before it (m. 15), because that D is going to move down to C. Handel disrupts the pattern by bringing the E♭ in out of turn, earlier than it ought to occur. The cumulative effect of these reachings-over is a stepwise ascent in the upper voice: C-D-E♭-F. And notice amid all of this the ubiquitous motif of the rising and falling fourth in the left hand: D-G-D (m. 15), G-C-G (m. 16), and C-F-C (m. 17).

Let's finish with the melodic line in the last three measures of the first reprise. We start with F (m. 17) and then descend F-E♭-D-C. But we have E♭ and D twice, so we have a choice to make. Either the D on the third beat of measure 18 is a neighbor note to the two E♭s and the main D in the line is the one in measure 19, or the E♭ on the first beat of measure 19 is a neighbor to the two Ds and the main D in the line is the one in measure 18. I prefer to think of the D in measure 18 as a neighbor note to the E♭s, simultaneously with the F in the bass as neighbor to the Gs. The harmony is the dominant, with a passing $^6_4$ within the dominant seventh chord starting on the second beat of measure 18 and lasting through the first beat of measure 19, at which point it moves to $^7_{\substack{5\\3}}$.

Now I want to digress for a moment to show you something really remarkable in the first movement of the Suite in F minor from which we've been studying the Courante. The first movement consists of a prelude plus a fugue, like the C-minor Cello Suite of J. S. Bach. The subject of Handel's fugue is F-G-A♭-B♭-C-F [Example 5.9].

EXAMPLE 5.9 *Handel, Suite No. 8 in F Minor for Harpsichord, Allegro, mm. 1–9, annotated score.*

You can see that the beginning of the Courante is very much prefigured in this subject, with its rising third, which is detached from the larger fifth-progression by the rest.

Now look at the passage from measure 93 to the downbeat of measure 105, beginning and ending on the subdominant, B♭ [Example 5.10].

EXAMPLE 5.10 *Handel, Suite No. 8, Allegro, mm. 90–105, annotated score.*

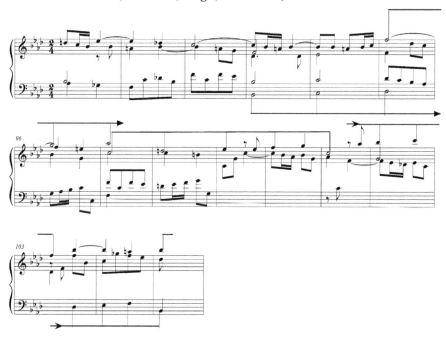

Let's follow each of the three main voices. The bass starts a statement of the subject in measure 93, B♭-C-D♭, then breaks off as the soprano enters in measure 95 with its statement of the subject, F-G-A♭. At the moment the soprano reaches A♭ (m. 96), it breaks off as the alto enters with a complete statement of the subject, C-D-E♭-E♭-F-G-C. This third statement manages to complete the entire subject. When the alto statement is complete (m. 101), the soprano re-enters and completes the statement it had previously broken off. When it ends (m. 103), the bass, which started first, gets to end last. The voices begin statements of the subject in the order bass-soprano-alto, and they complete their statements of the subject in reverse order: alto, soprano, bass. So you see it's a kind of fractured *stretto*, where the parts overlap and each one states the complete subject. I've not seen anything in Bach similar to what Handel does in this stretto.

Now let's go back to our Courante and see if we can make sense of the upper voice across the whole of the first reprise. The initial third-progression, F-G-A♭ (which we have three times, twice in the upper voice) represents, in Schenkerian terms, an *Anstieg*, or initial ascent (mm. 1–7). From there, the upper voice descends through the same third, A♭-G-F, arriving in measure 11 as the voice exchange with the bass is completed and we arrive on I⁶. The upper voice continues to descend to E♭ (m. 14). At that point, we jump down to C and ascend, C-D-E♭-F.

In English-language Schenkerian terms, that represents *motion from an inner voice*. Schenker's term for this is *Untergreifen*, which is not easily translatable, if indeed it's translatable at all. It literally means to grab or reach below. In that sense, it is the opposite of *Übergreifen*, which means to reach over—that's a concept and a term we have already used many times. One early translator of *Free Composition* [Kruger 1960] wanted to translate *Untergreifen* as "reaching under," which perhaps doesn't sound so very good in English.

Anyway, the ascending motion C-D-E♭-F (mm. 14–17) would be an *Untergreifszug,* that is, a reaching upward from below or underneath. Interestingly, that reaching-upward is itself created through reaching over—as we noted earlier, each step in the ascent is actually a reaching-over, until we finally reach the F in measure 17. But we're in C minor now, and so this motion up to F would actually represent motion up to a neighbor note—the main tone is E♭. We've reached E♭ in measure 14, ascended past it to the neighbor note F (m. 17), and we return to it in measure 18. From there the descent E♭-D-C completes the line.

Looking at the first reprise as a whole, this is one of those cases—they're not uncommon—where, above harmonic motion from tonic to dominant, the top line moves down a sixth from scale-degree 3̂ of the tonic (in this case, A♭) to scale-degree 1̂ of the dominant (in this case, C). The upper voice over the course of the first reprise is thus A♭-G-F-E♭-D-C [Example 5.11].

EXAMPLE 5.11 *Handel, Courante, mm. 1–20 (first reprise), analytical sketch of upper voice.*

Usually, a descending sixth of that kind is best analyzed with an implied scale-degree 2̂ at the end, so the upper-voice motion at the highest level would be 3̂-2̂ (A♭ to G). And very often you don't need to imply scale-degree 2̂ because it's literally present at the end. But that's not the case here, because the moment Handel leaves the key of C minor, at the double bar, he goes immediately to the key of the mediant, A♭ major, which does not contain G, the tone he would need to produce the 2̂.

As I suggested earlier, there's a somewhat different way of reading the first reprise of the Courante, taking the G in measure 13 as scale-degree 2̂ of the *Urlinie* [Example 5.12].

EXAMPLE 5.12 *Handel, Courante, mm. 1–20 (first reprise), alternative analytical sketch of upper voice.*

We start the same way, with an initial ascent F-G-A♭ and then a third-progression back down to F, coinciding with that large voice exchange we discussed earlier. Then, however, we take G in measure 13 as scale-degree 2̂—it comes in over the dominant of C minor, but it's a dominant that immediately goes to its tonic. Then we have an arpeggiation down into the inner voice (G-E♭-C), followed by the reaching-over and the motion out of the inner voice, taking us up to F in measure 17.

I think this reading gives us a better account of that F. Previously, we thought of it as just a neighbor note to E♭, not on a very high level. But there is something so climactic about the motion up to that F, and this alternative reading gives better emphasis to F as a passing note on the way from G down to C. It also wraps things up in a neater analytical package. All things considered, I think that this reading is better than the first one.

Now let's push past the double bar. After the arrival on the dominant (with a Picardy third) in measure 20, I think that Handel wants us to feel (and I apologize for the intentional fallacy here) a real disjunction with the A♭ major that begins the second section (m. 21). I think we hear the A♭ as coming from the F-minor beginning, rather than from the C in measure 20.

The second half begins with a passage in A♭ major, lasting until the downbeat of measure 29. The bass essentially goes from the A♭ to the C (m. 25), D♭ (m. 26), and E♭ (m. 27). Then we have a repetition of D♭-E♭ (m. 28), but the D♭ is a neighbor note of no real harmonic significance. So basically we have a I-IV-V-I progression in A♭ major, with the IV in measure 26 veering over into the territory of II.

In the melody, the subject comes in a free inversion, and we get a small third-progression, E♭-D♭-C. In measure 25, E♭ is still the main tone, moving to D♭ in measure 26, then to C, B♭, and A♭ (mm. 28–29). In measure 27, we have motion out of the inner voice, from G to C.

We move next to B♭ minor and cadence there in measure 32. The upper voice in the B♭-minor passage (mm. 29–32) is basically E♭ (mm. 29–30) to D♭ (mm. 32). Now let's trace the bass line from the cadence on B♭ minor in measure 32 until we reach our dominant (m. 36). I would say we have B♭ moving up chromatically through B♮ (m. 35) to C (m. 36). The F in measure 34, brought in by E♮ in measure 33, is actually the upper fifth of B♭, and not part of the main bass motion. To sum up in the simplest possible terms what happens from the double bar until the arrival of the dominant in measure 37, we have A♭ (m. 21) to B♭ (m. 32) to C (m. 37). The space between B♭ and C is filled in with the chromatic passing tone B♮ (m. 35). We might also say that the space between A♭ and B♭ is also filled in with a chromatic passing tone, namely, the A♮ in measure 30. There is thus latent in that progression a complete chromatic ascent from A♭ to C.

Now let's think a bit about the form of this piece as a whole. It seems pretty clearly to be an A-B-A form, with an A-section (mm. 1–20), a contrasting B-section (mm. 21–37), and a return of the A-section (mm. 37–end). But measures 37–38, where the A material returns, is a pretty tricky place. Tonic harmony returns in measure 37, but it's an anticipatory I: it anticipates the actual recapitulation, which is going to happen one measure later.

Look at the music that Handel is actually recapitulating here. At first glance, measures 38–48 would seem to present a fairly straightforward repetition of measures 3–5. A closer look, however, reveals that, starting in measure 38, we get pretty close to a note-by-note transposition *not* of the beginning, but rather of the music in C minor that starts in measure 14. Measures 38–43 are a literal transposition up a fourth of measures 14–19. We have here a situation of two wrongs making a right, so to speak. That is, the piece starts with something in F minor and then transposes that into C minor to make a prolongation of the dominant. When it comes time to recapitulate, Handel does so by recapitulating the C-minor music, now transposed to the tonic, F minor. So by recapitulating in the tonic the second part of the first reprise, we are also managing to recapitulate the opening of the piece.

Other parts of the first A-section are also recapitulated when the A-section returns. Measures 46–49 correspond closely with measures 7–10, harmonically and melodically. In that way, Handel has managed to recapitulate not only the C-minor music in the second half of the A-section, but also the second strain of the opening F-minor section, beginning in measure 7.

The only thing we haven't actually recapitulated is the opening of the movement, the thematic presentation in the first few measures. But look closely at measure 37 and at the ascending third there, F-G-A♭. Is this not a kind of digested version, you might say, of the fugue subject itself, with its rising third? If so, then every part of the first reprise has been at least alluded to, with measure 37 standing in for the point of imitation in measures 1–7, with its threefold statement of F-G-A♭.

Some of the things I've told you today I learned from a very dear friend and wonderful mentor, Ernst Oster. It was he who pointed out that incredible *stretto* in the F-minor fugue, with the sort of dislocated subject. My talking to him about this piece was occasioned by a review written by Saul Novack, a student of Felix Salzer's who taught for many years at Queens College and was one of the founding faculty members of the Ph.D. program in music here at the Graduate Center. Novack had written a review of some eighteenth-century-style theory books in which the authors, in Novack's view, had overlooked the possibility that the V at the end of the first reprise in pieces like the Courante might be a prolonging, dividing dominant [Novack 1964]. Novack preferred the idea that the dominant at the end of the first reprise is a back-relating, dividing dominant. If the second reprise begins on III, as in our Courante, the principal large-scale motion is from I to III (F to A♭), with the C as something secondary. In the Courante, that would seem like a pretty compelling view. I don't think any of us could deny the force of that F to A♭—for one thing, the bare octave at the beginning of those two moments (m. 1 and m. 21) creates a very strong bond between them, a bond reinforced by the fact that the theme returns right there in free inversion.

For a small-scale version of the sort of thing Novack has in mind, here's the opening of Mozart's D-major Piano Sonata, K. 576 [Example 5.13].

EXAMPLE 5.13 *Mozart, Piano Sonata in D major, K. 576, first movement, mm. 1–8, annotated score.*

The V in measure 4 is a back-relating dominant and does not connect directly to the II in measure 5. Rather than coming from V, the II in measure 5 connects to the I in measure 1, a connection that is strongly reinforced thematically. So what Novack was pointing out is something that happens very frequently on a small scale, and sometimes on a larger scale.

I asked Oster what he thought of Novack's idea, and he said, "No, I feel that that C minor is very significant. One has to find a way of incorporating the C minor, together with the A-flat, into a complete picture of the harmonic structure." Oster pointed out that the arrival on C minor as tonic (mm. 13–14), with those descending eighth-notes and downward leaping sixths in the right-hand part, is very similar to the arrival on C as dominant right before the recapitulation (mm. 35–36). For Oster, that spoke to some connection between the two dominants, the way they relate to and resemble each other.

That's as far as he went, but I found that idea very stimulating. Eventually, it led me to come up with the following [Example 5.14]. The background harmony, just like every other piece, is I-V-I.

EXAMPLE 5.14 *Handel, Courante, large-scale bass line.*

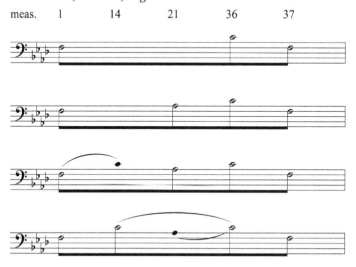

The next level would be I-III-V-I, but instead of going consecutively I-III-V-I, one does I-V-III-V-I. It is related to interruption, in that we are segmenting the progression, and we are also going back to a preliminary stage, conceptually, in between the I and the V, but we don't go back to the very beginning as in true, normal interruption. This is related to what Schenker in some of his analyses calls a "third divider."

The opening of Chopin's "Black Key" Etude (Op. 10, No. 5) gives a good example of a third divider [Example 5.15]. The first eight measures take us from G♭ major, the tonic, to B♭ major, a chromaticized version of the mediant (B♭ major instead of the diatonic B♭ minor). That would be a third divider. You could think of it as an applied dominant (V of VI), but I'd prefer to hear it as III with the third raised to make it more of a focal point. The B♭ major is preceded by an A♭-minor chord in first inversion (m. 7), creating a Phrygian cadence on B♭. So far, we've gone I-III.

The next eight measures start again on I (m. 9) but leading this time to V (m. 16). In the measure before the cadence, where we had a Phrygian cadence in measures 7–8 with C♭-B♭ in the bass, now we have C♮ to D♭ in the bass, creating a strong arrival on the dominant. Taking the sixteen measures as a whole, we have I-III and then I-V.

Schenker has a graph of third dividers in *Free Composition* [Example 5.16]. In *Meisterwerk*, in the Chopin article where he analyzes both the G♭-major and E♭-minor Etudes [Schenker 1997a], he slurs from the G♭ to the B♭, from the I to the III, and then from the B♭ directly to the D♭, even though there's a return to G♭ in between (Level b). It's as though he wants to have it both ways: the B♭ is both a third divider relating back to the initial G♭ and part of a tonic arpeggiation leading ahead to D♭.

What Handel does in the Courante is even more outrageous. He goes I-V and then III-V, and makes those two dominants motivically related, before starting again on the F, and this time actually having a progression that leads to closure.

EXAMPLE 5.15 *Chopin, Etude, Op. 10, No. 5 ("Black Key"), mm. 1–16, annotated score.*

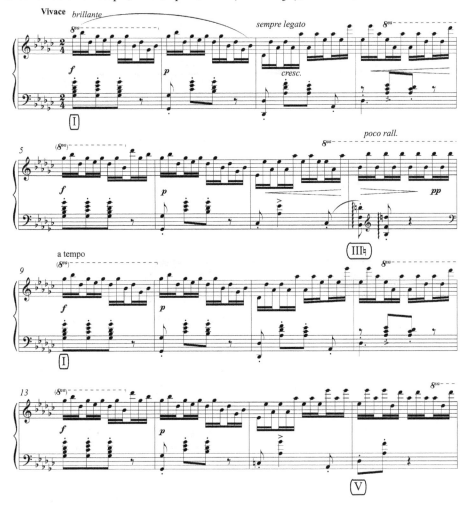

I want to conclude our discussion of the Handel Courante by pointing out one really incredible thing. Let's look again at the top line starting in measure 15, with that motion out of the inner voice. The line ascends a fourth, from C to F (m. 17) and then descends back to C (m. 20): C-D♯-E♭-F and F-E♭-D♯-C. Now go to the end of the piece, to the bass starting in measure 43. At that point, we're on the dominant and we expect a perfect authentic cadence, where measure 44 is going to provide the tonic. But instead, the bass ascends chromatically from C to F: C (m. 43)-D♭-D♮ (m. 44)-E♭-E♮ (m. 45)-F (m. 46). Then, having reached the F, it descends back to C: F (m. 46)-E♭ (m. 47)-D♭ (m. 48)-C (m. 49). Can you see the significance of this? We've talked about rising and falling fourths as a motive in this piece. The prime form of the rising and falling fourths is the one that goes C-F-C in the first three melodic notes of the piece. What we just looked at in the melody of measures 14–20 represents a huge augmentation and transformation of that motive at the same pitch level, C, despite the change of key. At the end of the piece, by putting in that deceptive cadence in measure 44, Handel is able to create another hugely augmented rising and falling fourth, C-F-C.

EXAMPLE 5.16 *Chopin, "Black Key" Etude, Schenker's analysis from* The Masterwork in Music, *Vol. 1.*

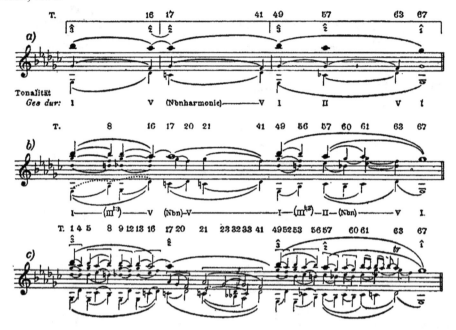

There is a tendency to think of Handel as a kind of wild man of Baroque composition, who, in a lot of his pieces, seemed unable to get inspiration unless he stole something from other composers. His music seems sometimes all over the map. But at other times it's quite astonishing, as in this piece, just how technically tight it is. Even if you don't entirely buy the derivation of these large-scale motions from the three little eighth-notes in measure 1, the integrative function of the perfect fourth, rising and falling, really can't be denied.

J. S. Bach, Gavotte en Rondeaux
from Violin Partita No. 3 in E major

We'll work on the Bach Gavotte en Rondeaux, including a discussion of Rondo form from a Schenkerian perspective. It's a very difficult piece, and we'll probably spend almost the entire class on it. At the end of the class, we'll talk a bit about the Classical rondo, especially in the music of Mozart, which is very different from the Bach Gavotte. [Editor's Note: Schachter discusses the Bach Gavotte at length in [Schachter 1987], an article published in Israel Studies in Musicology.

T HERE ARE A FEW ISSUES OF HISTORICAL BACKGROUND AND TERMINOLOGY I'd like to get out of the way before we begin to look closely at the Bach Gavotte en Rondeaux. It may seem surprising to some of you to find a rondo in the music of the Baroque period. In fact, rondos were extremely plentiful in the music of French composers. For example, a huge number of Couperin's harpsichord pieces are in rondo form, and his use of the form is not at all dissimilar to Bach's, although his music is less complex than Bach's. So rondos are rare in Bach's music, but not in Baroque music generally.

As for terminology, in their book, *Musical Morphology*, Siegmund Levarie and Ernst Levy make a useful distinction between a *refrain* and a *ritornello* [Levarie and Levy 1983]. For them, a refrain comes at the end of a segment of a piece, and it keeps coming back. A ritornello begins the piece and also ends it, and therefore seems to be more integral to the piece as a whole. For rondos, Levarie and Levy prefer the term ritornello, and that's the term I'm going to use (although it's not in general usage nowadays). For the music that comes between the ritornellos, I will generally use the terms episode or couplet.

Now I want to talk about the rhythms of a gavotte (and other pieces with similar rhythm), and especially about how performers should play them [Example 6.1]. Many performing musicians mistakenly think that a gavotte like this one just has an eccentric way of writing a normal $\frac{4}{4}$ or cut time piece—the barline is just shifted over two beats, and the main downbeat of the measure is the written beat 3. I concede that an emphasis accrues to those first two beats simply because they are the first sounds one hears. But that emphasis is what Lerdahl and Jackendoff call a *phenomenal accent*—an accent produced by sonic emphasis without regard for tonal or rhythmic function [Lerdahl and Jackendoff 1983]. I would maintain, however, that in this piece (and other gavottes) the *metric* accent falls on the notated

EXAMPLE 6.1 *Bach, Gavotte en Rondeaux from Violin Partita No. 3 in E major, annotated score.*

first beat, not the third. Scan the whole piece several times. I think you'll eventually find that the piece takes shape more satisfactorily if the metric accents fall on first beats. This is one of those pieces in which phrases tend to gravitate to an accented point at the end.

The co-author of my harmony textbook and great friend, Edward Aldwell, who was a wonderful Bach performer, said to me that he found it very helpful with gavottes—Bach's gavottes, anyway—to think of them in half-bars, beginning with half-bar 2. In the Gavotte en Rondeaux, we would start 2-3-4-1, and continue that way right through the opening ritornello [Example 6.2].

EXAMPLE 6.1 (*Continued*)

EXAMPLE 6.2 *Bach, Gavotte en Rondeaux, mm. 1–8, annotated score.*

The Gavottes from the English Suite No. 3 in G minor and the French Suite No. 5 in G major can be usefully counted out in the same way: in half-bars, starting on half-bar number 2. That works quite well, I find [Example 6.3].

EXAMPLE 6.3 *Gavottes from a) English Suite No. 3 in G minor and b) French Suite No. 5 in G major, annotated scores.*

I know very little about Baroque dancing, but my understanding is that in the eighteenth-century gavotte, the actual dance step starts on the first notated downbeat, and not on the opening third beat. This also lends plausibility to the idea that gavottes begin with a genuine upbeat.

There are many other examples, not gavottes, that present similar sorts of rhythmic issues. Consider, for example, the beginning of the Brahms Intermezzo in A minor, Op. 76, No. 7 [Example 6.4].

EXAMPLE 6.4 *Brahms, Intermezzo in A minor, Op. 76, No. 7, mm. 1–5, annotated score.*

The downbeat that you feel and play *has* to be the notated downbeat, not the first quarter-note you hear in the upbeat to measure 1. The way that Brahms's piece develops, it's quite clear that that's the way you have to think of the meter, right from the beginning of the piece.

In some later music (Mendelssohn is a prime example of this), there's a related tendency to organize melodic and harmonic ideas in groups of four impulses, and the question of which of the four is the metric downbeat can be an interesting one. Mendelssohn's beautiful *Song Without Words* (Op. 62, No. 1) is a good example [Example 6-5]. If you count out the half-bars, using the numbers purely to mark places, not to suggest accents, you start out with two phrases, each with four impulses. Mendelssohn writes an accent on the half-bar before measure 1, and he repeats the harmony over the barline into measure 1. He doesn't write an accent on the downbeat of measure 2 (the fourth half-bar); nevertheless it is a tonic resolution, in fact, the first tonic you hear in the piece. Using terminology from Lerdahl and Jackendoff [1983], the downbeat of measure 2 gets a *structural accent*, even though it would be played with a decrescendo by the pianist. A structural accent is caused by an emphasis on some event in the tonal structure. For instance, the final tonic in a cadence would attract a structural accent, even if it falls on a weak beat at the end of a diminuendo. So within these units of four impulses, we have different kinds of accents on 1 and 4. That's not an uncommon way to shape a phrase, with these sorts of accents at the beginning and the end, and with a transition between them in the middle. But that can never be put into a strictly metrical form, because the accented beats come unevenly.

The beginning of the second phrase is marked not with an accent, as the first one was, but with a *sforzando* sign, which is a stronger marking. It's quite clear, then, that one wants to give the main impulse to those beginning accents. Nevertheless, there is something slightly suspicious about the accents right from the beginning; they don't fall into equidistant units of time, but rather a long one, then a short one, then another long one, and so on. That's quite different from the gavotte situation, even though it's related to it.

Now let's get back to our Gavotte en Rondeaux and take a close look at the opening ritornello. The upper voice has two descents from G# (scale-degree $\hat{3}$) to E (scale-degree $\hat{1}$)— first leading to the downbeat of measure 4 and then to the downbeat of measure 8—but I don't like taking the first of those at face value. I prefer to say that the first one is a kind of motion into the inner voice of the tonic chord rather than a true resolution to scale-degree $\hat{1}$—it's too soon for that [Example 6.6]. One important harmonic detail: the chord on the downbeat of measure 1 might be analyzed as IV^7. But the sense of a 7-6 suspension is so strong, and its resolution so foreordained, that I think it makes more sense to hear it as II^6.

If we accept that the first top-voice motion down to the tonic note is not really a complete resolution, which comes only at the cadence in measure 8, then the basic harmonic plan of the ritornello would be a tonic prolongation in the first four measures, supporting a motion from $\hat{3}$ into an inner voice, and then a stronger I to II^6 to V to I supporting an upper voice that descends $\hat{3}$-$\hat{2}$-$\hat{1}$. In both halves of the ritornello, the upper-voice $\hat{3}$ is embellished by an upper neighbor (A), supported by II^6, that comes in through reaching-over.

Let's move ahead now to the first episode (or couplet). Harmonically, it gravitates toward C# minor. It connects with the preceding ritornello through a neighbor-note idea, namely, a motion 5-6 in relation to the overall tonic, E major [Example 6.7].

EXAMPLE 6.5 *Mendelssohn, Songs Without Words, Op. 62, No. 1, mm. 1–6, annotated score.*

EXAMPLE 6.6 *Bach, Gavotte en Rondeaux, opening ritornello, mm. 1–8, analytical sketch.*

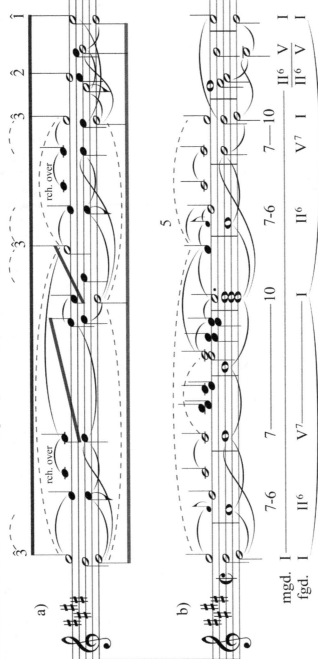

EXAMPLE 6.7 *Bach, Gavotte en Rondeaux, first episode (couplet), mm. 8–16, analytical sketch.*

Form: R₁   C₁   R₂

R = Ritornello; C = Couplet

Notice that whenever we get the possibility of the C♯-minor chord (as we do in measures 10 and 12), it's in first inversion, that is, with E in the bass and C♯ a sixth above it. The first time you get C♯ in what constitutes the bass in this texture is the very last note in the episode (m. 16). The single note there stands for a complete root-position C♯-minor triad, which goes right back to E major. That's where we return from scale-degree $\hat{6}$ to scale-degree $\hat{5}$ over E. In that way, Bach is able to stay very close to the E major of the ritornello—not only by going, as he does, to C♯ minor, but also in the way he goes there, with that large-scale 5-6-5 motion.

Look in measure 10 at the harmony in the first half of the measure. The B♯ in the upper voice is the leading tone, suspended from the previous measure. The C♯ on the second quarter note is not itself the resolution, but is an anticipation of the resolution, which comes on the third beat. That C♯ doesn't suggest any harmony other than the C♯-minor chord itself—that's why I think of the C♯ as properly coming on the third beat, but as being anticipated on the second beat.

Now let's talk about the voice leading starting on the resulting I⁶ chord in the second half of measure 10 [Example 6.8]. The bass has an ascending third-progression: E (m. 10)-F♯ (m. 11)-G♯ (m. 12). The underlying or expected placement of the G♯ would be on the downbeat of measure 12, although it doesn't actually occur until the second beat of the measure. There's a kind of hidden imitation there between the parts—they both have descending third-progressions: D♯-C♯-B♯ in the upper voice (mm. 11–12) and G♯-F♯-E in the bass (m. 12).

Now let's consider the top voice across the entire couplet (mm. 8–16). In the first four measures, we have $\hat{5}$ (m. 8 and m. 10)-$\hat{6}$ (m. 11)-$\hat{4}$ (m. 11)-$\hat{3}$ (m. 11)-$\hat{2}$ (m. 12). In the second four measures, we start again on $\hat{5}$ (m. 13), and descend $\hat{5}$-$\hat{4}$-$\hat{3}$-$\hat{2}$-$\hat{1}$, with the A in measure 14 as a neighbor note. So I would say we have a slightly disguised interruption in measure 12: $\hat{5}$-$\hat{4}$-$\hat{3}$-$\hat{2}$ before the interruption and $\hat{5}$-$\hat{4}$-$\hat{3}$-$\hat{2}$-$\hat{1}$ after it. The apparent resolution to the tonic in the second half of measure 12 is a very surface thing: the dominant on the first half of the measure is better understood as looking back to the opening tonic of the couplet, within the first branch of the interruption. The tonic in the second half of measure 12 is the beginning of the second branch.

In *Free Composition* [Schenker 1979], Schenker indicates that between the dividing or interrupting dominant (like the one on the first half of measure 12) and the tonic that comes at the beginning of the second branch (like the one on the second half of measure 12), we can have either a seventh of the dominant-seventh chord leading into a resumption of scale-degree $\hat{3}$, or we could have an 8-7 motion over the dominant [Example 6-9].

EXAMPLE 6.8 Bach, *Gavotte en Rondeaux*, first episode (couplet), mm. 8–16, more detailed analytical sketch.

EXAMPLE 6.9 *Two ways of connecting a dividing dominant with the tonic that follows (after Schenker).*

Usually that happens with a transfer of register, so the upper-voice tone can return in its proper register. Rather less frequently, the seventh ($\hat{4}$) is heard in the same register as the $\hat{5}$ it comes from. That's more natural in a way, but we lose the unity of register, because now the main upper-voice tone is returning an octave too low. But it's exactly that less common situation we have in measure 12 of the Gavotte. The 8-7 motion over the dividing dominant comes in the lower register and resolves there, but then it's immediately transferred up an octave, and the second branch resumes in the correct register.

It's important to understand that, in Schenkerian analysis, something can be tonally closed at one level but simultaneously open at another level. For example, if we have the interruption pattern $\hat{3}$-$\hat{2}$//$\hat{3}$-$\hat{2}$-$\hat{1}$, the first of those $\hat{2}$s does not resolve into the $\hat{3}$ that immediately follows it. That $\hat{2}$ wants to go to $\hat{1}$—that is its destiny. When $\hat{3}$ comes back again after the first $\hat{2}$, it comes back as a re-beginning or new beginning, rather than the ending or goal of something. Those two tones—the first $\hat{2}$ and the $\hat{3}$ that comes right after it—are divorced from each other. But just as we can have a river bisecting a river valley into two separate parts, you can still build a bridge over the river on another level, and that bridge can make a kind of connection. That's what we have here in measure 12 of the Gavotte.

After the first couplet, of course, the E-major ritornello returns, and I want to talk a bit about the ways in which Bach handles the return, here and elsewhere in the piece. The last two returns of the rondo theme of the ritornello in particular are a little bit different from the preceding ones, although these also vary somewhat. Look at the penultimate return of the ritornello in measure 64. This is the one place where Bach actually composes different notes—the ritornello begins with G♯ rather than E as the lowest note. The previous episode has ended on F♯ minor, which is II in E major, and it can be difficult to go directly from II to I (among other things, there's the danger of parallel fifths). I think that's why Bach makes the change he does—he is forced to by the circumstances.

But that change creates an opportunity for the player, because you can think of the E-major chord that comes on the second half of measure 64 as a passing chord rather than as a strong tonic that marks the return of the ritornello. Look at the harmony: we have F♯-minor (as tonic) in the first half of measure 64, followed by an E-major chord (that I want to think of as passing), followed immediately by another F♯-minor chord. By this time, of course, we've lost the key of F♯ minor, and the bass line is on its way up to B. So I would play the beginning of this ritornello, with G♯ in the bass, less as a new beginning and more as something that continues the line from F♯ up to B.

Something similar and yet a bit different happens at the end of the last episode leading to the final statement of the ritornello (m. 92). In this case, I would tend to hear the G♯ in the bass (marking a cadence in G♯ minor) as the first tone in a bass line that ascends G♯ (m. 92)-A (m. 93)-B (m. 94). Here, Bach doesn't have to change any notes in the beginning of the ritornello to create this musical bridge across a formal dividing line. So if you're playing it, you might want to bring out the continuity from the G♯ in measure 92 to the A in measure 93.

Now I want to say something about playing repeated things, like the repeated statements of the ritornello in this Gavotte. While I agree with C. P. E. Bach that in music there are no rules without exceptions, I think this is one that doesn't have too many exceptions: when we have something that repeats, we should bring out the differences. The similarities will often take care of themselves, but the differences are what we need.

Here's an illustrative story. There was a great violinist and gifted conductor, Szymon Goldberg, who played a lot from the 1920s through the 1950s. He was coaching some very gifted young musicians in a chamber music group when one of the players stopped a rehearsal to say, "Mr. Goldberg, this tune that I have here is the same as what another instrument had earlier. The notes are exactly the same. Should I play it the same or different?" And Goldberg said, "If it's exactly the same, make it different." That's a good philosophy for such things.

By the way, it's very often at places of recapitulation or reprise that something that is the same gets done differently, and something that one would expect doesn't actually happen. That's very often where a good composer especially is going to want to bridge over the beginning of a repeated section, specifically because it is so predictable. One wants to play with that predictability in various ways. A famous example is the first movement of Beethoven's *Appassionata*, where the whole first theme is repeated, but over a dominant pedal in the left hand. Or, something much less grandiose but equally great, the first movement of the G-minor Symphony of Mozart, where the opening upbeat figure is heard over tonic harmony at the beginning of the movement and over dominant harmony at the beginning of the recapitulation. This is something that Peter Smith has discussed quite a bit, and it happens a lot in the music of Brahms [Smith 1994]. That subtle thing makes a world of difference in the feeling. There are many places where you might have a thematic recapitulation, by where you've not yet fully arrived on the tonic. It's a ploy that you get with Beethoven, with Chopin, with Mozart, with all the great composers. Bach is in good company here.

Now let's look at the second couplet (mm. 24–40). Basically it moves from tonic to dominant, and the tonic music in measures 25–28 is literally transposed to the dominant in measures 29–32. Usually in Schenkerian analysis, if one has an immediate repetition of something, the first statement is considered the principal one. What happens in B major seems to be growing out of, or to be a result of, what happened in E major. But that principle of giving priority to the first statement of something creates some awkwardness in the analysis of this couplet. To show you why, let's focus on the B-major statement, starting in measure 29.

Our main upper-voice note in measure 29 is F♯, which is scale-degree $\hat{5}$ in B major. From there, we would seem to have a rather nice descending fifth-progression in the key of B: F♯ (m. 29)-E (m. 31)-D♯ (m. 36)-C♯ (m. 39)-B (m. 40). In light of that, we could imagine that the tonic statement in measures 25–28 is basically preparatory, and that the B-major statement has priority over the E-major statement. That actually works out very nicely in many ways. In the first two ritornellos, we had G♯ as the main upper voice tone. At the end of measure 28, still in the tonic key of E major, we regain G♯ in the proper register. At that point, G♯ ($\hat{3}$) moves down to F♯ ($\hat{2}$ in the main key and $\hat{5}$ in the dominant), and the F♯ is prolonged by the descending fifth-progression we discussed, moving into an inner voice.

That makes a very neat analysis, but I'm not quite prepared to abandon my conviction about giving priority to the first statement of something that is repeated, and so my reading of it is actually a little bit different [Example 6.10]. My reading is that all of this is in the shadow of E major. G♯ still goes to F♯ in measure 29, but I don't take that as an *Urlinie* tone. Instead, I take the F♯ in measure 29 as part of a long descending motion down a sixth from the G♯ (prolonged from the beginning of the piece until m. 29) down to the B in measure 40, at the end of the second couplet. When the

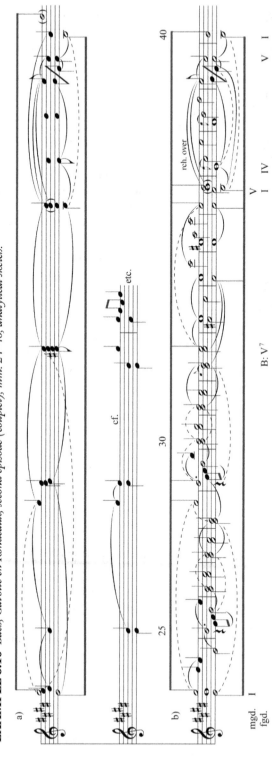

EXAMPLE 6.10 Bach, Gavotte en Rondeaux, second episode (couplet), mm. 24–40, analytical sketch.

B arrives in measure 40, there's an F♯ present by implication as a missing top-voice tone. Between the $\hat{3}$ over I (m. 24) and the $\hat{2}$ over V (m. 40) there would still be the initial segment of an interrupted progression, but not on the highest structural level. In this case, the highest-level $\hat{2}$ would be the implied F♯ in measure 40.

That's not as straightforward an analysis as the other one, and maybe not even as good an analysis. But while I don't want to be too principle-ridden, the principle of giving priority to the first occurrence of something is important to me. In this kind of analysis, you want to find a relationship between the elements of design—that is, the motivic things, the repetitions, the contrasts, all of those—and the underlying structure. One basic element of design is that there's a difference between the beginning of a process and the continuation of it. Usually, the beginning is going to be the main thing until you get to the goal of the process, which is also going to be of great importance.

If we make use of the concept of implied tones, and if we read an implied $\hat{2}$ (F♯) as the top voice of the second couplet (m. 40), we infer a large-scale interruption at the second couplet. We've been on G♯ as scale-degree $\hat{3}$, and now we follow it with F♯ as $\hat{2}$ over dominant harmony. So we have $\hat{3}$ over I and $\hat{2}$ over V. We know that this is a rondo, and we know that the E-major opening will return, so the necessary conditions for an interruption are present. We can therefore think of the first four sections of the piece (R1, C1, R2, and C2) as comprising a single large grouping that transcends the individual bits of this wonderful piece.

Let's look now at the third couplet (mm. 48–64). It goes to F♯-minor, which is II in the overall tonic, E major. That's something not uncommon in Bach, by the way, having as a secondary key area a composing-out of the II. It's not as common in later music, but it's very frequent with Bach. We get to F♯ minor within four measures, unlike going to C♯ minor in Couplet 1, which was a more laborious process, as was getting to the dominant in Couplet 2.

Starting right in measure 48, the bass ascends E-F♯ (m. 49)-G♯ (m. 49)-A (m. 50). Now look back to the very beginning of the piece—the first interval in the lower voice is E-A. The first couplet begins the same way (mm. 8–9): E-A. Also, at the beginning of the second couplet, the lower voice is essentially on E and G♯, but the first move away from the tonic takes us up to A. This seems to be a characteristic motive.

Now I want to use this third couplet to get us into a discussion about how measures are grouped [Example 6.11].

EXAMPLE 6.11 *Bach, Gavotte en Rondeaux, third episode (couplet), mm. 48–64, annotated score.*

We begin with a four-measure group (mm. 49–52) leading to a strong arrival on F♯ minor in measure 53, which begins another four-measure group (mm. 53–56). But look what happens in measure 56. It's simultaneously the fourth measure of one group and the first measure of the next. The expected four-measure group has been elided, and 4 has turned into 1. Measure 56 enters as though it is expected to be a fourth measure, but it is turned into a first measure of the next group, and the parallelism of measures 56–57 and 58–59 confirms the status of measure 56 as the first measure in a new four-measure group. As a result, we have one fewer measures than we would usually have. But we are actually compensated for that with an extra measure, namely, measure 64, which is added to the last four-measure group of the third episode. There are two places in this episode where there are really powerful F♯-minor chords (mm. 53 and 60). These are the local tonics when they come in, and I think they tend to emphasize and help to delineate the meter, which is based on this pattern of four-measure groups.

It is extremely important to understand that these groupings do not necessarily coincide with metrical strength. The relationship between what one emphasizes in performance—perhaps because something is an expressive dissonance you want to bring out—and the sorts of hypermetrical groupings we're talking about is not an easy or simple thing. Let's explore this relationship in the C-minor Prelude from the first book of the *Well-Tempered Clavier* [Example 6.12]. We start with four measures of tonic pedal. Measure 5 is where the right-hand part skips up so that the main note is now E♭ and not C. It's also where we have a 5-6 motion (G to A♭) over the bass C. I hear measure 5 as a hypermetrical downbeat, and it sets up a pattern of strong and weak measures, with measures 1 and 3 strong and measures 2 and 4 weak. However, interestingly, in this case the weak measures (like mm. 6 and 8) have dissonant harmonies that one might very well want to bring out. But I also would think that doesn't really disturb the hypermeter, which continues its alternation of strong and weak measures. At some point as one goes on, the cognitive dissonance of having the weak measures played strongly and the strong measures played weakly resolves itself.

In this Bach prelude, one very often hears or reads measures 6–7, 8–9, and 10–11 analyzed as 9-10 suspensions. *Counterpoint in Composition* (a book I co-authored) does exactly this, but I now think that's wrong [Salzer and Schachter 1969]. The pattern is actually not 9-10, but 10-9, grouping measures 5–6, 7–8, and 9–10 together. The dissonances are caused not by suspensions in the bass, but by anticipations in the top voice. That remains true regardless of whether one wants to emphasize the metrically strong measures or the metrically weak measures. In fact, it often makes the best sense to emphasize the measures that are hypermetrically weak.

Mozart very often has four-measure ideas in which the performer would naturally emphasize the metrically weak measures, as in the beginning of the first movement of his Piano Sonata in B♭ major, K. 333 [Example 6.13]. You would never play that phrase with an emphasis on measures 1 and 3. The music definitely moves toward measure 2, and then toward measure 4. But that does not mean that measure 2 or measure 4 is a hypermetrical beat 1. Even within measure 1 itself, beat 2 receives more emphasis than the actual downbeat. With hypermeasures as well as smaller measures, one brings out many different things, and one has to serve as the adjudicator for lots of conflicting demands. The harmony will point you one way, the voice leading will point you another, the melodic patterns will point you in yet another.

As a guide to the topics we are discussing, I highly recommend William Rothstein's wonderful book, *Phrase Rhythm in Tonal Music* [Rothstein 1989]. Its first chapter

EXAMPLE 6.12 *Bach, Prelude in C Minor from the* Well-Tempered Clavier, *Vol. 1, mm. 1–14, annotated score.*

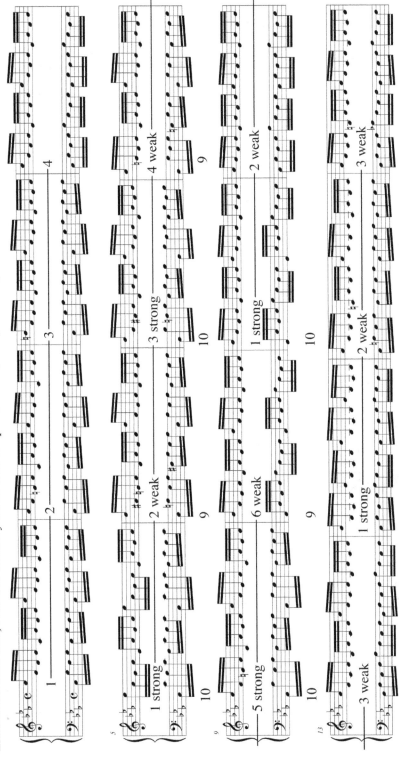

EXAMPLE 6.13 *Mozart, Piano Sonata in B♭ major, K. 333, first movement, mm. 1–4, annotated score.*

clarifies the difference between phrase or grouping on the one hand and hypermeasure on the other. One of his examples is the "Blue Danube" Waltz of Johann Strauss [Example 6.14].

EXAMPLE 6.14 *Johann Strauss, "Blue Danube" Waltz, mm. 1–17, annotated score (after Rothstein).*

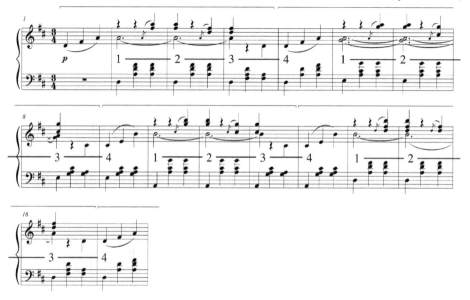

It's obviously in four-measure groups, and each group begins with an upbeat measure. But you would never project a downbeat quality for measure 1 (or mm. 5, 9, or 13) even though they are the first thing you hear in each group. Instead, you would bring out measures 2, 6, 10, and 14, because those are the hypermetrical downbeats. The grouping and the hypermeter are not the same. The hypermeter goes 1-2-3-4, 1-2-3-4, but the grouping might well go 4-1-2-3, 4-1-2-3 as in the Strauss waltz. It is very worthwhile to think about these things, especially for performers.

Now let's get back to the third couplet of our Gavotte [Example 6.15]. From the beginning of the section on E major (m. 48) to the arrival on F♯ minor in measure 53, I read the bass as moving up from E through E♯ (m. 52, actually in the upper register) to F♯. The upper voice ascends from G♯ to its upper neighbor A—there's that neighbor-note idea again—and the A is brought in via a reaching-over from B (m. 52). There's a strong connection between that F♯-minor arrival and the next big arrival in measure 60—the upper voice between them has a series of interesting reachings-over. From there, we have

EXAMPLE 6.15 *Bach, Gavotte en Rondeaux, third episode (couplet), mm. 48–64, analytical sketch.*

a descending third-span in the upper voice, A-G♯-F♯ (scale-degrees 3̂-2̂-1̂ in F♯ minor), prolonging the A. When the ritornello returns, the A moves back to G♯. In that sense, the whole third couplet involves prolonging an upper neighbor note (A) to the main melodic tone (G♯).

After the fourth ritornello (mm. 64–72), we get to the fourth couplet, which is not only the longest of the couplets but also the most complex and difficult part of the piece. To start right in the middle, I note that measures 80–88 are a kind of detour or insertion, an expansion of some sort between the D♯ in the first half of measure 80 and the D♯ at the beginning of measure 88. The greater length of this couplet is due in part to the insertion of these extra eight measures. If you play the fourth couplet without this insertion, going directly from measure 80 to measure 88, it actually goes quite smoothly. My feeling about this is that it's one of those places where we have to skip mentally. Schenker uses the term "the flying ear"—*das fliegende Ohr*—which he thought all the great composers had, and which other musicians should try to emulate as much as they can.

This episode begins in the tonic E major (m. 72) and then, as a kind of reference to the first episode, gravitates toward C♯ minor via the familiar 5-6 motion over E (mm. 73–74) [Example 6.16]. Then it goes briefly to F♯ minor (m. 76) and then to B major (m. 78) in a kind of descending fifths pattern: C♯-F♯-B. The whole basic idea so far is I-V, but to get there we go through some of the tonal areas of the previous episodes (C♯, F♯, and B), although not necessarily in the order in which they occur in the piece.

The music from the beginning of this couplet to the arrival in B major (mm. 72–78) sounds as though it could be a kind of eccentric antecedent phrase, and what happens next (mm. 78–90) sounds like the beginning of a consequent phrase. But the proportions are very odd: the consequent is so much longer, partly because of that big eight-measure interpolation (mm. 80–87). The A♯ in the upper voice in measure 80 connects eventually with the C♯ at the end of measure 90, moving down to B right before the cadence in G♯ minor.

Now I want to talk about some ways in which the music from the third ritornello to the end of the piece (mm. 40–end) is bound together [Example 6.17]. The third ritornello (mm. 40–48) is in E major, with G♯ as the upper voice. The third episode (mm. 48–64) then takes us to F♯ minor (via E♯ in the bass), and its upper-voice A is brought in via reaching-over. From there, I'd like to see the same pattern as continuing—the fourth episode (mm. 72–93) takes us to G♯ minor (via F𝄪), and its upper-voice B is similarly brought in via reaching-over. Then, in the final ritornello, we move to the dominant and then the tonic, with a resolution of the neighbor-note A to the primary melodic tone G♯, and then a final descent from G♯ to E.

But this description leaves the fourth ritornello (mm 64–72) out of the discussion. As in our discussion of the large-scale formal organization of the Handel Courante last week, it's important to learn to hear non-consecutively. One has to jump back and forth, and if the contour of the music seems to justify such jumping, none of us will fall into the river.

Bach's Two-Part Invention in F major gives a very small-scale version of what I'm talking about [Example 6.18]. You hear the returns to F on the second half of beats 2 and 3. But at the same time you also hear the motion up an octave, F-A-C-F. In hearing that larger motion, you skip over the F's, and hear them as interpolations.

I would like to maintain that in our Gavotte, you can similarly hear directly from F♯ minor in the third couplet to G♯ minor in the fourth couplet, skipping over the tonic return in the fourth ritornello. If so, it would be possible to hear the entire Gavotte in two large

EXAMPLE 6.16 *Bach, Gavotte en Rondeaux, fourth episode (couplet), mm. 72–92, analytical sketch.*

EXAMPLE 6.17 Bach, *Gavotte en Rondeaux, mm. 40–end, synoptic analytical sketch.*

EXAMPLE 6.18 *Bach, Two-Part Invention in F major, mm. 1–3, annotated score.*

groups, the first spanning from the first ritornello to the third ritornello, and the second from the third ritornello to the end of the piece [Example 6.19].

In anticipation of next week's lesson, let me talk briefly about Mozart's rondos. I want to emphasize an idea I've tried to present today, namely, that in a rondo, motion from one episode directly to the next one might actually coexist with motion from the episode to the theme and then to the next episode. For instance, Mozart very often uses a five-part rondo scheme: A^1-B-A^2-C-A^3. What I'm saying is that motion from B to C may coexist with motion from B to A^2 and A^2 to C.

The rondo theme, which is typically a kind of mini three-part form in itself, will be in the tonic. The episode that follows is very frequently, although by no means always, in VI. Let's take the second movement of Mozart's Piano Concerto in C minor (K. 491) as our example. The rondo theme is in E♭ major and the first episode is in C minor. Then there's a brief return to the ritornello, followed by a second episode in A♭ major. The second episode concludes on V^7/E♭, and that takes us back to the final statement of the ritornello.

A^1	B	A^2	C	A^3
Rit. 1	Episode 1	Rit. 2	Episode 2	Rit 3
E♭	c	E♭	A♭ → V^7/E♭	E♭

The dominant-seventh chord at the end of the second episode doesn't have a whole section to itself, but it's a chord of great structural importance.

That's an extremely important point: we can have important harmonic goals that are not prolonged at enormous length, that are not necessarily given a new theme, and that are not tonicized as a new key, but which are nonetheless of the greatest structural importance. In this Mozart rondo, the dominant-seventh chord at the end of the second episode is fully on a par with the tonicized VI and IV. In what I call "analysis by key"[Schachter 1999a] you might find a progression through the keys of E♭ major, C minor, E♭ major, A♭ major, and E♭ major, leaving out altogether the dominant B♭, which is just as vital to the piece as anything else in it. Furthermore, I think one can hear a direct connection between the C-minor and A♭-major episodes, with the return to tonic in the A^2 rondo theme as a sort of interpolation within a coherent progression that spans the movement: I (first A section)-VI (first episode)-IV (second episode)-V^7 (retransition)-I (third A section) [Example 6.20]. (I discuss this issue in my article, "Either/Or" [Schachter 1999b]).

EXAMPLE 6.19 *Bach, Gavotte en Rondeaux, analytical sketch of entire movement.*

EXAMPLE 6.20 *Mozart, Piano Concerto in C minor, K. 491, second movement, overview of bass line.*

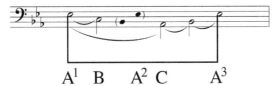

A^1 B A^2 C A^3

This idea of going I-VI-IV-V^7-I is very prevalent in music, especially in larger sonata-rondo forms. There, we might have an exposition that goes from tonic to dominant, followed by a return to tonic. Then we might have some kind of new episode that contains a development-like section, featuring VI and IV and culminating in a V^7 chord that leads to a recapitulation of the opening music in the home key. In the third movement of Mozart's A-major Concerto (K. 488), for example, we go to F♯ minor (VI) at the beginning of the new section. The F♯ minor goes to D major (IV), and the D goes to a big E (V^7)—again one of those dominants that doesn't get a key of its own but it's still part of the essential design. That's a scheme that Beethoven used quite frequently in his sonata forms, especially in some of the late pieces. The first movement of the Piano Sonata, Op. 111, for example, goes from C minor to A♭ major, strongly to F minor in the development section, and then V to I. The Ninth Symphony goes from D minor to B♭ major to G minor again, before returning to the tonic by way of V. The slow movement of Mozart's C-minor Concerto has the same scheme on a somewhat smaller (but still quite large) scale.

Mozart, Sonata for Violin and Piano, K. 481, Adagio

We'll spend the entire class on the Adagio from Mozart's Piano and Violin Sonata K. 481.

Let's work our way through this wonderful piece, starting with the first main section (mm. 1–16) [Example 7.1]. What is the inner form of this section? By that I mean the form of the section by itself, as distinct from the form of the entire movement. You might think of it as a *rounded binary* form; that would be correct, but not very specific. In many rounded binaries, if we have an eight-measure opening section, there will also be a return of those eight measures, but here there is a return of only four measures. I think a more exact description would be what is sometimes called *quatrain form*. That's a term that is not so widely used nowadays, although it was common among musicologists perhaps twenty years ago.

A quatrain is a verse form made of four lines. The musical quatrain works in the following way: a four-measure idea followed by another four measures of basically the same material; then four measures of contrasting material; then a return to the original four-measure idea. So, aaba, or if you prefer, aa'ba", because of the variation technique that might be applied. The musicologist who first pointed out quatrain form was Denes Bartha, who investigated its roots in central European folk music [Bartha 1969, 1971, 1975]. An amazing number of pieces can be classified this way well into the nineteenth century, and it's good to have a name for it.

"Au Claire de la Lune" is a simple example [Example 7.2]. The first two of those little sections belong in the tonic, the third one moves to the dominant, and then the first section returns. The most famous example of a quatrain is Beethoven's "Ode to Joy." The sixteen-measure rondo theme for our Mozart sonata movement can be thought of in similar terms: a (mm. 1–4)-a' (mm. 5–8)-b (mm. 9–12)-a" (mm. 13–16). Quite often, as in the Mozart, the two halves of the quatrain are repeated.

The tonal structure of the rondo theme is pretty straightforward [Example 7.3].

EXAMPLE 7.1 *Mozart, Sonata for Piano and Violin, K. 481, second movement (Adagio), annotated score.*

The first a-section takes us to V and the second a-section goes back to I, so we have tonic for eight measures. The b-section prolongs V for four measures, and then back to I for the last four measures. The upper voice involves a typical fifth-progression from E♭ down to A♭ in the final a-section, with the initial E♭ having been brought in as the first note in the pickup to measure 1 and prolonged through the first twelve measures. It seems pretty clear that E♭ (scale-degree $\hat{5}$) is the principal melodic tone, and that does turn out to be the case. But in principle I want to caution you against falling so in love with your preliminary analytical ideas that you remain too faithful to them, even though they betray you. Always have in reserve the idea that "this is what I now think may be the case, but I'm not sure I will always agree with that."

EXAMPLE 7.1 (*Continued*)

That brings us to the big B-section of the movement (mm. 17–34), but before we get into it in detail, we need to deal with one of the problems in this family of forms, including rondo and what is often called *compound ternary*. Let's say you have an A-section that consists of a little aba, which is a frequent thing in large-scale ternary forms. Sometimes, there are differences of opinion among analysts about whether that little b ought really to be a big B, in which case the section you had previously thought of as big-B is going to be promoted to big-C. In other words, we initially thought we had A (aba)-B, but now we're thinking it might be A-B-A-C.

Think, for instance, of the slow movement of Mozart's so-called "easy" piano Sonata in C major, K. 545, which many analysis students take as a rondo form [Example 7.4]. We have sixteen measures in the tonic (mm. 1–16), then eight measures of contrasting material in the dominant (mm. 17–24), and then eight more measures that return to the opening music in the tonic (mm. 25–32). That takes us to the double bar, after which there is music in G minor. Is the music that begins in measure 17 a small-b within a larger A-section? Or is it really a big-B, in which case the music after the double bar would be a big C-section,

EXAMPLE 7.1 (*Continued*)

and this movement would be basically a rondo, starting ABAC? I think it makes a better analysis to think of the first thirty-two measures as comprising a single A-section, with the G-major to D-major to G-major motion within it, and then the main contrast is with the B-section that begins in G minor in measure 33. Note especially the effect of the repetition of bars 17–32, which produces the inner form of a quatrain for those 32 bars. On the other hand, it is true that in many rondos, the C-section is more elaborately worked out than the B-section, and as a result, a lot of rondos verge on being large ternary forms. It can be difficult to draw a fixed boundary between a rondo, arranged as ABACA, and a large ternary, arranged as A (aba)-B-A.

In our Violin Sonata movement, however, I think we really do have a rondo, so let's return to its B-section, starting in measure 17. This section is obviously going to the dominant, though it doesn't get there right away—we start off with a little bit of F minor. After two measures we move to E♭ major, so the F becomes a kind of upper neighbor in the bass

EXAMPLE 7.1 (*Continued*)

to E♭. The defining cadence on E♭ major comes in measures 27–28, and the top voice there has a descending fifth-progression: B♭-A♭-G-F-E♭. By the way, what happens in the first half of measure 27 is very typical of tonal music. You can have a repeated motive, like the two groups of sixteenth-notes, where the first note (B♭) is the main note in the first statement, and the last note (A♭) is the main note of the last statement. A reinterpretation like that very often results from the way we privilege stepwise relationships. Something similar is happening with the two descending fifth-progressions in section A and in section B. In Section A we had E♭-D♭-C-B♭-A♭, and we said that it prolonged its first note (E♭). In Section B we have B♭-A♭-G-F-E♭, and its last note (also E♭) is the main tone. In other words, the two ideas meet on E flat.

Starting in measure 28, we have a seven-measure *codetta* and *retransition* to the return of the rondo theme in the tonic, A♭ major. That this is a codetta is proven by the fact that the same music is used toward the end of the piece (starting in m. 91), where Mozart is clearly

EXAMPLE 7.1 (*Continued*)

leading his listeners to expect a conclusion. Of course, there's a little surprise before the conclusion is reached, but the repeated I-V-I-V (similar to a pedal point) is a signal that in both passages we are in some kind of codetta.

At the end of the codetta (or retransition) in measures 32–34, there are some interesting motivic and voice-leading details to which I want to call your attention. The eighth-notes on the second half of measure 34 seem to represent, of course, the arpeggiation of the A♭-major triad that we had leading into measure 1—the notes of the triad are filled in with apparent passing notes: E♭-(D♭)-C-(B♭)-A♭. You might think that E♭ and C are the main notes, but they are not. D♭ and B♭ are the main notes locally, even though that seems to cut against the restatement of the motive. The upper voice is already on D♭ back in measure 32 over the dominant-seventh chord, and once the upper voice has gotten to the seventh, we've bit into the apple—we've already sinned and there is no going back. We can't un-sin, except by resolving that D♭, and its resolution to C takes place in measures 35–36, where the tonic A♭ major returns with C in the top voice.

EXAMPLE 7.1 (*Continued*)

EXAMPLE 7.2 *"Au Claire de la Lune" as an example of quatrain form.*

EXAMPLE 7.3 *Mozart, Violin Sonata, mm. 1–13, analytical sketch.*

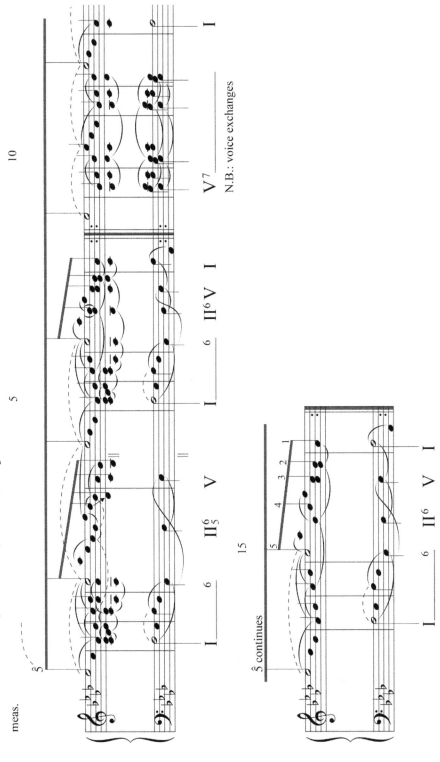

EXAMPLE 7.4 *Mozart, Piano Sonata in C major, K. 545, mm. 1–36, annotated score.*

But I don't want to give you the impression that every time you have 8-7 motion over the dominant, the seventh has to be heard as a passing tone as it is here. In many cases, it's the seventh that's the main tone, and the octave is a kind of consonant appoggiatura to a dissonant tone. The example that Ernst Oster liked to use to teach this point comes in the last movement of Beethoven's Sixth Symphony [Example 7.5]. Surely the upper voice ascends F-G-A-B♭, with B♭ as the main tone, and the C right before it, although it's an octave, is an appoggiatura to it!

There's something similar in Beethoven's Piano Sonata, Op. 101 [Example 7.6]. The E on the downbeat of measure 2, although it's an octave above the bass, is still an appoggiatura to D. There, the harmony also helps you hear it as an appoggiatura, because you have F♯ and A against it.

Back to the Mozart. Let's follow the upper voice, beginning with the arrival on E♭ in measure 28. The main upper-voice motion is from E♭ (m. 28) through D♭ (m. 32) to C (m 36) [Example 7.7].

EXAMPLE 7.4 (*Continued*)

EXAMPLE 7.5 *Beethoven, Symphony No. 6 ("Pastoral"), last movement, mm. 34–36, annotated score.*

EXAMPLE 7.6 *Beethoven's Piano Sonata, Op. 101, first movement, mm. 1–2, annotated score.*

EXAMPLE 7.7 Mozart, *Violin Sonata, mm. 17–35, analytical sketch.*

We stay around E♭ until the end of measure 30, then D-F-A♭ in measure 31. Then in measure 32, an octave lower, the A♭ goes down to G, then G-A♭-B♭-C-D♭, with D♭ as the seventh of the V⁷ chord over E♭. The piano in measure 33 extends above the D♭ to F—that's the ninth above the E♭, which is often used as a kind of accompaniment to the seventh, so clearly we're in seventh territory here, not triad territory. As I said before, the main upper voice motion is 8-7 over the dominant, and the seventh resolves into the third of the A♭ chord in measure 36. We could also say that it resolves into the violin double stops in measure 35, but the resolution is much more vivid when it comes in the melodic line in measure 36.

What follows is a return of the A-section, but abbreviated to only eight measures (mm. 35–42). Schenker claims that the shortening of a rondo theme does not prevent it from being a full thematic return. That is true in this piece, but I do sometimes question it. We talked about this issue in the previous lesson with reference to the second movement of Mozart's Piano Concerto, K. 491, with all of its marvelous wind writing. I argued that it would be hard, and actually wrong, not to hear a continuous motion from E♭ (Ritornello 1), through C minor (Episode 1, dominated by winds), directly to A♭ (Episode 2, again dominated by winds), with the brief return to the Ritornello between the episodes understood within parentheses. We had a very similar thing in our Bach Gavotte en Rondeaux, where we considered the possibility that the next-to-last return of the rondo theme, despite its return to the tonic (E major), was nonetheless parenthetical with respect to a stepwise rising line in the lowest voice.

After that brief return of the rondo theme in the tonic (mm. 35–42), we get to our C-section, which is in the subdominant. As is very often the case in ternary forms and in rondo forms—not an inevitable but certainly a very frequent, very typical way of creating a kind of tonal image for that formal design—we will have, in the upper voice, an upper neighbor (always an upper neighbor, never lower neighbor) to scale-degree $\hat{5}$ or to scale-degree $\hat{3}$, whichever of these was the main upper-voice tone in the rondo theme or A-section. In this case, the C-section has F in the upper voice supported by subdominant harmony, and that tells us that we probably weren't wrong to think, at the beginning of the piece, that the E♭ is in fact scale-degree $\hat{5}$ of the *Urlinie*.

Compared to the A- and B-sections, the music takes on quite a different character in this heavenly D♭ section. It's a little bit reminiscent—I shouldn't say reminiscent, but anticipatory—of the "Priest's March" in *The Magic Flute*. It has a hymn-like character, which is not uncommon in slow movements of this period. The magnificent slow movement of Haydn's String Quartet, Op. 76, No. 1—that great C-major movement—has a similar quality.

The C-section begins very much as though it is going to be a period, but what is unusual is that, instead of going from I to V, the music goes from I to III (i.e., F minor in the key of D♭ major, arriving in m. 50). This kind of large-scale use of III in major is not terribly characteristic of the Classical period, though there are other examples in Haydn and Mozart—it's rather a rarity. Many aspects of the music enhance its unusualness, and the music gets curiouser and curiouser as it goes on.

The C-section seems to be aiming for a kind of closed form. We have a small a-section in the local tonic (D♭ major, mm. 43–46), a modified repeat of the a-section taking us to the mediant (F minor, mm. 47–50), a contrasting b-section (mm. 51–56), followed by a return of the a-section back in D♭ major (mm. 57–60). At this point, I think we expect a continuation that would end with a strong cadence in D♭, giving us basically a small ternary form: A(aa)-B(b)-A(aa) [Example 7.8].

EXAMPLE 7.8 *Mozart, Violin Sonata, mm. 57–60, analytical sketch and hypothetical recomposition.*

But that is not at all what Mozart does, and what happens instead is the crux of the whole movement.

Let's get into it by talking a bit about the dramatic roles of the piano and violin, not only in this section, but throughout the movement. There are certain possibilities that a duo sonata naturally affords that you would not find either in a solo sonata or a larger ensemble such as a quartet. That is to say, you have these two characters, and the composer has to provide them with appropriate material. The most typical thing would be to rely a lot on the repetition of themes: the piano will have the theme in the first place and then the violin will have the theme, and then the next time the piano will have it, and so forth. But what Mozart is doing here is something different. Instead of repetitions within the theme, he relies on the contrasting character of the themes, set off by being given either to the piano or the violin.

Up to this point in the movement, the rondo theme has been given completely to the piano, and the violin plays only an accompaniment. In the episodes, in contrast, in both in the A- and B-sections, the violin takes over and the piano accompanies. The piano has a very chaste and innocent character. The violin is much more passionate, and its passion sometimes has a kind of religious quality, as in the D♭ section. I think of Blake's poems, *Songs of Innocence and of Experience*. The piano is the innocent, and the experienced one is the violin. But the violin is not terribly happy at being excluded from that ritornello theme. So, when she gets the chance, she tries to take over the opening theme. She gets her chance in measures 65–68 and she takes it, presenting a four-measure antecedent phrase in A (!) major. The piano, however, gets a little bit agitated by this, and responds with an increasingly nervous passage with sixteenth-note accompaniments, a passage that goes in register from the middle of the piano to very near the top. It's marked with a big crescendo, one that is perhaps not intended to get to its *forte* as quickly as Mozart shows.

From a formal standpoint, the return of the rondo theme in A major in measures 65–68 is a false return. Its falsity is demonstrated right away, not only by its being in the wrong key, but also because the wrong instrument is playing it. There is thus a sort of drama that is being constructed around the medium of the duo sonata, and that is something one should very much keep in mind. By the way, there's an important dissertation by David Gagné on the influence of medium on Mozart's compositions, although he does not talk about the violin and piano sonatas [Gagné 1988].

Now let's step back and consider this part of the C-section as a whole (mm. 57–75). I'm going to argue that what we have here is a huge chromaticized voice exchange, which starts with the D♭ chord in measure 57 and finishes with the augmented-sixth chord in measure 73, right before the dominant of A♭ major [Example 7.9].

EXAMPLE 7.9 *Mozart, Violin Sonata, mm. 57–75, analytical sketch (overview).*

Our augmented-sixth chord (m. 73) has F♭ in the bass and D♮ in the top voice. Compare that to the initial D♭-major chord (m. 57), which had D♭ in the bass and F♮ in the top voice. The F is exchanged into the bass as an F♭ (written as E), and the D♭, which was in the bass, becomes D♮, which is an augmented-sixth above F♭. Both D and F♭ resolve in the normal way, into the octave E♭. We saw something similar in the Handel Courante—there, too, there was a voice exchange that spanned a big section of music, but that was a diatonic, not a chromatic, voice exchange.

Between the D♭ chord (m. 57) and the augmented-sixth chord (m. 73), there is a passing motion. In the upper voice, we're moving from F to D, and the space between them is filled in with passing notes: F♭ (spelled as E in mm. 61–72) and E♭ (spelled as D♯, in m. 73). To make the connection smoother, the first thing Mozart does is to turn the D♭ major into D♭ minor (spelled as C♯ minor in m. 61). That's the harmony that supports the passing-note F♭ (spelled as E). In fact, that whole false recapitulation in A major (really, B♭ major) can be thought of as support for a passing tone within the large chromaticized voice exchange.

I'd like to say a few words about these sorts of large-scale voice exchanges, especially chromaticized voice exchanges. I consider them part of a wider phenomenon, which is the destabilizing of tonic (or, sometimes, subdominant) harmony as a way of moving to some kind of goal. This destabilization of tonic harmony is something that may happen in the exposition of a sonata form. In the first movement of Mozart's Piano Sonata in F major, K. 332, for example, there's a large-scale chromaticized voice exchange that destabilizes the tonic, F major, and leads to the second theme in C major [Example 7.10]. The A-over-F in the opening becomes F♯-over-A♭ in measures 35–36. That takes us to the V of C major, the dominant key, which is where we want to go.

Here's another possibility, from the development section of the first movement of the Mozart Piano Sonata in A minor, K. 310 [Example 7.11].

EXAMPLE 7.10 *Mozart, Piano Sonata in F major, K. 332, first movement, mm. 1–44, annotated score.*

EXAMPLE 7.10 (*Continued*)

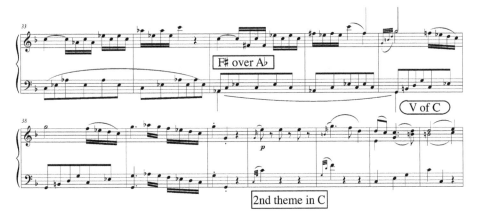

The development section begins in C major (III), but at this point we're in D minor (IV). The goal of the development section is V, and to get there with greater intensity, Mozart chromaticizes the IV within a voice exchange. In measure 70, we have F over D within D minor. The D in the bass descends stepwise (the A minor at the beginning of measure 73 is not yet the functioning tonic) to F, and at the end of measure 73, we have D♯ over F within an augmented-sixth chord that resolves to V. There are a lot of people who are otherwise sympathetic to Schenker who seem not to believe in these chromaticized voice exchanges. But I find them extremely important, and I'm quite convinced they exist. But they do require what Schenker called *Fernhören*, or "distant hearing."

Here's a diatonic voice exchange for comparison, from the development section of the first movement of Scarlatti's Keyboard Sonata in C major, K. 159 [Example 7.12]. The "development" section starts on the dominant, G, then moves to the minor subdominant, F (mm. 30–35). (This Scarlatti piece is similar in many respects to a classical sonata movement, hence my use of a somewhat anachronistic terminology.) Then we move down in tenths to a different position of the F-minor triad, now with A♭ in the bass and F in the upper voice (mm. 39–41), and that's the chord that leads to V at the end of the development section (mm. 42–43). It's very similar to the Handel Courante, and really not all that different from the Mozart A-minor Sonata, except that it ends up on a minor triad, not an augmented sixth chord.

In our Mozart Violin Sonata, by emphasizing the chromaticized voice exchange, it may seem disturbing to some of you that I appear to be devaluing the A-major music that starts in measure 61 by seeing it as something passing within the voice exchange. People sometimes feel that their favorite parts of the music are somehow going to be neglected because they're not at a certain level of structure in the graph. One of the things I like to quote in this connection comes from a not-very-good book by Lewis Carroll, called *Sylvie and Bruno*. Lewis Carroll is the genius author of *Alice in Wonderland* and *Through the Looking Glass* and *The Hunting of the Snark*, but he did have one or two bombs, and this is one of them. But it has good things in it, as you expect from a genius like that. There is a professor who is one of the characters, and he talks about how, in his country, the mapmakers were making maps that were larger and larger and larger, until finally they made a map in which one square mile of the countryside was represented by a square

EXAMPLE 7.11 *Mozart, Piano Sonata in A minor, K. 310, first movement, mm. 70–81, annotated score.*

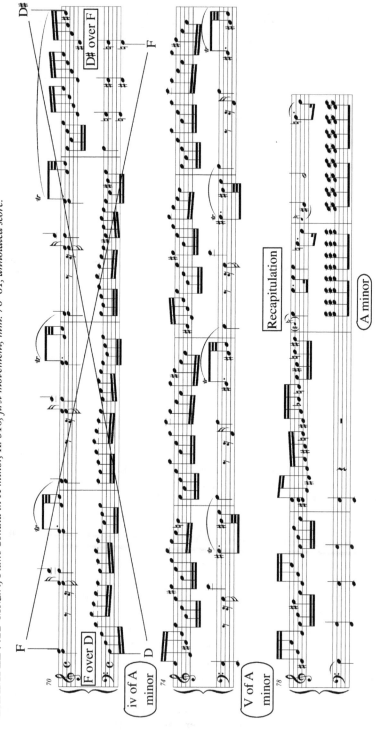

EXAMPLE 7.12 *Scarlatti's Keyboard Sonata in C major, K. 159, first movement, mm. 26–44, annotated score.*

mile on the map. However, that map was never used, because the farmers complained that if it were opened, it would block out the sun, and their crops wouldn't grow. The point is that mapmaking, good mapmaking, requires you to adopt a reasonable scale, and to prioritize some things over others.

In order to find the hidden kernel of meaning and connectedness in a passage of music, it's necessary to relegate certain elements to lower levels of structure. The A-major harmony actually appears at quite a high level of structure, but not as high as the D♭-major chord or the augmented-sixth chord. I don't think anyone should think that we are somehow impoverishing A major by treating it in this way. We're saying that, out of a few passing tones and chromatic alterations, this whole fantastic thing emerges. Can it not even be something like a dream? It has not very much foundation in reality, but is incredibly meaningful to us in other ways. I wouldn't feel sorry for the A major, or feel that it's being given short shrift. No, what's remarkable is that this chord, which comes about in such an improbable way, then comes to dominate the piece so much.

Within the A-major section, I want to call your attention to the chord on the second half of measures 62 and 63, marked with *sforzandi*. The chord is V⁷ of A, and represents the same sound as the augmented-sixth chord in measure 73, although in a different context. That is, V⁷ of A (or B♭) is equivalent to a German augmented-sixth chord in A♭. This is a way in which the music tells you what it wants to do, or perhaps even what it will do at some point—there is a sense of futurity in a moment like this.

Ernst Oster once pointed out to me a similar example of futurity, this one again from the development section of the first movement of the Mozart A-minor Sonata [Example 7-13]. The development section starts in C major. The seventh, B♭, gets added to the chord, and then C⁷ gets reinterpreted as an augmented-sixth chord leading to B in measure 58—that's the first big move. The C⁷ is embellished by a neighboring harmony, namely, the diminished-seventh chord we hear first in measure 53. In the bass we have D♭-C (mm. 53–54), again D♭-C (mm. 54–55), and then something really unusual. The third statement of the diminished-seventh chord, in the second half of measure 55, has C♯ instead of D♭ in the bass. It does go back to C, just as the D♭s did, but the spelling is strange. Oster encouraged me to think about it in terms of where the music wants to go, namely, from C major to D minor, which we get to in measure 70. So it's as though the C♯ is telling us what we're being pulled toward, even though from the point of view of its immediate voice leading, the notation of D♭ as C♯ is actually meaningless—it really is a D♭. But its notation as C♯ is not arbitrary and embodies a notion of futurity and the potential for connection on a large scale.

EXAMPLE 7.13 *Mozart, Piano Sonata in A minor, K. 310, first movement, mm 50–70, annotated score.*

EXAMPLE 7.13 (*Continued*)

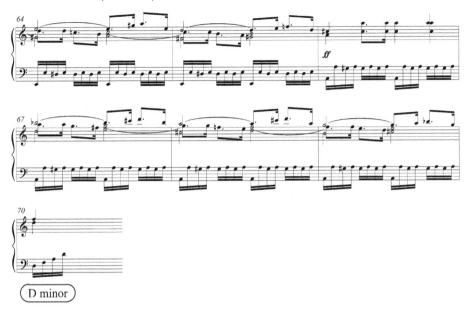

D minor

Another example of a moment in a piece that might point to something far ahead is from the fugal development section of the last movement of Beethoven's Piano Sonata Op. 101 [Example 7.14]. Right before the fugue begins, we have a ⁶₄chord above E (m. 89). The fugue culminates on a big dominant (m. 195), as we would expect it to, and that dominant leads to the recapitulation in measure 200. There's a strong association between the ⁶₄ chord and the dominant chord: both involve groups of three notes in each of the hands. What Beethoven is showing us is that the dominant chord is a long-range resolution of the ⁶₄ chord. The ⁶₄chord is really a cadential ⁶₄, with the entire fugue interpolated, in the manner of a cadenza, between the ⁶₄chord and its resolution. That beautiful idea comes from Oswald Jonas, who was a pupil of Schenker's.

Now back to Mozart Violin Sonata, and to a possible reading of the first part of the B-section (mm. 17–28) [Example 7.15]. So what I have here is two measures of F minor (mm. 17–18) and then immediately to E♭ major, so that the F becomes a kind of upper neighbor to E♭ in the bass. At that point, the upper voice has the first of three descending fifth-progressions from B♭ down to E♭.

I'm not entirely happy with that reading, however, so let's look at something I consider a better reading [Example 7.16]. Instead of showing an arrival on E♭ in measure 20, I defer it to measure 24, and I focus instead on the parallel tenths between the outer voices (an idea originally suggested to me by Eric Wen). In measure 17, we have A♭ over F. The next tenth in the series is in measure 19: B♭ over G. The apparent arrival on E♭ in measure 20 is actually on the way to the next tenth: C over A♮ in measure 22. And there's also a harmonic connection between the F-minor chord in measure 17 and the F seventh chord in measure 22 (although with A♮ replacing A♭). That harmonic connection reinforces my sense that the apparent tonic arrival in measure 20 is actually in the middle of an ongoing process.

EXAMPLE 7.14 *Beethoven, Piano Sonata, Op. 101, last movement, mm. 88–97 and 190–200, annotated score.*

EXAMPLE 7.15 *Mozart, Violin Sonata, mm. 17–28, analytical sketch.*

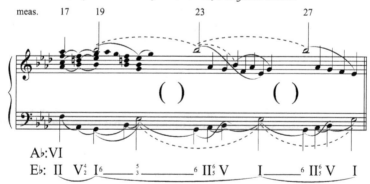

In both readings, the descending fifth in the upper voice in measures 23–24 is somewhat covered over by a line a third above it. I tried to show that in my graphs by a slur from the half-note B♭ to A♭ and G, and then a snakelike curve to the F-E♭ of the middle voice. In the next descent, in measure 27, there's nothing above the 5̂-4̂-3̂-2̂-1̂.

EXAMPLE 7.16 *Mozart, Violin Sonata, mm. 17–28, a better analytical sketch for the same passage.*

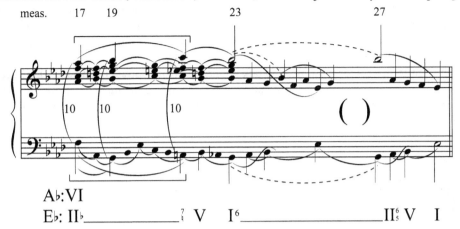

The next graph I want to show you places the whole B-section (mm. 17–28) in a larger context [Example 7.17].

EXAMPLE 7.17 *Mozart, Violin Sonata, mm. 1–35, analytical sketch (synoptic overview of the B section).*

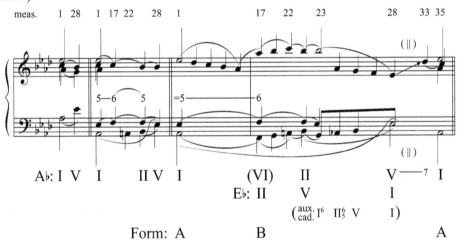

The first part of the graph gives a synoptic overview, from the beginning of the movement to the arrival on the dominant at the end of the B-section (mm. 28–34), with the upper E♭ as a common tone between the two harmonies. The next level, shown after the double bar in the graph, has first a 5-6 motion over A♭ (that refers to the F-minor music at m. 17), then a bass ascent through A♮ (m. 22) to B♭, which is V of V. The next level of the graph fleshes things out a bit more, and aligns the voice leading with the formal sections of the movement: A-B-A. At the end of this graph, I'm showing the arrival on V as indicating an interruption. The arrow shows the origin of the D♭, the main upper tone at that point, and then the slur shows its resolution to C as the A-section returns in the tonic. As D♭ resolves to C, the E♭ is once again established as the main upper voice tone. Note that the harmony in measures 23–29 takes the form of an *auxiliary cadence*: I⁶-II⁶₅-V-I. For Schenker, an auxiliary cadence is a progression of chords with a V and I (closing tonic), but without a structural opening tonic. For Schenker, I⁶ is a possible initial chord in an auxiliary cadence. Poundie Burstein has written a whole dissertation on this topic [Burstein 1988].

I want to digress for a moment to talk about the great contrast in character between the rondo theme in this Violin Sonata and the corresponding theme in the great A-minor Rondo for piano, K. 511. It's a contrast in character that strangely goes together with a lot of similarity in layout [Example 7.18].

EXAMPLE 7.18 *Mozart, Rondo in A minor, K. 511, mm. 1–8.*

Both melodies begin by arpeggiating down from scale-degree $\hat{5}$ to scale-degree $\hat{1}$, although the arpeggiation is a complete $\hat{5}$-$\hat{3}$-$\hat{1}$ in the sonata and just $\hat{5}$-$\hat{1}$ in the rondo. Both melodies then ascend right back to $\hat{5}$. Then, after a leap up to the tonic in the higher octave, both melodies descend $\hat{6}$-$\hat{4}$-$\hat{2}$ over II⁶ and then $\hat{8}$-$\hat{7}$ over V. There is an almost note-for-note correspondence.

There are differences, too, of course. One important difference is evident in the consequent phrase, where the descent from $\hat{5}$ in the rondo omits scale-degree $\hat{4}$. In fact, when I analyze the Rondo, I actually analyze the main upper voice as E-F-E, with inner-voice motion that descends to the tonic without completely filling in the descent with stepwise motion.

An additional significant difference is the way in which the sonata movement emphasizes symmetry in its phrasing. The first four measures divide neatly into 2 + 2, with the climax of the phrase coming right at the midpoint. In the Rondo, however, the division is 1 + 2 + 1: a one-measure statement of an idea, then two measures of chromatic ascent, and then a cadential measure. There's thus an asymmetry in the basic layout. And I think we inevitably hear the 1 + 2 + 1 against a background of expectation that the usual arrangement would be 2 + 2. I think a pianist would be well advised to play through the downbeat of measure 3 to emphasize the asymmetry of the layout—that's more true to the character of the theme than a more conventional 2 + 2 would be. It's interesting that the structural similarities of these two pieces are susceptible to being executed in such contrasting ways.

Returning to the C-section of the sonata, in Db-major, I want to point out that there is something anomalous in the beautiful melody that starts in measure 43. The melody descends from F to Bb, but what is the function of that Bb (m. 45)? In a linear descent like this, unless the highest note is an appoggiatura or some other sort of decorative note, the corner notes (that is, the lowest and the highest notes) are usually faithful to the prolonged harmony, in this case, the Db major. And yet the Bb, which is very much emphasized, somehow doesn't fit into our Db chord [Example 7.19].

EXAMPLE 7.19 *Mozart, Violin Sonata, mm. 43–46, analytical sketch.*

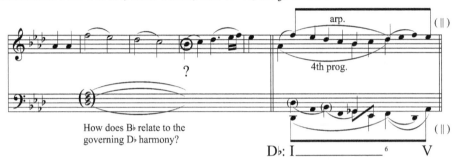

My solution is to suggest that the Bb grows out of the Ab in the inner voice: the upper voice descends from F to Db and the inner voice ascends via a fourth-progression from Ab to Db. Like Schenker, I am using the term "arpeggiation" to apply to the chordal skip from F to Db in the upper voice. So the F doesn't go directly to Eb, but first skips down to Db before moving to Eb (m. 46). In the same passage, the left-hand part goes down in thirds from an implied upper Db. The Eb it arrives on becomes part of an ascending stepwise line in the bass: Db-Eb-F.

The next graph I want to show you covers most of the C-section (mm. 43–56), and let's focus on the b-level graph, starting in measure 47 [Example 7.20]. As you can see, I'm showing a very large progression of a descending sixth, from F all the way to Ab. It goes F-Eb (m. 47)-Db (with a diminished third below it, m. 48)-C (prolonged through the beginning of m. 50). Then we go to Cb at the end of measure 50, beautifully recalling and contrasting with the B♮ of the augmented-sixth chord in measure 48, and then to Bb (m. 51), prolonged by a third descent (Bb-Ab-G, as the harmony changes from II⁶ to II⁷), and finally to Ab (m. 56).

We've already talked about the chromatic voice exchange that spans the rest of the C-section (mm. 57–75). The next graph gives a somewhat detailed account of that passage, and I hope that it's reasonably self-explanatory [Example 7.21].

Finally, I want to talk about the structural close of the movement (mm. 77–end), and I offer two rather different readings of it [Example 7.22]. One way of reading the structural close is to say that it comes at the end of the last statement of the Rondo theme. In other words, all of the many descending fifths that we've had up to this point (Eb-Db-C-Bb-Ab) are understood as offshoots of the *Urlinie* Eb, from which the final descent occurs in measure 91. Everything after that is coda, following the Schenkerian definition of coda as "whatever happens after you arrive at a tonic harmony with scale-degree 1̂ in the melody as a structural note." In *Free Composition*, Schenker quite explicitly defines coda in just this way.

There's a lot to be said for that way of thinking, but there are some things to be said against it, too. That is, the normal sense we have of what a coda does is not with regard only

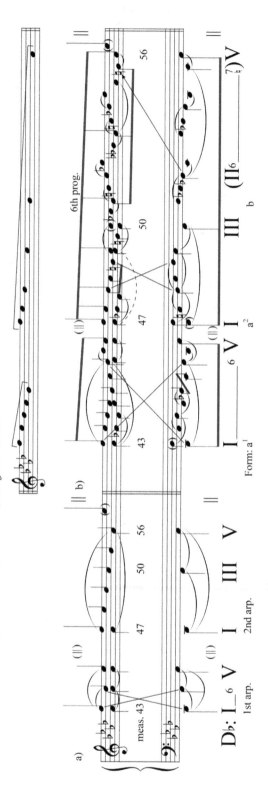

EXAMPLE 7.20 *Mozart, Violin Sonata, mm. 43–56, analytical sketch.*

EXAMPLE 7.21 *Mozart, Violin Sonata, mm. 57–75, analytical sketch.*

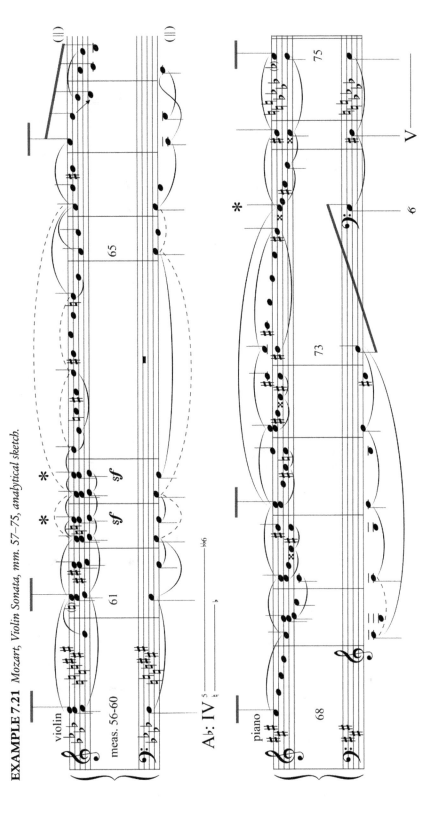

*Note associative connection between V_5^6 of A (Bᵇᵇ) and augmented 6th.

EXAMPLE 7.22 *Mozart, Violin Sonata, mm. 75–end, analytical sketch.*

3rd A Section, Coda

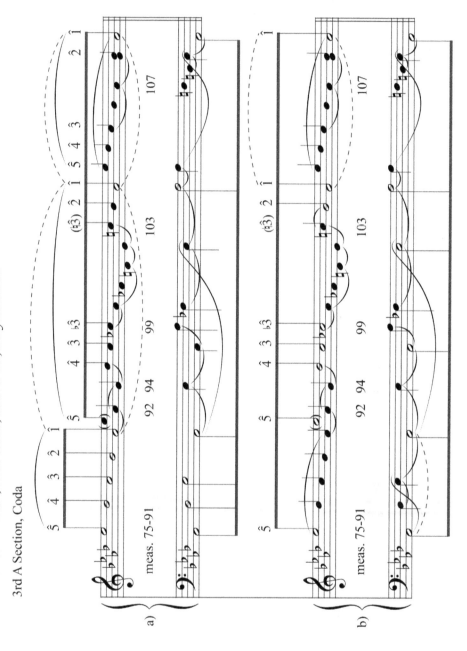

to tonal structure, but also to form and design. In particular, if we have a piece in which something repeats and repeats and repeats (as our rondo theme does here), there is a less definite sense of conclusion about the final statement of it than there might be in another piece of equal length and complexity where there is not so much repetition. The repetition that we have so lavishly displayed here weakens the sense of closure at any given instant, because we never know if there's going to be yet another statement of the rondo theme. Of course in a certain way we do know that it's not going to go on forever, but nonetheless, we can't help but react to those repetitions.

I think there may be a tendency in recent scholarship to relax Schenker's stricture about codas. For example, John Rink has an analysis of Chopin's famous Nocturne in E♭, Op. 9, No. 2, in which he argues that the structural close takes place in the coda [Rink 1999]. Schenker and others who have analyzed that piece take the resolution to scale-degree $\hat{1}$ in the melody just at the end of the last statement of the nocturne theme. But the coda that follows contains not only roughly one-third of the piece but also its big climax. So Rink argues that the structural close occurs in the coda, even though it's outside the formal boundary of the ABA form. And I tend to agree with Rink.

Interestingly, Schenker himself published a rather incomplete analysis of Mozart's A-minor Rondo in *Free Composition* [Schenker 1979]. In it he shows the descent $\hat{5}$-$\hat{4}$-$\hat{3}$-$\hat{2}$-$\hat{1}$ coming in the coda. I think that may be because scale-degree $\hat{4}$, as we discussed, is neglected in the rondo theme, but is very much included in the coda.

If we pursue that logic in our Mozart Violin Sonata, we might decide that the final descent of the *Urlinie* and the definitive arrival on the tonic come not in measure 91, at the end of the last statement of the rondo theme, but rather in measure 105. That would mean that, as Schenkerians, we have to accept the double meaning of *coda*. It has one meaning that derives from the tonal structure and another meaning in terms of the layout of the form. Certainly the idea of a strong resolution to scale-degree $\hat{1}$ is much more effectively conveyed for this piece if we show it as coming in the coda. And that final descent of the upper voice coincides with the resolution of other issues in the movement. Note the return of the hymn theme of the C section and the final reference to the tonal issue of A major, with the associated enharmonic reinterpretation of V⁷ of A as German $\substack{6 \\ 5}$ of A♭. In many respects, the coda is typical, in that it offers a backward look at the movement as a whole.

Beethoven, String Quartet, Op. 18, No. 6, first movement

We'll analyze the whole first movement of Beethoven's String Quartet, Op. 18, No. 6. [Editors Note: Only the exposition of the movement is reprinted here.]

THE CHARACTER OF THE OPENING OF THIS MOVEMENT IS VERY MUCH IN THE STYLE of comic opera (this was an idea suggested to me by Stephen Slottow) [Example 8.1]. One can almost imagine the hero of the comic opera singing at the pickup to measure 6 without letting his soprano girlfriend finish her line. There is certainly a *buffo* element to it.

As far as the voice leading goes, the main idea in the opening of the top voice is an ascending third-progression, B♭ (m. 1)-C (m. 8)-D (m. 9), which is an *Anstieg* to scale-degree 3̂ of the *Urlinie*. The B♭ is prolonged by a rising arpeggio that takes you up two octaves, and then from that higher B♭—which is certainly the obligatory register of this movement—we ascend through C to D. The cello actually anticipates the ascent in measures 5–7 and then echoes it in measures 9–11.

In *Free Composition* [Schenker 1979], Ernst Oster translates *Anstieg* as *initial ascent*. *Anstieg* in itself simply means *ascent*, but since these things always lead up to the first *Urlinie* tone, I think Oster's change to *initial ascent* is a valid one. Of course, we don't know at the very beginning whether this particular ascent, B♭-C-D, is in fact going to lead to the first *Urlinie* tone, because it's quite possible that the line will continue in a subsequent phrase and go up to F as scale-degree 5̂. But in this case, it doesn't continue up, and the Fs we do get (in mm. 14 and 16) come in a quite different way, not as a result of stepwise motion.

It's not too uncommon to have a first theme in a sonata exposition take the form of an initial ascent. Sometimes the initial ascent can be very large scale. A fantastic example is the first movement of the Sonata Op. 13 of Beethoven ("Pathétique"). There's a wonderful article by Ernst Oster on register and the long-range connection [Oster 1961/1977], in which he sees the exposition as going from C (m. 15) to D (m. 45)—D is supported by the dominant of E♭ and preceded by an ascending third, B (m. 37) to C (m. 41) to D (m. 45)—and then E♭ arrives in the second part, the non-tonic part, of the exposition (m. 98) [Example 8.2].

There's nothing like that in Op. 18, No. 6—just the modest *Anstieg* we have discussed.

EXAMPLE 8.1 *Beethoven, String Quartet in B♭ major, Op. 18, No. 6, first movement, exposition (mm. 1–91), annotated score.*

From the point of view of tonal structure, this first theme is almost all tonic prolongation, with very simple dominants helping to expand the tonic. The cello's half notes in measures 11–12 give us a kind of $\hat{3}$-$\hat{2}$, with the C retained over the dominant in a sort of interruption. But this is still part of the first theme, and you shouldn't overvalue the structural level of that C. The real scale-degree $\hat{2}$ doesn't happen until later.

So we have a sonata exposition where the first big chunk of music ends on a half cadence (m. 13), and then starts over again the same way, but this time modulates to the second key area. When he analyzes a sonata exposition of this sort, Schenker calls the first part an antecedent and the second part a modulating consequent (in *Tonwille* [Schenker 2004], he calls it a "consequent and modulation").

EXAMPLE 8.1 (*Continued*)

This is a rather frequent thing with Mozart and Haydn, as well as with Beethoven. The opening theme is cast in the form of a phrase, ending with a half cadence, and thus giving the impression of being the antecedent phrase of a period. This is followed by a phrase that begins the same way, but then begins to modulate and is very often expanded, which is actually what happens in Op. 18, No. 6. Scale-degree $\hat{2}$ of the *Urlinie* arrives in the phrase that actually effects the modulation (m. 33), not the earlier half cadence (m. 13)—these two $\hat{2}$s are not on the same level.

It is possible to have an interruption where the $\hat{3}$-$\hat{2}$ (or $\hat{5}$-$\hat{4}$-$\hat{3}$-$\hat{2}$) comes more than once before the eventual $\hat{3}$-$\hat{2}$-$\hat{1}$ (or $\hat{5}$-$\hat{4}$-$\hat{3}$-$\hat{2}$-$\hat{1}$). The wonderful little Brahms song (Op. 84, No. 4) called "Vergebliches Ständchen," which means "Useless Serenade" or "Serenade in Vain," is a particularly clear example of that [Example 8.3]. The melody descends two times to $\hat{2}$ over the dominant, and then there's a complete descent, $\hat{5}$-$\hat{4}$-$\hat{3}$-$\hat{2}$-$\hat{1}$.

EXAMPLE 8.1 (*Continued*)

The modulatory part of a sonata exposition obviously has the task of connecting the first and second themes or thematic complexes. Of course, one can't give any kind of recipe or prescription for how that has to be done. Perhaps the most frequent group of ways would be that the transition is going to lead to some sonority that has something in common with the initial tonic, but has actually transformed that initial tonic into something that is less stable. The simplest way of doing what I've previously referred to as "detonicizing the tonic" is with the interval succession 5-6.

So let's say we're in C major and we're going to the dominant key of G [Example 8.4]. From your C-G-E, you might very well then get yourself to C-A-E. The motion from G to A with a sustained C underneath will give you 5-6, of course. But the presence of the A already means that the C, the foundation of the harmony, has been a little bit shaken off of its pedestal, and is about to be replaced. That would be simplest way of doing it, although it's not necessarily the most common way.

EXAMPLE 8.2 *Beeethoven, Piano Sonata, Opus 13 ("Pathetique"), first movement,* Allegro molto e con brio, *mm. 1–19, 38–49, and 89–99, annotated score excerpts.*

EXAMPLE 8.3 *Brahms, "Vergebliches Ständchen," Op. 84, No. 4, mm. 1–21, annotated score.*

EXAMPLE 8.4 *5-6 motion in C major.*

The 5-6 motion over the tonic might lead to V/V (the dominant of the new key), and you could have what Hepokoski and Darcy [2006] call a "medial caesura" there, if you like [Example 8.5].

EXAMPLE 8.5 *5-6 leads to V/V.*

Or, you could chromaticize the tonic note, keeping the 6, as before, but having a 5 with it, so we get a seventh chord in $^6_5$ position as an applied dominant to V-of-V [Example 8.6].

EXAMPLE 8.6 *Tonic note chromaticized to create applied dominant to V/V.*

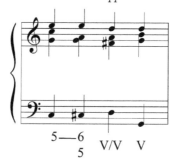

The main effect of that is that our main tonic dips below the horizon, as Tovey might have said. Because our new applied dominant tonicizes V/V (that is, D major), the V itself then comes with a sense of resolution to a new tonic. So even before the second theme starts, that sense of resolution to the new key acts as a kind of stabilizing force for the second theme.

I could intensify this further by replacing the 6 with a diminished seventh [Example 8.7].

EXAMPLE 8.7 *Diminished-seventh chord instead of $^6_5$.*

I could even have a whole little passage commencing on the tonic chord and, just before returning there, moving instead to that applied diminished-seventh chord [Example 8.8].

EXAMPLE 8.8 *A passage connects the tonic to the diminished-seventh chord.*

That emphasizes the affinity between the tonic chord and the applied diminished-seventh chord: they share two notes (E and G), and the C♯ is just a chromatic alteration of C (the only thing we are adding is the diminished seventh, which replaces the 6 we had before).

If we swap the registers, so that what was on top is now on bottom, and vice versa, we create a voice exchange [Example 8.9].

EXAMPLE 8.9 *Chromaticized voice exchange.*

This is a chromaticized voice exchange, because the C♮ has become C♯ to create that applied diminished-seventh chord, resolving to V/V.

A closely related move would be to have an augmented-sixth chord instead of the diminished-seventh chord, still part of a chromaticized voice exchange with the initial tonic [Example 8.10].

EXAMPLE 8.10 *Augmented-sixth chord instead of diminished-seventh chord.*

So we have a whole family of possibilities arising out of the simple 5-6 above the tonic: a chromaticized 5-$^6_3$; a diminished-seventh chord retaining the chromaticized version of scale-degree $\hat{1}$; and an augmented-sixth chord, within the same voice exchange. These are some very natural ways of connecting the first and second themes, by preserving elements of the first theme at the end of the bridge section, but making them unstable, so that they resolve into the dominant of the second theme area.

I think you could argue that something similar happens in our quartet movement. Look at measure 29, the last moment we're clearly in B♭, with B♭ in the bass and D in the upper voice. Right before the big arrival on V/V in measure 33, with the *Urlinie* $\hat{2}$ in the top voice, we have first D in the bass (first half of m. 32) and then B♮ in the upper voice (second half of m. 32). If you are willing to put together the D on the downbeat, which is actually supporting a D-minor chord at first, and the B♮ in the second half of the measure, you get a chromaticized voice exchange. I find that very convincing, although it's not the most obvious way of doing it.

Then, at measure 33, we come to the sort of passage that William Caplin and others call "standing on the dominant" (mm. 33–44) [Caplin 1998]. With that strong scale-degree $\hat{2}$ on top, I think we can feel that our hypothesis that this piece has a $\hat{3}$-line has been pretty well proven. The high G in the first violin part is heavily emphasized locally, and you might even say it has a registral connection to the high F in measure 14, but there is really no voice-leading connection between them and neither of them enters into important long-range linear connections.

Following the medial caesura (mm. 43–44), we enter a somewhat more problematic part in what is in general a very clear sonata form, with an almost textbook-like clarity in shaping the form to coincide with the harmonic and voice-leading structure. It certainly seems as though the second theme begins on scale-degree $\hat{3}$ (A in F major) starting in measure 45. But according to Schenkerian convention, it's supposed to begin on scale-degree $\hat{5}$ (C in F major). That is, the normal procedure is for scale-degree $\hat{2}$ in the original tonic to be prolonged through the second theme, now locally scale-degree $\hat{5}$ in the key of the dominant—that's how a strong connection is made between the first and second themes.

We could try to make it conform by saying that the main note in the second theme is really the C in measure 49. But you'll recall my mistrust of analyses where, if we have the continuation of a pattern, we take the second statement as the predominant thing; I almost always prefer to take the first statement as the main thing, with the second statement as a weaker echo. Here, the C does sound more like an echo than an arrival point. The simultaneous shift to F minor perhaps further weakens the structural role of the passage and of the melodic C. So I don't think we've solved our problem.

Here's another alternative. Acknowledge that the A at the beginning of the second theme is the main tone locally (and indicate it as a quarter-note in your graph). Show it coming from the B♭ as an inner voice tone of the initial tonic. Slur it to the C in measure 49 (and indicate it also as a quarter-note in your graph). We jump up to F in measure 54, but it leads back down to C in measure 60, repeated in measure 62. Then, where you see the *sforzando* in measure 64, that's the scale-degree $\hat{2}$ of the *Urlinie* (and you would indicate it with a half-note in your graph). Use dotted slurs or some other kind of connection to indicate that we've been on C all along, but its structural status is not made explicit until measure 64.

I can think of two movements by Mozart that start their second subject with $\hat{3}$ of the dominant key, just as our Beethoven quartet movement does. The first of these is the Piano Sonata, K. 332 [Example 8.11].

EXAMPLE 8.11 *Mozart, Piano Sonata in F major, K. 332, first movement, exposition (mm. 1–93), annotated score.*

The first subject moves from $\hat{3}$ (A, mm. 1–16) to $\hat{2}$ (G, mm. 37–40). But the second subject, instead of beginning on G, begins on scale-degree $\hat{3}$ of the dominant key, namely, E (m. 41). Ernst Oster, one of the great Schenkerian analysts of a previous generation, suggested to me that the scale-degree $\hat{5}$ of the dominant (that is, the G) comes in measure 42, and for a long time I agreed with him. But really the main note in measure 42 is F, not G—the F is a neighbor to E, and the G is a neighbor to F. The main motions in these measures involve thirds ascending and descending (E-D-C, C-D-E) and these connect with motivic thirds in the first subject (mm. 5–9, mm. 12–16). These voice-leading and motivic considerations would argue strongly against taking the G in measure 42 as scale-degree $\hat{2}$ of the *Urlinie*.

Scale-degree $\hat{2}$ comes later, starting in measure 56. It's embellished by a chromatic upper neighbor (A♭, m. 61) and by a diatonic upper neighbor (A, m. 71), and then we get strong descents from G, $\hat{5}$-$\hat{4}$-$\hat{3}$-$\hat{2}$-$\hat{1}$ in C major, toward the end of the exposition (mm. 78–86). The second Mozart example of a second theme that starts on $\hat{3}$ of the dominant key is the "Kegelstatt" Trio, K. 498, for Clarinet, Viola, and Piano; I'm not going to take the time to talk about that now, but I'll come back to another aspect of it in a moment.

Now, back to the Beethoven. Between measures 53 and 64, we start on C (m. 53), then jump up to F. C is the main note—I think of the F as a superposition, that is, an

EXAMPLE 8.11 (*Continued*)

inner voice shifted to the top. Then comes a descent, F-E♭-D♭-C, counterpointed in paral-lel tenths with the bass line of the cello, and thereby ending up on a I⁶ (first in F minor and then in F major). It is a linear progression of a fourth, but the C, not the F, is the main tone. In the bass, there's a linear progression of a sixth, from F down to A♭, which is then corrected to A♮.

At that point (m. 64), we start getting strong descending fifth-progressions from the high C. The first one (mm. 64–67) looks like a fourth-progression (C-B♭-A-G) but it's really a frustrated fifth—the terminal F is missing. Then we get the big, definitive descent, starting in measure 68. It might seem possible to read measures 64–70 as an instance of interruption, but it is clear that the complete descent that starts in measure 68 is on a dif-ferent and much higher level than the incomplete one starting in measure 64. The incom-plete descent counts as a motion into the inner voice of the prolonged F-major chord.

Let's look more closely at the complete descent [Example 8.12]. First we get C (m. 68)-B♭ (m. 69)-A (m. 70), and then things get a bit complicated. There's an octave descent to a lower A (m. 75) and then down to G in the original octave (m. 76). The G is decorated with an upper neighbor A, but in the second violin (m. 78)—what the first violin has at that point covers the main line. Then the first violin takes over again

EXAMPLE 8.11 (*Continued*)

EXAMPLE 8.12 *Beethoven, Quartet, mm. 68–80, analytical sketch.*

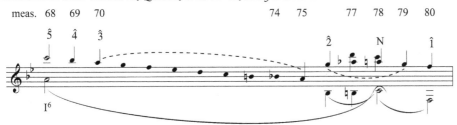

at measure 79 and brings the line down to F (m. 80). Starting in measure 68, where the descent begins, we could imagine that the bass is going in parallel tenths with the first violin part, but Beethoven prefers the much more expressive use of accented neighbor notes, rather than passing tones, which would blend into the landscape there.

There's very often a tendency, in a classical sonata form exposition, to have a certain rhythmic character of acceleration from the beginning and deceleration toward the end. While this movement is far from the most outstanding example, it does have something of that character. The very long, sustained tonic harmony at the beginning of the movement is something that one is not likely to get later on in such a movement. Beethoven keeps it relatively static like that for a quite long time. When we get to the modulating transition at measures 29–33, the rhythm of chord changes has definitely sped up, until we get the place where we stand on the dominant (mm. 33–44), where it slows down again. The beginning of the second theme is perhaps more static than is quite usual, but once we get around measure 54 or so, the pace definitely picks up, as it does through this whole rest of the second theme, leading to the big cadence in measure 80. When we get to the codetta (mm. 80–91), everything slows down again. The harmony is pretty much V-I-V-I in whole bars, and then a long F-major tonic in the last few bars.

Look, from that point of view, at the first movement of Mozart's "Kegelstatt" Trio, K. 498 [Example 8.13].

EXAMPLE 8.13 *Mozart, Trio for Clarinet (in B♭), Viola, and Piano, K. 498 ("Kegelstatt"), first movement, mm. 25–47, annotated score.*

EXAMPLE 8.13 (*Continued*)

What Mozart often does toward the end of an exposition is to drastically slow things down. When the second theme begins (m. 25), the chords are mostly changing every half bar. At the cadence in measures 33–34, it's still one chord per half-bar. Now look at the cadence near the end of the exposition (mm. 43–47), and you can see how drastically the previous cadence has been expanded.

The *development section* in most major-key sonatas in major will be, of course, a prolongation of the dominant, but it is a prolongation designed to destabilize the dominant harmony
so that it no longer sounds like a local tonic. This is often accomplished at or near the end
of the development, with a motion to the seventh of the dominant chord—that's probably
the single most frequent strategy that composers use. There will often be a key area explored
other than the dominant itself, and certainly other than the global tonic of the piece. For a
piece in B♭ major, there might be a modulation to E♭ major. That can be a lower neighbor of
the dominant (F), and when we get back to F, it is not going to sound like the tonic anymore,
precisely because of that E♭. Similarly, one could tonicize a C-minor chord, the II of B♭. But
perhaps the most frequent thing that happens is a modulation to VI. This is especially true in
the proto-sonatas of the early eighteenth century, where it became a kind of cliché.

And that's exactly what Beethoven does in this quartet movement: the first main goal is G
minor (VI in B♭ major). We get there via contrary motion in the outer voices: the first violin
rises C-C♯-D and the cello descends F-E♭-D (mm. 100–102). The C♯ over E♭ gives us a familiar
augmented-sixth chord. You will find that in any kind of normal Classical sonata movement,
the most prominent melodic tone at the beginning of the development section is likely to be
either the scale-degree $\hat{2}$ that was the structural note at the beginning of the second theme, or
the dominant note itself ($\hat{5}$), which will be the last emphasized thing that one hears at the end
of the exposition. In this case we start with F (the dominant note), arpeggiate upward from F
(mm. 93 and 95) through A (mm. 96–99) to C (m. 100). That C is our scale-degree $\hat{2}$. Then
comes the ascent C-C♯-D we already talked about. From the D, we go up to E♭ as the upper
neighbor to D (mm. 108–109) and then back to D (m. 110). That D moves down to C (m.
111), and where that C goes is one of the mysteries of this development section. It probably
does resolve somewhere in the G-minor music after measure 111, but not in any explicit way.

Then we have a massive sequential passage that begins with the pickup to measure 114,
and this passage goes very determinedly downward. From G minor we go first to F major
(m. 121), shading to F minor (m. 125), then to E♭ major (m. 127), shading to E♭ minor
(m. 131), and then to D♭ major (m. 133) [Example 8.14].

EXAMPLE 8.14 *Beethoven, Quartet, development section (mm. 100–139), analytical sketch.*

The unison passage in measures 137–138 leads to an implied augmented-sixth chord
(m. 138) that resolves to F, as V of B♭. That's one of the wonderful things that tonal music
can do, namely create structures that are purely imaginary, but are nevertheless real.

Over the course of this whole passage then (mm. 114–139), the bass goes F♯ to G, E to F, D to E♭, C to D♭, B♭ to C, and then finally A to B♭, then our imaginary G♭ for the augmented-sixth chord, then F [Example 8.15].

EXAMPLE 8.15 *Beethoven, Quartet, development section (mm. 114–139), bassline sketch.*

Looking at the development section up to this point in its broadest sense, we might say that we start on F, move to G, and from G we go back to F through that implied augmented-sixth chord on G♭ [Example 8.16].

EXAMPLE 8.16 *Beethoven, Quartet, development (mm. 100–139), analytical sketch in three stages.*

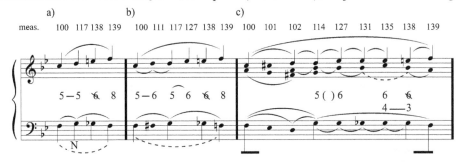

The upper voice starts on C over F, then up to D over G (the parallel fifths are broken up by the intervening 6). From D, the upper voice ascends through E♭ to E♮ (as part of that augmented-sixth chord) and finally up to F. That counterpoint would be the Schenkerian core for this development section.

Just a word about analytical graphing in a passage like this, with all of its repetitions. You could simply write out every repetition, but instead, you could do the first instance in as much detail as you like, and then do a pretty radical reduction, or even use just barlines with empty bars to indicate the repetition. There are various levels of completeness that you can strive for. But the one thing you don't want to do is burden an analytical graph with so many notes that nobody's going to see the larger connections.

The next portion of the development section—the retransition—is for me one of the most perplexing passages in Beethoven's quartets: an extremely long retransition, in which very little happens. The effect is comical in some ways, but I can't help feeling that the proportions of this movement are not ideal. This retransition feels overly long, and the end of the recapitulation (from m. 237 on) strikes me as abrupt and short, given what has happened earlier in the piece.

In the retransition, the top voice basically arpeggiates F major: F (m. 139) through G to A (m. 141), then to C (m. 143), and F (m. 144). The arrival on E♭ in the second violin in measure 147 seems to motivate the first violin to continue its ascent up to its own E♭ (second half of m. 152). There's also a G above the E♭ (m. 156), but in the music of Beethoven and other composers, the ninth is often used as an associate of the seventh over the dominant harmony. In this case, the G doesn't actually go so strongly to an F when the tonic returns, but the E♭ resolves strongly to D as the *Kopfton*.

But notice that the resolution of the E♭ at the end of the development to D at the beginning of the recapitulation is not direct or immediate: we get to the E♭ in measure 152 (and again in m. 171), but the D does not arrive until measure 183. It is fundamental to Schenkerian analysis that you can have connections between tones that are not consecutive. That sort of thing happens so much in tonal music. Here's an example from Mozart's Piano Concerto, K. 467 [Example 8.17].

EXAMPLE 8.17 *Mozart, Piano Concerto in C major, K. 467, first movement, mm. 84–87, annotated score.*

In the second measure of the passage, we have a dominant-seventh chord in $^6_5$ position with the seventh of the chord, F, in the top voice. We expect it to resolve to E. But instead it starts on C and works its way back up until it finally gets to the tone it should have gone to a measure earlier. The tonic chord in the third measure of the passage is interposed before the tonic chord that actually brings us the melodic goal that we wanted. That's Schenker's idea of *das fliegende Ohr*, the flying ear that is able to move instantaneously from one place to another and trace distant connections.

Returning to the Beethoven, you'll note that the development ends with C in the first violin (mm. 173–174), moving to B♭ as the recapitulation begins. But in a very deep sense, that B♭ is an inner voice of the tonic harmony; the upper voice is D (although it hasn't yet arrived).

Interruption raises related issues, because it often creates a feeling of disconnection. Schenker's term is "cut off," by which he means that the voice leading is cut off at the deepest level that the interruption affects. On more superficial levels, all kinds of connections can be forged that bridge across the interruption. That's exactly what happens here as the development ends and the recapitulation begins. At a very deep level, the E♭ goes to D, which arises from the repeat of the opening *Anstieg*, but underneath it, the C in measure 174 goes to the B♭ in measure 175.

A metaphor I like to use in such situations is that of a valley that has been devastated by an earthquake, so that what was one valley now becomes two, with a big canyon in the middle separating the two parts—that's the interruption. Over the centuries, the canyon becomes filled with water, and there's a big river, and the people living in the valley are very unhappy about this, because they can't trade or see their friends. So they build a bridge. Well, the valley in its original state of complete unity is the *Ursatz*. The earthquake is the interruption that divides the one into two. But the division is somewhat mitigated by the bridge. That doesn't mean that there is still not a division into two parts, but there's a connection, though not on the highest level. That's the kind of situation we have here.

In the recapitulation, there is significant emphasis on the subdominant—we get there in measure 195. The harmony right before it is V, so it appears that we have a direct motion from V to IV, but of course these are on different levels. The V that we have in measures 187–192 is actually part of the opening theme and looks back to the tonic, B♭. The IV, starting measure 195, looks ahead to a bigger dominant, namely, the one that comes before the second theme (m. 206) [Example 8.18].

EXAMPLE 8.18 *Beethoven, Quartet, recapitulation (mm. 175–218), analytical sketch.*

When the E♭ is confirmed in the bass in measure 198, the first violin rises E♭-F-G, which creates some resonance with the rising third in the first theme, B♭-C-D. The A♭ in measure 201 is a neighbor to G. Then we start again on E♭ (m. 202) and ascend, but this time to G♭ (m. 204). The G♭ is transferred to the bass (m. 205), and the harmony there is a French augmented-sixth chord.

That augmented-sixth chord marks the end of a chromaticized voice exchange, which unfolds in gradual stages. First we have E♭ major with G on top (m. 200); then there's the modal inflection of G♮ to G♭; then the G♭ moves into the bass and the E♭, now inflected to E♮, moves to an upper voice. If it were a more conventional voice exchange, the E♮ would come in the highest voice, but here it comes instead in the viola. So what we have here is the very common use of a chromaticized voice exchange in the motion from IV to V, something we have discussed previously. In this case, it brings in F as the main dominant (m. 206).

It's very common for subdominant harmony to be emphasized in recapitulations. In this case, by making it the goal of a brief modulation, Beethoven can later make the tonic sound fresh. Thinking about the recapitulation as a whole, from the beginning to the end of the bridge to the second theme, the upper voice has gone B♭-C-D in the first theme, then to E♭ over the subdominant. The E♭ moves up to E♮ over the augmented-sixth chord in measure 205, and from there to F, the dominant [Example 8.19].

EXAMPLE 8.19 *Beethoven, Quartet, recapitulation (mm. 175–218), synoptic analytical sketch.*

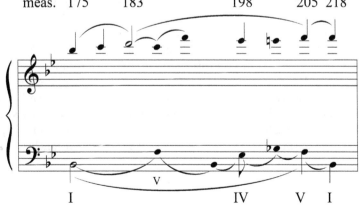

In analyzing the second theme in the recapitulation, we are confronted with a basic question of analytic ethics, namely, whether or not it is okay to analyze the same music differently at two different places in a movement. When the second subject begins in the recapitulation (m. 218), we're on scale-degree $\hat{3}$ (D). Four measures later (m. 222), we get to scale-degree $\hat{5}$. In the exposition, C (scale-degree $\hat{5}$ in the dominant) took over as the main top voice tone of the second subject, and we decided that the beginning of the second theme on A (scale-degree $\hat{3}$ in the dominant) was subordinate to it. Here, in the recapitulation, how do we evaluate the relative position of the D, the main tone at the beginning of the second theme (and, of course, the *Kopfton* of the whole movement), and the F (in m. 237)?

It's actually a reasonably common situation. If scale-degree $\hat{2}$ is the main tone in the second theme in the exposition, when the second theme is transposed to the tonic in the recapitulation, now scale-degree $\hat{5}$ will seem to be the main tone. As a result, even in movements whose *Kopfton* is $\hat{3}$, the final descent will seem to be $\hat{5}$-$\hat{4}$-$\hat{3}$-$\hat{2}$-$\hat{1}$ instead of $\hat{3}$-$\hat{2}$-$\hat{1}$. Schenker alludes briefly to that situation, calling it a kind of *Überhöhung*, a going-above, of scale-degree $\hat{3}$ to scale-degree $\hat{5}$. He didn't make a big fuss about it, and I try not to make a big fuss about it either.

But I know that some of my colleagues feel that in those cases (and this is a very strong example of such a case), where bringing the material of the exposition into the tonic emphasizes scale-degree $\hat{5}$ rather than the *Kopfton*, scale-degree $\hat{3}$, it may not be right to analyze the second theme differently, and insist that, in the recapitulation, the descent is from $\hat{3}$. I had this discussion many years ago with Charles Burkhart, who is a wonderful Schenkerian analyst. He was very skeptical about changing the evaluation of the second subject between the exposition and the recapitulation. The more I think about it, the more I'm *not* skeptical about it. In this particular recapitulation, the second subject begins with D as the top voice tone, and I see no reason not to connect it with the *Kopfton* D, and to say that D remains the main tone even when we have scale-degree $\hat{5}$ (F) coming in above it and initiating a $\hat{5}$-$\hat{4}$-$\hat{3}$-$\hat{2}$-1 descent, and even though we did not analyze it that way in the exposition. Therefore, in a graph of this piece, I would make the D a half-note, and not improperly devalue it in order to get an unnecessary consistency between the exposition and the recapitulation. With regard to the analysis of second subjects in sonata forms, I think almost all decent Schenkerian analysts would, at least on some occasions, analyze similar material differently, because the context is different. The whole point is that if the context is different, the material is also different.

There is one magnificent example that may shed a little bit of light on this, namely, the last movement of Beethoven's "Moonlight" Sonata, Op. 27, No. 2. In that movement (in C♯ minor), the *Kopfton* (scale-degree $\hat{3}$) is achieved through an arpeggio, G♯-C♯-E, which ultimately derives from the first three notes of the entire sonata. In the exposition of the last movement, the second key area is minor V (and there are very few earlier sonata movements that do this). In the recapitulation, Beethoven goes to G♯, then C♯—he doesn't go up to the E, but actually gets to G♯ in the second part of the recap. At that point, the piece becomes sort of a fantasy, and it doesn't recapitulate anymore.

Anyway, what then happens is that the big climax of the movement is in the coda, with a huge E going to D♯ and C♯. (This is explained beautifully in a wonderful article by Ernst Oster [1983]). So it was one of those cases of the curious incident of the dog in the nighttime, where something that doesn't happen has extreme importance. The missing E is then taken up to be the crux of the whole movement later on. That would be a case where one would really have to have a heart of stone to not see that the second theme simply doesn't have the same meaning in the recap. It doesn't bring us to the kind of conclusion one thinks it does, because the E itself has been missing until the coda.

Beethoven, String Quartet, Op. 18, No. 6, fourth movement ("La Malinconia")

We'll work on "La Malinconia" (the slow introduction to the last movement of Beethoven's String Quartet, Op. 18, No. 6). We'll discuss musical narrativity and the concept of the compositional idea from a Schenkerian perspective. In the course of this essay, I'll have occasion to refer to a most interesting and valuable article on "La Malinconia" by the noted American theorist William J. Mitchell.

IT'S NOT KNOWN WHERE BEETHOVEN GOT THE IDEA OF ENTITLING A MOVE-ment "Melancholy," or whether that corresponded to something in his life. There is, however, a long tradition, starting long before Beethoven and continuing long after him, of creating pieces of music or other works of art based on the "four humors" or "four temperaments" (in addition to melancholic, these are sanguine, choleric, and phlegmatic). In the twentieth century, both Carl Nielsen and Paul Hindemith wrote pieces called *The Four Temperaments*—Nielsen's was his second symphony and Hindemith's was commissioned by George Balanchine for the New York City Ballet. Of the four humors, melancholy seems the best disposed to inspire literature, art, or music. In my extensive researches on this topic, I have not run across many "Anatomies of Choler" or "Odes on Phlegm."

Looking back before Beethoven's time for artistic representations of melancholy, one thinks first of Albrecht Dürer's famous engraving, and *The Anatomy of Melancholy* by Robert Burton. As is clear from Burton's discussion, melancholy at one time was understood to encompass much more than just being sad. Nowadays, we think of melancholy as involving wistful sadness, but it would at one time have also included tragic sadness. There is an interesting duet for two solo violins by C. P. E. Bach, which Bach describes as a conversation between two men, one of them melancholy, and the other of them sanguine. Then, of course there is the magnificent ode by John Keats, called "On Melancholy." Keats was a contemporary of Beethoven; indeed, his life was more or less enclosed within Beethoven's (he died when he was only twenty-six). Keats's poem is quite obscure and difficult to come to grips with, but he clearly allies melancholy with the energy of inspiration. He pursues the notion that in order to really experience great joy, one has to also be open to experience great sorrow.

Ay, in the very temple of Delight
Veil'd Melancholy has her sovran shrine,

Though seen of none save him whose strenuous tongue
Can burst Joy's grape against his palate fine;
His soul shall taste the sadness of her might,
And be among her cloudy trophies hung.

Melancholy is usually regarded as the most adverse of the four temperaments. But there is a current of thought that maintains a more positive attitude to the melancholic temperament. This goes back centuries—indeed, millennia. An anonymous ancient writer, one of several given the name "Pseudo-Aristotle," states that when the heroic frenzy of inspiration combines with the black bile of melancholy, great men—geniuses, heroes, and philosophers—result. This was an idea taken up by Renaissance neo-Platonists, notably Marsilio Ficino. Keats's Ode falls within this tradition. Close to our own time, the great historian Frances Yates [1991] relates the Dürer print to this tradition of inspired melancholy, through which the inquiring mind gains all sorts of esoteric knowledge.

The opening of Beethoven's slow introduction doesn't really sound all that melancholy in its familiar connotation of sadness [Example 9.1].

EXAMPLE 9.1 *Beethoven, String Quartet, Op. 18, No. 6, fourth movement ("La Malinconia"), annotated score.*

EXAMPLE 9.1 (*Continued*)

It sounds rather solemn, but not particularly sad, and certainly not deranged, which can be another aspect of melancholy.

I want to focus on a special moment in the music: the place where it seems to start to lose its way. Look at measures 9–11, the beginning of the third statement of the main idea of this movement. The music seems to be very clearly leading to C minor, and ends on V⁷ of C. What we expect on the downbeat of measure 12 is a C-minor chord, which would most probably function as II in a progression that leads back to the tonic key of B♭ major. But that's not what happens. Instead, V⁷/C is reinterpreted as an augmented-sixth chord, and we suddenly find ourselves (m. 12) on a cadential ⁶₄ chord over the dominant of B minor (instead of the expected C minor). And, of course, B minor is not at all a diatonic key area or chord in the key of B♭ major. This is where the piece starts to go off the rails.

There are lots of examples in the literature of reinterpreting a dominant-seventh chord as an augmented-sixth chord. Here's a particularly notable one from the final movement of Beethoven's Piano Sonata, Op. 110 [Example 9.2]. We're in A♭ major and we arrive on V⁷ (mm. 110–113). But instead of resolving as expected to A♭ major, the harmony is reinterpreted as an augmented-sixth chord in G minor, and it resolves to the dominant of G minor (with a cadential ⁶₄ chord over it).

One of the most astonishing passages in all of music occurs at the beginning of the development section in the first movement of Mozart's String Quartet in D minor, K. 421 [Example 9.3]. The exposition has ended, as it should have, in F. We go from there to E♭ major, as the development begins with a quotation of the opening theme, a half-step away from the tonic of the piece. The bass leads down to F supporting what sounds like V⁷ of B♭ (m. 45). But it is reinterpreted as an augmented-sixth chord and resolves instead to the dominant of A minor (again with a cadential ⁶₄). Thus Mozart moves from F major to A minor by way of E♭—as circuitous a path as you can possibly find. So Beethoven is in very good company, including his own, in reinterpreting a dominant-seventh chord in this way.

EXAMPLE 9.2 *Beethoven, Piano Sonata, Op. 110, third movement, mm. 112–118, annotated score.*

Perhaps for a normal person who is not addicted to the melancholy aspects of life, one could make something positive out of this confusion of measures 11–12, where instead of going to C minor, we seem to be going to B minor. But the confusion only seems to deepen in the music that follows. If you play just the individual parts without ornaments in measures 12–16, it sounds more like Webern than Beethoven.

The chords are all diminished-seventh chords, and their spelling is interesting. Initially, there is a push toward the sharp side, outspokenly on the sharp side, with the E♯ in the ornamentation in the first violin in measure 12. But the diminished-seventh chords in measures 14 and 16, which are both F♯-A-C-E♭, sound as though there is still some impetus toward G, the dominant of C minor. It's quite curious. The alternation of loud and soft measures adds to our sense of disorientation. It's as though the wrong step we took in measures 11–12 has led us to a strange and unexpected place. There is a kind of reaction out of all proportion by the members of the quartet, when they see what they have done.

In measure 12, we have the dominant of B (a cadential $^6_4$ to an implied $^5_3$). The disorienting passage that follows, with all of its leaps and diminished-seventh chords, leads down a fifth to B, now as V of E (mm. 18–20). So we've gone from our F♯, which resulted from a misstep you might say, to a B that is implied by its dominant (m. 12), to a very real B (mm. 18–20), and then to E minor. In that sense, the progression is a very logical one, and the motion from each chord to the next is very comprehensible. The larger direction of the progression, however, is not so easy to understand, because it takes us to E minor, a tritone away from the B♭-major tonic. In its mixture of clarity and disorientation, logic and apparent illogic, the progression seems to reflect the neurotic aspects of melancholy.

For the next section of the piece (mm. 21–29), let's follow the analysis in William Mitchell's article about "La Malinconia" [Mitchell 1973] [Example 9.4].

EXAMPLE 9.3 *Mozart, String Quartet in D minor, K. 421, first movement, mm. 40–47.*

EXAMPLE 9.4 *Beethoven, "La Malinconia," mm. 21–29, analysis from William Mitchell (Example 5).*

His Level A is simply a reduction to two voices, with the material in each of the voices labeled 1 or 2. It's simple double counterpoint, and Mitchell uninverts the voices in his Level B to make the larger connections easier to follow. In his Level C, Mitchell constructs an extremely convincing imaginary continuo. What he shows there is a sequence of rising fifths, which goes E-B-F♯-C♯-A♭-E♭-B♭-F-C (with the enharmonic change at some convenient point).

Whether we're thinking diatonically or chromatically, passages of ascending fifths certainly give a very different impression from passages of descending fifths. Most people feel that there's something lacking in direction about a passage like this that goes in an extended way up in fifths. When you have a progression in rising fifths, like I-V-II-VI-III, Schenker would probably analyze the basic progression as I-II-III, with the other chords inserted to prevent parallel fifths and octaves. Schenker did not consider rising fifths to be on a par with falling fifths. One must bear in mind, however, that the first rising fifth, from I to V, is a privileged creature, because that's the rising fifth of the bass arpeggio in the *Ursatz*. So that's a rising fifth of the greatest structural importance, but in general, rising fifths are less impressive. In this regard, you might take a look at the Chopin Prelude in D major. It goes D-A-E-B-F♯, but it's very clear that the underlying progression is D-E-F♯. In our Beethoven quartet, Mitchell very beautifully shows the motion that underlies these ascending fifths, namely, a stepwise ascending sixth from E to C (Mitchell's Level D). In Mitchell's imaginary continuo, you can hear the rational model behind the disordered impression that Beethoven's actual writing gives.

It's interesting to think about why extended passages in rising fifths are so problematic, and why so few of them occur, compared to descending fifths. I think it's at least in part because when you ascend by a fifth, the new bass note is already present in the previous chord, whereas in a descending fifth, you bring in a new bass note. And that is also why descending thirds are stronger than ascending thirds, because they give you a new bass note rather than repeating something from the previous chord. So when you progress by ascending fifth or ascending third, you're not progressing to something sufficiently new. Descending fifths, however, as in the progression III-VI-II-V-I, are a strong way of clinching a motion to some new place. Beethoven's music is so strongly future oriented and directed that it is particularly striking to find, as we do here, an extended progression of ascending fifths. It's even more striking when you note, as Mitchell's Level D makes clear, that these ascending fifths actually project an ascent through most of a whole-tone scale: E-F♯-A♭-B♭-C.

Looking at the structure of "La Malinconia" as a whole, I would certainly identify F as the main melodic tone [Example 9.5]. There is no *Urlinie* in this piece, because it is not a complete piece, just the introduction to a more complete piece. But if we have a kind of *Ersatzurlinie*, a substitute *Urlinie*, it would definitely move from F. In fact, I would take F-G♭-F as the main top voice of the whole thing. The G♭ arrives at the climax, two measures before the end, just before the return of the tonic (now as B♭ minor).

In my graph of measures 21–28, you can see the whole-tone ascent in the bass from E to C, unfolding an interval within the C-major triad that arrives *sforzando* in the second half of measure 28. This is a section of music in which Mitchell goes seriously astray, I think [Example 9.6]. The passage starts in E minor, and Mitchell shows G as the main top voice tone, which is undoubtedly correct. But Mitchell wants to connect directly from the bass-note E in measure 21 to the bass-note E in the second half of measure 27, and I think that's a problem. That's because the E in measure 27 is impossible to understand as part of a long-range connection. The E that Mitchell wants actually leads to F, just as in the immediately preceding measures D led to E♭ and A led to B♭. The leading tones are subordinate to the main tones they go to. The E in measure 27 is just such a leading tone, and it goes to F. Unfortunately, that's a very vital connection to his whole analysis, and it's a sign that there is something misconceived in the analysis, brilliant as it is in other respects.

EXAMPLE 9.5 Beethoven, "La Malinconia," complete analytical sketch of linear/harmonic structure.

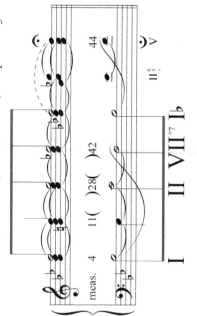

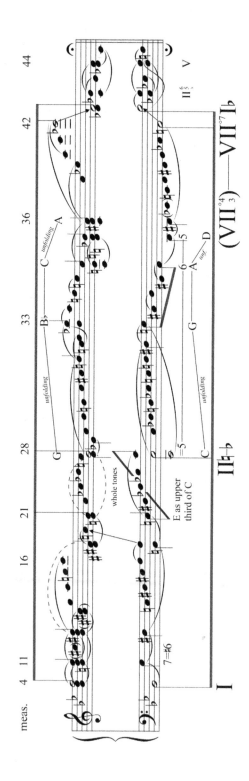

EXAMPLE 9.6 *Beethoven, "La Malinconia," mm. 21–33, analysis from William Mitchell (Example 6).*

The sequence in measures 25–28, at the end of the long progression of ascending fifths that we've been talking about, breaks in an interesting way. The bass alternates descending diminished fifths with ascending semitones, leading us to F minor (m. 28): Ab-D-Eb-A-Bb-E-F. To continue the sequence, the next note in the cello should be a low B, but the cello would need to have a low B string. Instead, we go immediately to C, without a leading-tone B. And that C-chord is very much emphasized. It comes in after a crescendo of almost four measures, and it's marked with a *sforzando* at the peak of the crescendo. Also, it is held for two beats (with the second violin changing from E to Eb). That C is thus a heavily foregrounded event.

I think the emphasized C in measures 28–29 connects back to the events that we discussed in measure 11. There, we had a dominant seventh of C that should have gone to C, but instead got reinterpreted as an augmented-sixth chord in B minor, and the music took a serious wrong turn. Now, in measure 28, the C comes in almost by accident: it sort of falls in the lap of the melancholy person. You can see this spelled out in a graph that I think of as a sort of road map for the piece [Example 9.7].

EXAMPLE 9.7 Beethoven, "La Malinconia," complete analytical sketch ("road map").

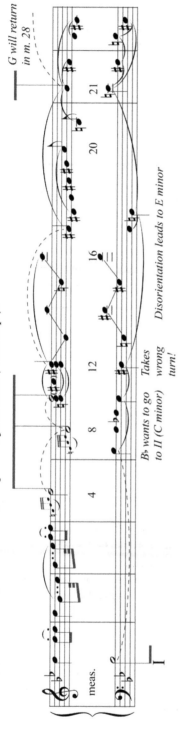

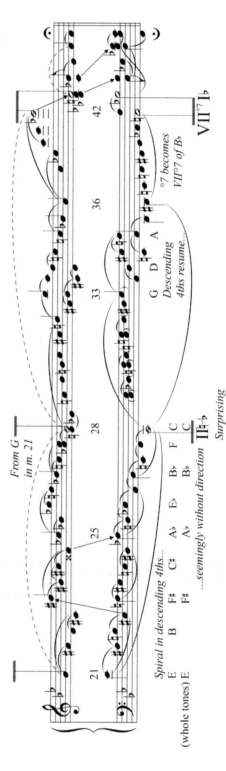

I'll return to this road map in a moment, but first I want to consider some motivic issues. In his very first example, Mitchell draws attention to the motivic use of the diminished fifth [Example 9.8].

EXAMPLE 9.8 *Beethoven, "La Malinconia," motivic issues, from William Mitchell (Example 1).*

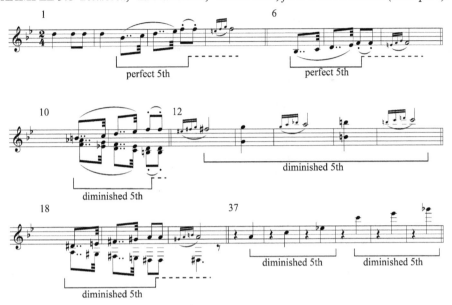

Some of this has to do simply with the frequent diminished-seventh chords in this movement, but I think Mitchell is certainly onto something here. Yet he does not try to relate his motivic diminished fifths to the fact that the second important key in this music, E minor, is a diminished fifth away from the tonic of B♭. I think that reflects a certain caution (perhaps a praiseworthy caution) in analytic procedure, which a little bit characterizes the way that an older generation of Schenkerians dealt with motivic relationships. They were more inclined to insist that for two motives to be equivalent they had to have the same harmonic function and consist of the same scale degrees. So, for example, if in one case it was the first note of the diminished fifth that was dissonant and in another case the second note was the dissonant one, I'm not sure if Mitchell would have recognized that as a parallelism. John Rothgeb, who is (together with Hedi Siegel) one of Schenker's best translators, goes perhaps a bit too far in demanding an almost one-to-one correspondence between model and derivative [Rothgeb 1971]. On the other hand, it's probably good to exercise a bit of caution, because one can go a little wild with these things, and show connections to the point where they become meaningless.

Curiously, at one stage in the production of Mitchell's article—it may have been while it was still in manuscript—I was doing a certain amount of assistant editorial work for the *Music Forum*. Where the finished article now says "diminished fifth," Mitchell had originally written "depressed fifth." Salzer refused to print it that way, feeling it was too cute for a serious article like this. That was an interesting and rare attempt by Mitchell to get into the emotional character of the music, and he had to cut it out.

In his own analyses, Schenker doesn't take very obscure melodic connections and make them into significant parallelisms, but he also doesn't completely disallow giving significance to similarities in sound that are not grounded structurally. Schenker sometimes calls attention to successions of notes even if they are not connected by voice leading, especially patterns of the highest notes in phrases. Look, for example, at the high notes in the beginning of the melody of the slow movement in Haydn's Symphony No. 104: B-C-D-E [Example 9.9].

EXAMPLE 9.9 *Haydn, Symphony No. 104, second movement, mm. 1–8.*

That is in no sense a linear progression of a fourth, but part of the effect of the beautiful melody has to do with the fact that these tones, although they are ornamental in their local context, nonetheless join together to form that stepwise motion.

　　Now let's go back to my road map. I did something like this in an article I wrote about Beethoven's Sixth Symphony [Schachter 1995/1999]. It's a simplified graph together with foreground features, including those that are programmatic or dramatic in nature. So you can see comments like "B♭ wants to go to II (C minor)—Takes wrong turn!—Disorientation leads to E minor." Although the graph is simplified in some respects, it does show a few large-scale voice-leading things. For example, look at the connection I draw (with a dotted slur) between the G in measure 21 (part of E-minor harmony) and the return of the G in measure 28 (now part of C-major harmony). One familiar harmonic aspect of Schenkerian analysis involves understanding certain harmonies as the "upper third" of more basic, fundamental harmonies. For example, a III chord (E-G-B) can function as the upper third of a I chord (C-E-G); III could be used in place of I, and possibly combined with I into a large-scale harmony. One of the wonderful things about Schenker's way of dealing with harmony is that a *Stufe*, a harmonic unit, can be a triad, it can be something derived from a triad like a seventh chord, it can be a single note that implies a triad, it can be a two-part counterpoint, it can be a linear progression, and it can also be a rather different chord (as when you have VII in place of V).

　　My feeling is that the E-minor harmony in measure 21 is best understood as the upper third of the C chord which arrives in measure 28. That's one reason, by the way, why it has to be a C-major rather than a C-minor chord when it first comes in. Though we do have upper thirds that also involve chromaticism, it doesn't usually happen in a context where everything else is so disorienting that it would be almost impossible to hear. Here, there is enough similarity in sound between the C major and E minor to make it, at least for me, a plausible analysis.

　　In that sense, I don't take the motion from B♭ major to E minor totally at face value. It is true that B♭ and E are juxtaposed as the two main key areas in the first half of the movement, but the E is not on the same level as the C that is going to follow. For me, the arrival on C is the turning point of this piece, and the key for what is to follow. And it arises from the initial desire of B♭ to go to its II chord, and its inability or unwillingness to do so. The music then goes astray and seems to take a wrong turn down the wrong path, until its apparent mistake is corrected by the arrival on C in measure 28. Once we get to that C, we are in a situation where we can actually complete the movement in a rational way. This would be an example of a foreground that misleads about the background: the foreground seems to be to some extent incoherent, but there is coherence in the larger pattern.

Some people might question the validity of seeing long-range connections like the one from the E in measure 21 to the C in measure 28, especially because there are so many foreign elements between the E and the C that are both intriguing and disturbing to the ear. Furthermore, in this case, we cannot draw on a storehouse of memories of lots of other pieces that do something similar, because there's really nothing quite like this in any other piece that I know of. To make matters even more challenging, there's a long lapse of time between the E and the C: it's only a few measures in the score, but at this very slow tempo, it's like events in a faster tempo that might be a half-page or even a full page apart.

There are people working in the field of music cognition who might deny the validity of large-scale connections like this. And certainly these are not things that college freshmen in the psychology lab are likely to grasp on a first hearing. But it's important to recognize that these pieces are not meant only to be listened to, but also to be studied and pondered over. And it's possible that one can bring to one's hearing of a piece a lot of information that one would never be able to hear the first time, or even the fifth time.

It puts me in mind of a discussion by William Empson, in *Seven Types of Ambiguity* [Empson 1966], of a strange speech in the third scene of Shakespeare's *Macbeth*. Macbeth has just distinguished himself in battle, and a nobleman named Ross praises him by saying:

Nothing afeard of what thyself didst make,
Strange images of death.

In other words, he praises Macbeth for not being afraid of dead people, namely, people he had killed on the battlefield. But, as Empson points out, the *last* thing that a practiced soldier and a rather brutal person like Macbeth would be disturbed by would be the sight of dead enemies on a battlefield. Much later in the play, however, he *is* haunted by the dead people whom he has killed or ordered to be killed, and he *is* brought to ruin by it. So we have a speech that nobody pays any attention to near the beginning of the play, and then something very closely related to it near the end of the play. The two things are widely separated in time, and the first is practically unnoticed in its context, but they are nonetheless closely bound together.

One finds such things in music, too. We have already talked about Oswald Jonas's idea about the last movement of Beethoven's Op. 101 Piano Sonata, where the exposition ends on a $^6_4$ chord that is resolved pages of music later, after the whole development section, including a quite substantial fugue. The similarity in texture binds together the two widely separated events, making the whole of the fugue seem like a kind of gigantic interpolation. But who is going to catch that? Which college freshman in a cognition experiment is going to hear that? And are we then to say that it's not important? One really has not only to study the music, but one has also to be someone like Jonas, with that kind of keenness of perception, to be able to make such a connection.

Sometimes significant large-scale connections can occur to you in a sudden flash, even while listening to a performance. I can't say this happens very often, but I do remember hearing a recital by Murray Perahia, where he played the Chopin Fantasy, Op. 49. There was one place where I suddenly realized that there was a gigantic chromaticized voice exchange, with a whole *Lento* section interpolated between the elements of the voice exchange. That came to me in the concert, and it was the key to my understanding of the piece as I do, and that analytical insight became the basis for an article I wrote about this work [Schachter 1999e].

Studying a piece like "La Malinconia" raises important questions about the ethics and the aesthetics both of creating and judging a work of art. The playwright Anton Chekhov allegedly said that it's perfectly all right to write a play whose central character is a boring man, but that would not justify writing a boring play. In other words, the work of art need not take on the qualities of the things it is describing, and that is something that most artists appear to believe. One vivid example is the music of Mozart, which remains so beautiful even when it is describing unbeautiful things and situations. Mozart wanted music always to be music, not just sounds, even when extreme emotional states are involved. When we get to the latter part of the nineteenth century, that idea is no longer generally held. Think about something like Edvard Munch's painting, "The Scream," where he deliberately creates something quite distorted and ugly looking (to great expressive effect by the way). But Beethoven's representation of craziness in "La Malinconia" does not sound totally crazy at all. Rather, he writes something that is notably restrained in the way in which it depicts an extreme emotional disorganization.

Let's conclude our discussion of this remarkable piece by looking at the final twelve measures, starting with the turn toward A-minor in measure 37. The passage seems to move toward the $^6_4$ chord in measure 37 as a goal. That $^6_4$ chord is preceded by a Neapolitan sixth chord (m. 35), which seems to pass through a diminished-seventh chord with D♯ in the bass (m. 36) to what sounds like a cadential $^6_4$ chord over the dominant of A minor (m. 37). But when the music goes on, what we thought was a cadential $^6_4$ is now heard retrospectively as a passing $^6_4$ chord, and the diminished-seventh chord in measure 36, which we thought was passing, now is heard as the prolonged harmony.

What is actually happening here is that we are prolonging a diminished-seventh chord through passing motions and quasi-voice exchanges. We've previously seen similar situations in the Chopin E-major Prelude and in Beethoven's Second Symphony in which a diminished-seventh chord is prolonged by passing motions and voice exchanges. Here, we first think that the diminished-seventh chord on D♯ (m. 36) is passing to E, but it turns out in fact that the E is passing from that D♯ up to F♯. The $^6_4$ chords are not cadential $^6_4$ chords, but passing $^6_4$ chords. So this is another passage where the foreground is misleading or deceptive with respect to the background—an extreme example of such a thing.

Rhythm, Hypermeter, and Phrase

We'll focus today on rhythm and phrase organization. We'll look at several pieces, including the Adagio from Mozart's String Quartet, K 458.

W E'LL TALK TODAY MOSTLY ABOUT PHRASES AND PHRASE ORGANIZATION, topics of interest for everyone, but especially for performers. It's a truism that phrases in music are roughly analogous to sentences in language. But it can be quite difficult to define precisely what a phrase is, or indeed what a sentence in language is. (When I was a kid, we were taught that a sentence is a group of words containing a subject and a predicate, and expressing a complete thought. But who can tell me what a complete thought is?) Instead of offering general and mostly useless definitions, let's start by looking at a piece: the Trio section of the Scherzo movement of Beethoven's Piano Sonata, Op. 2, No. 3 [Example 10.1].

In the graph, I identify measures 1–8 as a "provisionally closed phrase." I make a distinction, which is not original with me at all, between open phrases and closed phrases, the closed ones being those that end with a perfect authentic cadence. I call this phrase "provisionally closed" because, while it does end with a perfect authentic cadence, it does so in the wrong key, the key of the dominant.

This provisionally closed phrase is followed by two "transitional phrases" (mm. 9–12 and 13–16). These are phrases that have no real independent existence, but instead are totally dependent on context. Really, they are meaningless by themselves—you have to know what comes before them to make any sense of them.

That's something that is analogous to language. If I say something like, "Yesterday, I didn't see Steve," that's definitely a closed sentence. But if I say, "Did you?," it has absolutely no meaning apart from the sentence before it. It means, in this context, "Did you see Steve?" The next phrase of the piece, measures 17–24, I identify as "definitively closed." I should add that it's a bit misleading to call this phrase "definitively closed" because it is followed by a repetition of the Trio's second strain, which changes course at the end to lead us back to C major, the key of the scherzo as a whole.

Many phrases are organized around a motion to a climactic point and away from it. This is not universal—there are plenty of phrases without climaxes—but especially in nineteenth-century music, the idea of building up to a climax is quite important, although it's not always entirely obvious where the climax is. For instance, at the beginning of this

EXAMPLE 10.1 *Beethoven, Piano Sonata, Op. 2, No. 3, third movement (Trio section of the Scherzo), score and analytical sketch.*

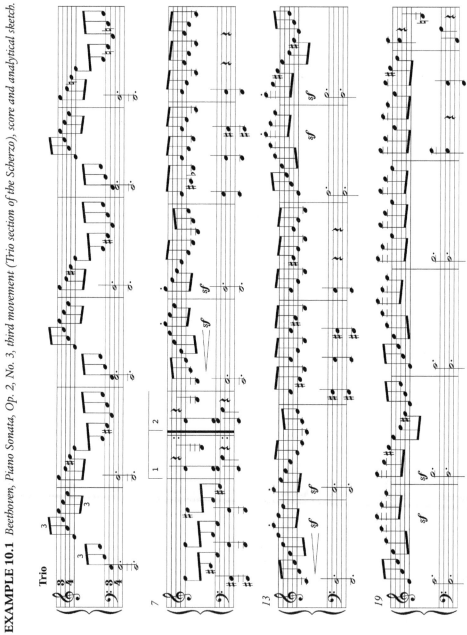

EXAMPLE 10.1 (*Continued*)

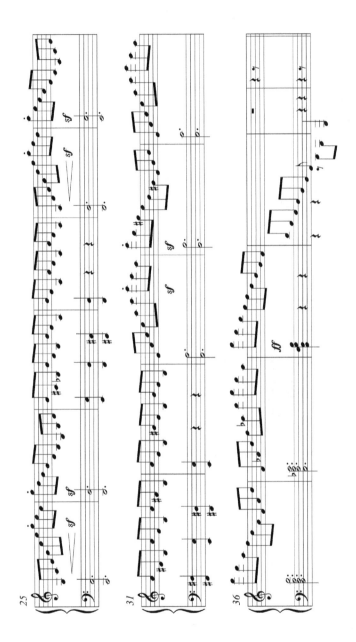

EXAMPLE 10.1 (*Continued*)

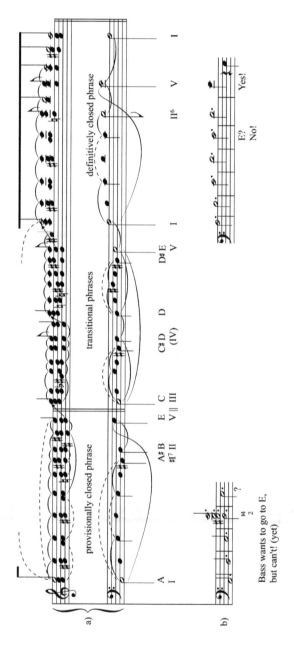

Trio, the melodic interest is all in the bass, but the bass still maintains the character of a bass line—it's not trying to be a *bel canto* melody at all. Initially, you might be tempted to take the highest note as the climactic point, which indeed it often is, but I'm not sure that's the best choice here. My own feeling is that the melody reaches a turning point with the A♯ in measure 7 and, in playing the piece, I would drive it up to that note.

The norm for the performance of dissonant and chromatic notes in the time of Beethoven was that they should be emphasized by being played more loudly, with a decrescendo into whatever consonant or diatonic notes come after. The bass line of measures 1–8 can be understood as an unfolding of the opening tonic through rising and falling thirds, but the second third becomes diminished: A-B-C, then C-B-A♯. The larger motion is from A (m. 1) passing upward through A♯ to B (m. 7) and then E (m. 8). The A♯ is thus both a chromatic note and an important melodic goal.

Each of the four-measure phrases after the double bar (mm. 9–12 and 13–16) is a compression of the opening eight-measure phrase. They provide additional evidence for making the A♯ in measure 7 the focal point of the first phrase, because they are organized in similar fashion, leading to the C♯ in measure 11 and to the D♯ in measure 15.

The bass line in the first eight measures presents an interesting sort of musical problem. When you have a melody in A minor that ascends A-B-C-D, you naturally expect it to continue up to E. That's a basic principle of Gestalt psychology, namely, that if you start a process of some kind, you would normally try to take it to a point of closure. But the harmony in measure 4 does not allow the bass to continue up to E; instead, the $\frac{4}{2}$ chord forces the line down again. In the last phrase (mm. 17–24), we again hit the barrier of a $\frac{4}{2}$ chord (m. 20), pushing the line back down to C (m. 21), but now there's a second attempt, pushing up through D to E (m. 23) and completing the motion that had been thwarted in the first phrase. That creates a climax not just for measures 17–24, but for the whole 24-measure passage. So phrases can stand alone to varying degrees and can be organized around climaxes also, in varying degrees.

The next piece I want to look at is the Chopin Prelude in C minor, Op. 28, No. 20, and I want to deal with a question that arises frequently, namely, "How long is a phrase?" [Example 10-2]. For example, in the Chopin Prelude, do the first four measures constitute one phrase or four phrases? Rather unusually, this prelude is written so that the first measure actually has the contents of an entire phrase.

The beautiful F♯-minor Prelude from the same opus is another one where you can read a whole phrase in the first measure, or you can make it part of something larger, or you can do both [Example 10.3].

EXAMPLE 10.2 *Chopin, Prelude in C minor, Op. 28, No. 20, mm. 1–4, score and analytical sketch.*

EXAMPLE 10.2 (*Continued*)

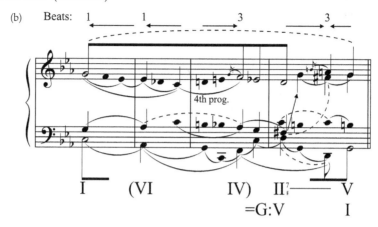

It's analogous to Caesar's famous declaration to the Roman Senate: "I came, I saw, I con-quered" ("*Veni, vidi, vici*"). Is that one sentence or three? It is actually both. We have a name for that—it's called a "compound sentence." The same sort of thing comes up all the time in music. If you have an eight-measure stretch of music that takes a breath after four measures and a bigger breath after eight, should one think of it as one eight-measure phrase or two four-measure phrases?

Taking the beginning of the second movement of Mozart's Piano Sonata, K. 545, as an example, I think you would all agree that the first eight measures make up one eight-measure phrase [Example 10.4]. There is certainly a little breathing pause after four measures, but it would be better to think of measures 1–4 and 5–8 as comprising two sub-phrases within a basic structure of eight measures. That eight-measure phrase itself turns out to be the ante-cedent in a parallel period of sixteen measures.

Returning to the Chopin C-minor Prelude, I am perfectly happy to think that there are small phrases inside large phrases, and to think that the first measure of this Prelude is simultaneously a little phrase on its own and also part of a larger four-measure structure. And four measures at the tempo of this piece lasts for quite as long as a sixteen-measure phrase might in a fast *allegro* in $\frac{2}{4}$ time, so in actual duration, Chopin's four-measure phrase represents a considerable stretch of music.

Within that stretch, measures 3 and 4 present a beautiful kind of problem. Measure 2 is a normal continuation of measure 1, related to it sequentially a major third lower, and tonicizing the sixth scale degree (A♭). Thus whatever we say about measure 1 will also most probably be true of measure 2. But measures 3 and 4 present a different situation.

The problem I'm referring to turns on the melody note on the fourth beat of measure 3. As you probably know, there are two different versions reflected in the many different edi-tions of this piece: some have it as E♮ (like the second beat of the same measure) and oth-ers have it as E♭. The manuscript of Op. 28 does not have a flat sign before the fourth beat, suggesting that the natural is still in force from the second beat. But a flat sign is inserted, in Chopin's handwriting, in a copy of the music belonging to a student of his. I think without any question that the E♭ is ever so much more powerful and beautiful than the E♮.

The E♭ also has a much more compelling logic to it than the E♮. If it really were E♮, then it would have made much more sense for measure 4 to follow measure 3 sequentially, just as measure 2 followed measure 1 [Example 10.5].

EXAMPLE 10.3 *Chopin, Prelude in F♯ minor, Op. 28, No. 8, mm. 1–4.*

Molto agitato.

EXAMPLE 10.4 *Mozart, Piano Sonata, K. 545 in C major, second movement, mm. 1–16.*

EXAMPLE 10.5 *Chopin, Prelude in C minor, Op. 28, No. 20, mm. 1–4, hypothetical recomposition.*

In that hypothetical version, starting measure 4 on F♯ gives meaning to the E♮ at the end of measure 3. But the fourth measure actually begins on D, and that argues strongly for an E♭ at the end of measure 3 to lead down to it. The connection between measures 3 and 4 is reflected by Chopin's slurs: he has one slur for measure 1, one slur for measure 2, and then a single slur for measures 3 and 4 together. Pianists often play measures 1–4 as though there are four equal one-measure segments. But it's better to think of this as one measure, plus one measure, plus two measures. Incidentally, there is a very important phrase type characterized (among other things) by the proportions 1 measure, 1 measure, 2 measures. As we shall see presently, this type of phrase is called a "sentence." This type of musical phrase has nothing in common with the linguistic sentence except the name.

Some passages are propelled toward a future goal, and others seem to be reacting to something that happened previously: they have either prospective or retrospective tendencies. I think of measures 1 and 2 as receding away from their downbeats, rather than moving forward to a goal. But in the second half of the phrase (mm. 3–4), the motion is directed toward the third beat, and undoubtedly the climactic moment of the whole four-measure phrase is in fact the third beat of measure 4. Mind you, that climactic moment is not part of the structural background of the piece, because the harmony is an applied dominant to the dominant, and the melody is a suspension.

Notice that I'm not insisting that the end of every phrase be marked with a cadence. Rather, phrases involve motion from one musical place to another, ending with a feeling of breathing or stopping—this is something William Rothstein discusses persuasively in his wonderful book on phrase rhythm [Rothstein 1989]. A formal cadence is the strongest way of conveying that sense of breathing or stopping, but it's not by any means universal in what one would call a phrase. Along these lines, I think it is possible to distinguish between a sub-phrase and a small phrase inside a larger one. A small phrase has a claim to independent existence, whereas a sub-phrase doesn't really cut it by itself.

Sometimes, the point of articulation at the end of a phrase can be bridged over musically, somewhat in the manner of a conjunction like "and" in a compound sentence. In Chopin's Prelude in E minor, also from Op. 28, there's a phrase that ends in a cadence on the first beat of measure 12, but then there's a connective idea, a magnificently composed connective idea [Example 10.6].

An important aspect of musical phrases is their degree of symmetry. Here are two interestingly similar melodies by Mozart, which we discussed a few weeks ago—from the Violin Sonata, K. 481, and the Rondo, K. 511 [Example 10.7]. These pieces were written at around the same time and, although there are obvious and important differences between them, there are striking similarities also, including the surprisingly similar endings of the two phrases. But one of the things that make the two so different from each other is their very different attitude toward symmetry. The Violin Sonata melody is highly symmetrical, and its symmetry is reinforced by the rhythmic stress placed on the notes of the tonic triad. (I've used arrows to indicate notes that belong to the tonic triad). In the Violin Sonata, those triadic notes are in very prominent positions: the first downbeat and the two subsequent downbeats. In the Rondo, the first triadic note is on the downbeat, but the next two are not on the downbeat. The four measures of the Violin Sonata melody divide neatly into 2 + 2. The Rondo begins with a one-measure idea followed by two measures of chromatic ascent and then a measure of cadence. So whereas the four measures of the Violin Sonata divide into 2 + 2, the four measures of the Rondo divide into 1 + 2 + 1, creating a kind of large-scale syncopated rhythm. There is a much greater sense of tension in the Rondo, and that is due in part to its being in minor rather than major, and in part because it is chromatic rather than diatonic, but also because it is asymmetrical rather than symmetrical in its design.

In the first eight measures of the Finale of Beethoven's Violin Sonata, Op. 24, the "Spring" Sonata, we have a two-measure idea (mm. 1–2), a continuation of the same idea

EXAMPLE 10.6 *Chopin, Prelude in E minor, Op. 28, No. 4, mm. 1–14.*

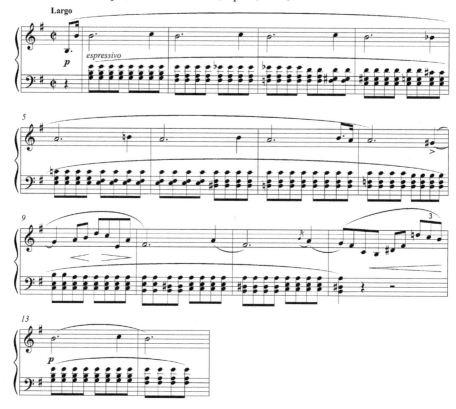

EXAMPLE 10.7 *Mozart, Sonata for Violin and Piano, K. 481, second movement, and Rondo, K. 511, analytical comparison of two melodies.*

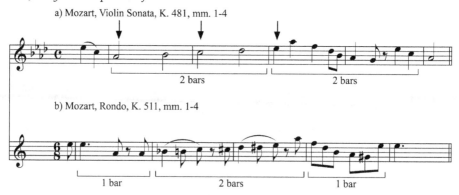

(mm. 3–4), and then four measures with an acceleration of rhythmic values leading to a cadence (mm. 5–8)—I'm showing you both the score and my own two-voice reduction [Example 10.8].

It's the sort of arrangement that is commonly called a sentence. It's very symmetrical, with the two-measure groups being subsumed into a larger four-measure group. In the

EXAMPLE 10.8 *Beethoven, Violin Sonata, Op. 24 ("Spring"), Finale, mm. 1–18, score and analytical sketch.*

second four-measure group we also have two-measure groups, but the individual measures are not emphasized because of the motivic fragmentation that one often gets in a sentence. So we have (2 + 2) + (2 + 2), in which some of the two-measure groups divide clearly into 1 + 1, whereas in others the boundary is indistinct. Overall, the phrase is arranged in a typically symmetrical way. In the consequent phrase (mm. 9–18), there's an expansion that extends the second hypermeasure from four to six bars, but the underlying symmetry remains.

In all of this, it's important to take note of the great importance of two-measure units in the phrase structure of a great deal of Classical and nineteenth-century music, and also in a lot of high Baroque music, especially dance music. In his operas, for example, Mozart will very typically set each line of verse to two measures of music. That means that if the verse has only four or five syllables per line, they will be spread out across two measures, and if the verse has ten syllables, as is sometimes the case, they will be packed into two measures, although the measures themselves

EXAMPLE 10.8 (*Continued*)

(b) hypermeasures:

may be longer in such a case. The two-measure length is a norm; there are exceptions, of course. Similarly, in Schubert's songs, each line of verse is frequently set to a two-measure musical unit.

When we think about phrase organization, often one of the first things to deal with is the prevalence of two-measure groups—how they are joined together and to what extent they are submerged as elements of larger groupings. If I were performing the last movement of the "Spring" Sonata, either as a violinist or pianist, I would rejoice in the two-measure ideas, and in their dancelike quality of the rhythm. I would want to delineate and articulate the smaller groupings—the half-measures, the measures, and the two-measure units—in a clearly perceptible way. In the first movement, in contrast, you would probably want to let the smaller units recede into the larger outline of the ten-measure phrase as a whole. The extent to which you want to allow the smaller symmetries to intrude on the larger structure is an important consideration in musical performance.

The first movement of the "Spring" Sonata starts out as though it's going to be a symmetrical eight-measure phrase [Example 10.9].

EXAMPLE 10.9 *Beethoven, Violin Sonata, Op. 24 ("Spring"), first movement, mm. 1–10.*

We have one two-measure idea (mm. 1–2) followed by another two-measure idea (mm. 3–4), and these sound like the four-measure beginning of an eight-measure phrase. But it turns out instead that the idea of measures 3–4 is repeated in measures 5–6, and then again in measures 7–8, and that pattern conflicts with what we had expected to be a four-measure unit. One can scan that beginning in various ways, but in no way is it going to be symmetrical. You certainly couldn't divide the ten measures into five-plus-five! And imagine how terrible it would be to delete measures 5–6 and go directly from the end of measure 4 to the beginning of measure 7. From a durational standpoint, that would fit the eight measures very well, but we would have eviscerated a vital part of the living tissue of that phrase. We need each new little sub-phrase, starting on the last note of the previous one, and building this glorious theme, one of the most beautiful themes in music, I think.

It might be possible to regularize this a bit by saying that we have a four-measure phrase, then another four-measure phrase, and then another two measures of cadence $(4 + 4 + 2)$, but I am not at all satisfied with that. For me, the repeated motivic pattern links measures 3–4, 5–6, and 7–8 into a single six-measure idea $(2 + 6 + 2)$. The harmony corroborates that view: the harmony at the beginning of measure 7 is the same as at the end of measure 6, so there is nothing to suggest that a new unit of time is being born at the beginning of measure 7.

Getting back to the last movement of this sonata, the piano plays a quite normal eight-measure antecedent phrase, divided easily into four-plus-four. The violin then plays the consequent phrase, but it's a ten-measure consequent to an eight-measure antecedent. The elongation of the consequent phrase results from the chromatically inflected deceptive cadence in measures 14–15, with V leading to VI instead of to I. If measures 15 and 16 were eliminated, the music would move perfectly nicely from measure 14 to measure 17, and we would have a more normal eight-measure consequent phrase. That is certainly what Beethoven expected his listeners to expect.

This raises the notion of phrase expansion. Composers use a variety of devices to break up the surface symmetry of eight-measure phrases, as Beethoven does with his deceptive cadence. They break up the symmetry, but at the same time, they evoke a comparison to an underlying symmetrical model, and permit us to hear the surface of the music as a modification of an underlying model. There is a valuable analogy here to the bilateral symmetry of the human body. Our two sides are mirror images of each other, and we thus have an intrinsic binary organization, which is particularly evident when we stand upright. But bodies can be presented in many other ways. In talking about sculpture, Italians have what they call *contrapposto*, which refers to the asymmetric and irregular presentation of what is essentially a symmetrical structure. And that is very different from a structure that is deeply and intrinsically asymmetrical.

Schenker talked about these sorts of issues when he talked about expansion. He used the term expansion in a more restricted sense than many people do nowadays. For example, if we have a one-measure upbeat formation that precedes and is not part of a metrical pattern of, say, $2 + 2 = 4$, Schenker did not call that an expansion. He also made a distinction between expansions that are taken at face value and irregular groupings of measures that result from a diminution.

For example, the first six measures of the Minuet of Mozart's G-minor Symphony, K. 550, are famously divided into $3 + 3$ [Example 10.10].

EXAMPLE 10.10 *Mozart, Symphony No. 40 in G minor, K. 550, Minuet, mm. 1–6.*

Schenker pointed out that the two three-measure groups arise from the diminutions: two descending third-progressions (B♭-A-G and D-C-B♭). The linear progressions thus generate the three-measure phrases. The phrases are not expansions or contractions of something else—they're just three-measure groups. Riemann, on the other hand, had the idea that those three-measure groups actually are the compression of implicit, underlying four-measure groups. That's something Schenker would not agree with at all. For Schenker, some three- or five- or seven-measure phrases are simply born that way, while others result from an expansion or some other manipulation of time.

Expansions can result from many different causes. For instance, in the "Spring" Sonata, fourth movement, it is definitely the deceptive cadence in measure 15 that gives us the feeling that two additional measures have been inserted into a phrase that we've already heard in its eight-measure antecedent version. It's the digression toward D minor that adds the two extra measures. Instead of calling the added two measures an insertion, we can say that they're parenthetical, as though that deceptive cadence and the elements surrounding it are enclosed within brackets, and that there is a larger continuity available if you skip over those two measures.

These are things for performers especially to ponder. If you have, say, two extra measures, that will disturb the hypermeter without destroying it altogether. What the performer has to ask herself is, "Do I go on playing in strict time"—which might very well be the proper or desirable course—"or should I use some kind of freedom to reflect that it belongs, in a certain way, in a different universe of discourse from the rest of the phrase? And if I do want to make some difference, what should that difference be?" It would seem to me in the case of the Spring Sonata finale, if you do want to make a difference, you might want to slow down a little bit, particularly in the left-hand part, going from the C♯ to the D (mm. 15–16), and then when things are back on their proper course, to go in strict time.

So we have three large categories here. First, we have constructions that are intrinsically symmetrical. Second, we have constructions that are entirely asymmetrical. (In fact, total asymmetry is not possible, and even the Hunchback of Notre Dame still has a kind of symmetry in his body, even though it's very much disguised). Finally, we have constructions that are derived from symmetrical ones, but that become asymmetric, as in the case of the "Spring" Sonata and the Hunchback of Notre Dame, through insertion, parenthetical statement, or other sort of expansion or alteration.

There are many devices that composers use to increase the length of a phrase. We've just spoken about parenthetical insertions. Simple repetition or enlargement of note values is also possible. The beginning of the duet "La ci darem la mano" (from Mozart's *Don Giovanni*) has wonderful examples of expansions and contractions of phrases as Zerlina tries to slow things down while Giovanni tries to speed things up. This, and other ways that rhythm tells a dramatic story in this music, are things that Charles Burkhart discusses in a wonderful article [Burkhart 1991] [Example 10.11].

Giovanni starts with an eight-measure phrase divided into 4 + 4. Zerlina starts in the same way, but just at the point where she might have been expected to end her own eight-measure phrase (downbeat of m. 16), the orchestra, instead of supporting her with a root-position tonic chord gives her only a I⁶ chord, thus withholding any real harmonic conclusion. That requires her to back up and get onto the road again, and it takes her two additional measures to do so. Just as in Beethoven's Spring Sonata, the two parenthetical measures (mm. 16–17) could have been removed and the underlying eight-measure model restored.

EXAMPLE 10.11 *Mozart, "Là ci darem la mano" from* Don Giovanni, *mm. 1–39.*

As the music continues, Giovanni sings two measures (mm. 19–20), Zerlina sings two measures (mm. 21–22), Giovanni sings two more measures (mm. 23–24), and then Zerlina sings not two but four measures. She stretches things out by repetition. We don't get the sort of insertion or parentheses we've been talking about—it's more just a swelling of the tissues, you might say, through repetition.

One can also, of course, cut things short. When we are deviating from symmetry, it's not always in the direction of making something longer, but mostly it is, actually. Schenker makes a very important related observation in *Meisterwerk* [Schenker 1996], where he is talking about the differences between the visual arts and music. He says that the visual artist is confronted with an enormous, infinite number of things, and his—forgive my sexist language, but Schenker says "his"—task is therefore to abbreviate and select. But the basic materials of music for Schenker—just the third, fifth, and octave that create the tonic harmony—are very small and restricted. The composer therefore has the task of fleshing it out, expanding it, doing more with it. In the same way, the prototypes in the underlying rhythmic structures are usually modified in the direction of expanding them rather

EXAMPLE 10.11 (*Continued*)

than in the direction of abbreviating them, though the other happens also, and can be very important.

In fact, we can see an example of contraction in the phrases as this duet continues. In measures 30–33, Giovanni and Zerlina share a four-measure phrase, as 2 + 2. In the four-measure phrase that follows, however, Giovanni takes what we expect to be the fourth measure of the phrase (m. 37) and turns it into the first measure of a new phrase. He wants to get things going, and Zerlina is not cooperating quite as he would like. This abbreviation of a phrase by taking the last measure of an expected group of measures and turning it into the first measure of a new group, as Giovanni is doing here, is a very important possibility.

The beginning of Beethoven's Piano Sonata, Op. 110, shows two ways of joining phrases together, both of which can be characterized as overlaps. (We already discussed this passage a bit in Lesson 4) [Example 10.12]. In the first type of overlap, you have what seems to be a complete group of measures durationally, but it does not arrive at its tonal goal on time. The tonal goal, instead of occurring within the group, is shifted over to the beginning of the next group. The first four measures of this piece are obviously a four-measure span, but the

EXAMPLE 10.11 (*Continued*)

resolution, both in the bass and the upper voice, doesn't occur until after the four-measure span has completed itself (i.e., in m. 5). For situations like this, Tovey uses the expression, "four measures closing into . . .," which I find a very expressive and beautiful way of thinking about this. Tovey uses this expression throughout his book about Beethoven's piano sonatas [Tovey 1931]. We do hear the four-measure group as a meaningful thing on its own, but it's not closed; rather, it *closes into* the first measure of the next group.

The second type of overlap works in a somewhat different way. Starting in measure 5, we have an eight-measure phrase. But the last measure of that eight-measure phrase is omitted, and something new begins in measure 12. The last measure of the eight-measure phrase and the first measure of the new musical idea are collapsed into a single measure. Or, to put it in a slightly different way, the eighth measure of one phrase is reinterpreted as the first measure of the next.

This is a kind of overlap that is also correctly characterized as an elision. People sometimes use the word elision for the kind of thing that happens in measures 1–5, but I don't think that's correct. Elision means that something is removed or taken out, and nothing is removed or taken out in measures 1–5, but something is elided in measure 12. The German

EXAMPLE 10.12 *Beethoven, Piano Sonata, Op. 110, first movement, mm. 1–12, score and ana-lytical reduction.*

(a)

expression *Takterstickung* ("suppression of a measure") is sometimes used for a situation like the one in measure 12. Schenker's term for the phenomenon is *Umdeutung* ("reinter-pretation"), because what is expected to be the final measure of one phrase is reinterpreted as the first measure of the next phrase. In my reduction, I show how the overlap, the "closing into" measure 5, works with the harmonic and melodic structure, whereas in measure 12, the eighth measure of one phrase is "suppressed" and the first measure of the next phrase takes its place. This sort of reinterpretation is a much more radical technique than overlap, and that's because it disturbs the hypermeter. (Incidentally, the word *Ersticken* is often used to mean "suffocate" or "smother.")

The first example in William Rothstein's book on phrase rhythm [Rothstein 1989] is Strauss's *Blue Danube Waltz*, which is a very good example for showing the difference between phrases and hypermeasures. As we discussed in Lesson 6, the musical phrases begin with the first note, but the hypermeter begins with the first hyperbeat that is perceived as a downbeat. The *Waltz* is always starting its phrases on beat four of the hypermeter.

It's also possible to have extended upbeats that take up a whole measure or more, and have them inserted into what is otherwise a metrically regular setting. My favorite example is the main theme of the first movement from the "Clock" Symphony of Haydn (Symphony No. 101) [Example 10.13].

EXAMPLE 10.12 (*Continued*)

(b) meas.

EXAMPLE 10.13 *Haydn, Symphony No. 101 ("Clock"), first movement (Presto), mm. 1–10.*

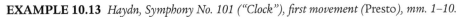

It is in $\frac{6}{8}$ time and begins with an upbeat measure. It would be terribly wrong to count that first upbeat measure as an accented beat 1 of a hypermeasure.

We've been speaking of extended upbeats, which are reasonably common. But there are also extended downbeat formations, either at the beginning or end of phrases, although these are less commonly acknowledged and less commonly found. I'm referring to a single downbeat measure, and Schenker actually does talk about that possibility. It might happen like this: 1-2-3-4, 1-2-3-4, 1, 1-2-3-4. That is, two four-measure phrases leading to what you think will be the downbeat of a new phrase. Instead, that downbeat measure is isolated, and then a new four-measure phrase begins.

A situation like that might arise in a mixed-media composition, like a piano concerto, where the music for one of the media stops and the other one starts. Here's an example from Mozart's Piano Concerto, K. 491 [Example 10.14]. The orchestra has an eight-measure phrase, leading to the downbeat of what might be the beginning of a new phrase. Instead, that downbeat measure remains isolated, and the piano starts with its own new four-measure phrase.

Something similar happens in "Der Wegweiser" from Schubert's *Winterreise*, a song we have already talked about a bit [Example 10.15]. The piano introduction makes perfectly acceptable sense as a four-measure phrase ending with the half cadence in measure 4. That's followed by a single downbeat measure, and then the singer enters with his own four-measure phrase, leading to a half cadence in measure 9. Then we get another isolated downbeat measure (m. 10). Note that the vocal line, and therefore also the text, ends in measure 9. Only the piano part continues into measure 10. This confirms the impression that measure 10 and also measure 5 lie outside the basic pattern of 4-measure phrases. Also note that the "extra" measures 5 and 10 contain tonic chords, thus converting the half cadences into authentic cadences. I believe that the tonic chords of measures 5 and 10 represent the normal roads that the "other travelers" take, and the very chromatic events that follow represent the climbs through snowy mountain passes that our narrator describes.

The extra downbeat formations we have been talking about come at the end of a phrase. But there is another type of downbeat formation, one that Schenker doesn't talk about, namely, one that occurs at the beginning of a phrase. Normally, this involves one (or even two) measures of tonic harmony in the bass or accompaniment, and then the melody comes in to begin a new phrase. Here's an example from "Dalla sua pace," Don Ottavio's first-act aria from Mozart's *Don Giovanni* [Example 10.16].

EXAMPLE 10.14 *Mozart, Piano Concerto No. 24 in C major, K. 491, first movement, mm. 101–113, annotated score (piano and strings only).*

EXAMPLE 10.15 *Schubert, "Der Wegweiser" from* Winterreise, *mm. 1–14, annotated score.*

EXAMPLE 10.16 *Mozart, "Dalla sua pace" from* Don Giovanni, *mm. 1–5, annotated score.*

The music begins with a measure of tonic harmony in the orchestra. That doesn't sound like an upbeat to me, particularly because of its tonic quality, so I take it as a bass downbeat. Then the voice enters in measure 2 with its own downbeat to the melodic phrase that follows. That sort of thing is not so uncommon.

A very controversial and exceedingly famous example of the same thing can be found in the opening measures of the Beethoven Violin Concerto [Example 10.17].

EXAMPLE 10.17 *Beethoven, Violin Concerto in D major, Op. 61, first movement, mm. 1–5, annotated score.*

Measure 1, with its four timpani strokes, is very often called an upbeat. I don't exactly object to that, but when the same music comes at the beginning of the recapitulation, now played fortissimo by the whole orchestra, it no longer sounds to me too much like an upbeat. And that makes me wonder about the opening—perhaps it would be better to say that measure 1 is a preparatory downbeat, rather than an upbeat.

One final example of the same thing: the beginning of Chopin's Prelude in G major, Op. 28 [Example 10.18].

EXAMPLE 10.18 *Chopin, Prelude in G major, Op. 28, No. 3, mm. 1–6, annotated score.*

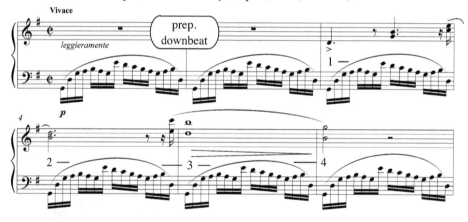

We have two measures of tonic harmony before the right hand comes in with the melody. This is very frequent in textures where there is a melody and an accompaniment, or where a characteristic rhythm wants to be heard. I think of these two measures as a preparatory downbeat rather than as an upbeat.

The Adagio movement from Mozart's String Quartet in B♭ major, K. 458, is a particularly wonderful movement. The whole quartet is great, but this movement is the glory of the quartet—I'm giving you both a score and my own rhythmic reduction of measures 1–25 [Example 10.19]. One of the first things you'll notice is that melodic ideas and phrases begin sometimes on first beats and other times on third beats of the measure, and that those third beats have very much the character of first beats. Right at the beginning of the piece, the first musical idea begins on beat 1. But already in measure 5 we have the same

EXAMPLE 10.19 *Mozart, String Quartet in B♭ major, K. 458, third movement (Adagio), mm. 1–25, annotated score and rhythmic reduction.*

(a)

idea starting on beat 3. Similarly, the musical idea that begins with the C-minor chord in measure 2 begins on the third beat, although it has an obvious downbeat quality to it. What produces these rhythmic (or metrical) dislocations is the upbeat quality of the rising arpeggio in measures 2 and 5.

Normally, extended upbeats are considered to be those that last for one whole measure or more, but these upbeats apparently last for only half a measure. But that's actually an illusion, because the meter of this movement is what is known as "compound $\frac{4}{4}$ time."

EXAMPLE 10.19 *(Continued)*

That is, one measure of the notated $\frac{4}{4}$ is equivalent to two measures of an unnotated but perceived $\frac{2}{4}$ time. The eighteenth-century theorist Johann Philipp Kirnberger said that in compound $\frac{4}{4}$ time, the first of the two downbeats (beat 1) should be relatively strong compared to the second downbeat (beat 3) [Kirnberger 1982].

But in practice this is not what always happens in Bach's music, Mozart's music, or the music of other composers. They sometimes take advantage of the downbeat quality of the third beat to let it outweigh the first beat and become what feels like the true downbeat. In

EXAMPLE 10.19 (*Continued*)

(b)

Alternate barring:

upbeat

*

Original barring:

5

*

* upbeat in 16th notes does not
stretch the time, but fits into the
prevailing meter

EXAMPLE 10.19 (*Continued*)

Reduction with expansions (*) removed:

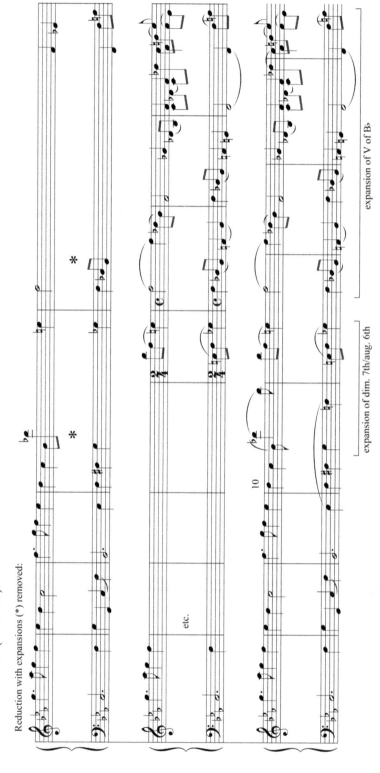

EXAMPLE 10.19 (Continued)

EXAMPLE 10.19 (*Continued*)

Reduction with expansion removed:

this passage, if we think of the $\frac{4}{4}$ as compound—that is, as containing two $\frac{2}{4}$ bars—the arpeggio figure in measure 2 really is an extended upbeat because it lasts for a full ($\frac{2}{4}$) measure. The arpeggio in measure 5, however, is in sixteenth-notes and therefore does not affect the hypermeter at all. If Mozart had written it in eighth-notes instead of sixteenths, then the theme would have entered on the first beat of the next measure (as it did in measure 1), but instead the theme starts on the third beat, as we noted. The upbeat figure in measure 6, however, is in eighth-notes and thus shifts things so that the half-bar that was taken away in measure 2 is now restored to us, and the mid-bar downbeats give way to first-beat downbeats, as in the downbeat of measure 7. At this point, the music once again sounds the way it is written.

If measures 1–6 are a first theme area, measure 7 marks the beginning of the bridge or transition in what turns out to be a sonata form without development. It's not at all uncommon in Mozart to have a sort of "bridge theme," you might say, very often (as here) in a key other than the tonic, that will eventually modulate to the second key area. When we get to measure 9, we might imagine that we have already reached our goal, namely, B♭, which is V in the original key and thus the likely key area for the second theme. I daresay many analysts, including possibly some in this very room, would consider measure 9 the beginning of the second theme and the fulfillment of the modulation to the dominant. But I would beg you to remember what I said some weeks ago: when you have an initial statement and a modified repeat of it, unless there are unusual and compelling reasons, the first statement is the main event and the second one is not a goal but lies in the middle of a larger motion initiated by the first statement. The main motion here is not to the B♭ in measure 9, but from the C minor in measure 7 all the way to the V of V (F) in measure 11. That V of B♭ is then extended through measure 13.

That V of V is preceded by an augmented-sixth chord (m. 11), which completes a very large-scale voice exchange. It is just as large as the one in the Violin Sonata that we looked at a few weeks ago, but more typical because it happens at this particular juncture in the sonata form. In this case, it is a chromaticized voice exchange that takes us from G over E♭ in the opening tonic (m. 1 and m. 5) to E♮ over G♭ in the augmented-sixth chord (m. 11) [Example 10.20].

EXAMPLE 10.20 *Mozart, String Quartet in B♭ major, K. 458, third movement (Adagio), mm. 1–11, analytical sketch.*

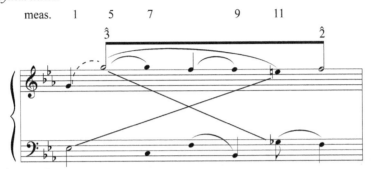

Within that voice exchange, the B♭ harmony in measure 9, which might have been taken for an arrival on the dominant, is shown to support the F in the upper voice which is a passing note between G and E♮.

Looking back at my rhythmic reduction, notice the expansion of diminished-seventh and augmented-sixth harmonies from the third beat of measure 10 through the second beat of measure 11. These two chords are very closely related: G-B♭-D♭-E and G♭-B♭-D♭-E. Lowering G to G♭ changes the harmony from a diminished seventh to an augmented sixth, so this passage is really like an expansion of one harmony.

That harmony resolves to the definitive V of B♭ on the third beat of measure 11, and it's expanded through the first half of measure 14. To me, that arrival on V of B♭ creates a metric realignment, and in the middle level of my rhythmic reduction, I position it on a downbeat. On the top level, I have taken out the expansions of both the diminished-seventh/augmented-sixth harmony and the standing on the dominant of B♭. Eight measures of Mozart's music (mm. 7–15) have thus been reduced to five-and-a-half measures. That rhythmic reduction gives a picture of the piece as it might have existed, in a sense, before Mozart begins to manipulate time with expansions and metric shifts. Within Mozart's expansions, we get the feeling that the wheels are turning, but the car isn't moving. That is, the expansions introduce a sense of timelessness into the music, or at least a sense that time has been enormously stretched out.

That brings us to the second theme in B♭ major, starting in measure 15. Right before it begins, in the second half of measure 14, we get a half-measure of locally tonic harmony. The hypermetric function of that harmony is as one of the preparatory downbeats we were just discussing. The melodic downbeat at the beginning of measure 15 is that incredible, unbelievably beautiful ⁶₄ chord—I often feel that if there were a beauty contest for ⁶₄ chords, this one would be "Miss ⁶₄." You notice that all the important thematic things in this piece start with G on top, including this ⁶₄ chord. At that point, and also on the first beat of the next measure (m. 16), the perceived downbeats are actually the first beats of the measure.

Then something really unusual happens: the fourth beat of measure 16 becomes a temporary, local downbeat, introducing a new musical idea that lasts for four beats. But there is a precedent for it in the beginning of this movement. One could easily group the first nine beats of this movement into three groups of three, with a thematic idea that lasts for three beats, an upbeat figure that lasts for three beats, and a modified repeat of the thematic idea that lasts for three beats. I'm not saying that's what most people would hear, but it is a kind of secondary implication, derived from the fact that the actual musical sounds occupy three, not four, beats. So what happens in measure 16, when a four-beat idea is reduced to three beats (when the fourth beat of the measure is reinterpreted as a first beat), is related to what happens at the beginning. Mozart is taking an implication in the opening and realizing it later.

Something similar happens in the first movement of Mozart's Piano Sonata in C minor, K. 457 [Example 10.21].

EXAMPLE 10.21 *Mozart's Piano Sonata in C minor, K. 457, first movement, mm. 1–8 and 118–122, annotated score.*

The opening theme lasts for three beats, and then a silence. Much later in the movement (mm. 118–119), there is suddenly an eruption of $\frac{3}{2}$ meter, which realizes the potential that was there from the beginning in the opening gesture, but untouched until then.

Back in the quartet, similar sorts of metrical things persist until the end of the exposition. The cello has the tune starting in measure 18. In its second measure (m. 19), its four-beat group is cut short by a new idea arriving on the fourth beat of the measure. That realignment lasts until measure 21, where a fourth beat is reinterpreted as a first beat, and the downbeats remain on beat 3 thereafter.

This is one of those sonata movements without a development section. The recapitulation begins in measure 25, and starts out exactly the same as in the exposition—in fact, it's mostly pretty regular throughout. But something very important that we had in the exposition is now missing. The music in measures 3–5, which had seemed to make this theme go to sleep a bit by relaxing it, is initially omitted. But in measures 47–50, just before the end of the movement, that music does return, and not just once, but twice. And, incidentally, it starts on the first beat of the measure, whereas it started on the third beat back in measure 3. I don't think this is necessarily something in the nature of a rhythmic resolution, but that is something worth pondering. One may have a feeling of tension when a musical idea begins on the third beat, even though third beats mostly sound quite normal as downbeats. What Mozart is doing here thematically is something he does a lot in the concertos, namely, to omit something from the recapitulation that had been heard in either the orchestral ritornello or the exposition, and then bring it back at the last minute, in the coda.

Let's turn now to the Scherzo from Haydn's String Quartet, Op. 33, No. 5, and I'm giving you both an annotated score and a rhythmic reduction (which breaks off in m. 34, where the opening music returns) [Example 10.22].

EXAMPLE 10.22 *Haydn, String Quartet, Op. 33, No. 5, third movement (Scherzo), mm. 1–42, annotated score and rhythmic reduction.*

EXAMPLE 10.22 (*Continued*)

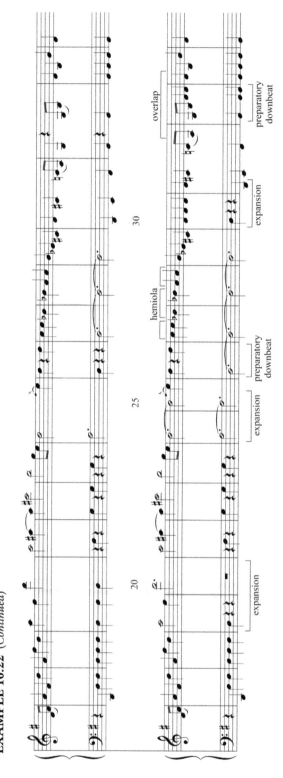

The first four measures are extremely asymmetric in their structure, because we have a kind of hemiola stuck in the middle. It's a little bit like the Mozart A-minor Rondo in that the four measures scan as 1 + 2 + 1, except that in the Haydn, the middle two measures have a rhythmically dissonant hemiola design.

Hans Keller has a book on the performance of the great Haydn quartets [Keller 1986], and it's worth reading, even though he's quite insufferable sometimes. What he says about the beginning of this quartet is that the whole thing should be played as an upbeat, until you get to measure 4. If by that he means "without any differentiation," then I disagree. I would like to play it with a strong beginning and then a slight acceleration through the hemiola, giving emphasis to its main notes. If you can do all of that and still give it an upbeat feeling, that is good, but some inner differentiation is certainly needed.

There's a wonderful stroke of humor in the remaining measures of this first strain. I think everyone would expect a tonic chord right on the downbeat of measure 8, concluding a four-measure group that balances the first four-measure group. You'd expect a full measure of tonic harmony with the tonic note on top, but what you get is a measure of silence. So Haydn fools us. In the passage after the fermata (mm. 17–21), Haydn composes a deceleration, like a windup toy that runs around, but then slows down more and more. It's also a rhythmic expansion: where we had four-bar groups at the beginning, now we have a five-bar group.

At measure 26, we have a metric reinterpretation of the sort we have already seen many times: the measure is simultaneously the last measure of one group and the first measure of the next—the beginning of the long D in the cello clearly suggests a hypermetric downbeat, while the upper parts are gently concluding what came before. At the same time, measure 26 also sounds like a preparatory downbeat—a measure of tonic harmony before the melody gets going (the four-measure group in the melody begins with the pickup to measure 27).

Something wonderful happens in measure 32. The original two-note pickup to measure 1 has now been expanded to an entire measure. At the same time, its original upbeat quality is contradicted, and it becomes a downbeat. So not only does it become much longer, but also its rhythmic function changes. I would say that measure 32 is now functioning like one of the preparatory downbeats we have discussed so much today.

Haydn, Symphony No. 99, Adagio

We'll work on the Adagio movement from Haydn's Symphony No. 99. [Editor's Note: Only the exposition and coda of the movement are reprinted here.]

I T MATTERS WHAT EDITION OF A SCORE YOU USE, BECAUSE THE DYNAMIC INDI-cations, slurs, accent marks, and the like can have a lot of analytic value. For example, look at the accent mark in all of the instruments in measure 8—it is authentically Haydn's own indication [Example 11.1]. To understand its significance, let's talk first about the harmony and voice leading in measures 1–2.

The first measure has tonic harmony with the upper voice moving from $\hat{1}$ (G) up to $\hat{3}$ (B). There are two plausible ways of understanding the harmony in measure 2. The first possibility is to read the main harmony in the measure as the tonic (I^6) on the third beat. If we take the B in measure 1 as the main note in that measure, which eventually it turns out to be, we would also have a voice exchange—G in the bass and B on top in measure 1 as against G on top and B in the bass in measure 2. The other possibility would be to read the first beat of measure 2 as a suspension into the A-minor chord on the second beat. We might decide that the II^6 chord on the second beat is the main harmony of the measure, passing through the apparent I^6 on the third beat (a chord that resembles I, but does not have tonic function), to V on the first beat of measure 3. Of those two interpretations—that measure 2 is either tonic harmony (within a voice exchange) or supertonic harmony (with the apparent I^6 as a passing chord)—it seems to me pretty clear that the first one is correct. To substantiate this claim, look at measure 8, whose G♯ connects back to the G♮ in measure 2.

And that brings us back to the accent signs in measure 8. There, I read another voice exchange, just as in measures 1–2, but now with an emphasis on the chromaticized tonic note: B over G moving to G♯ over B. Looking at the first eight measures as a whole, we could say that the most significant dramatic gesture is just that move, from G to G♯. The accent signs seem to me to corroborate the voice exchange, both in measures 7–8 and, retrospectively, in measures 1–2. The accents are telling you that this is not just a passing chord—there would be something aesthetically questionable in reading it that way.

Now I want to point out something that has more to do with sonority than with harmony or voice leading. By sonority I mean just the *sound* of certain chords, and the resonance that one chord might have with another, where some parts of the chords are

EXAMPLE 11.1 *Haydn, Symphony No. 99 in E♭ major, second movement (Adagio), exposition (mm. 1–34), annotated score.*

the same and others are not. I am thinking in particular of the sonority on the downbeat of measure 2, where we have that 7-6 suspension, producing the notes C-E-B. That's not a harmony, but it is a distinctive sound. Now look at the downbeat of measure 10. There we have another seventh (F♯-E, part of a whole seventh chord) with C and E belonging to the chord. That harmony occupies a climactic position within the larger context of the first ten measures, just as the similar sounding sonority in measure 2 did in the smaller context of the first two measures. On the downbeat of measure 15, we have a wonderful climax on a dominant-ninth chord: A-C♯-E-G-B. The seventh C♯-B within that chord recalls the seventh C-B in measure 2 (the E is also present in both chords). I think of the dominant-ninth chord in measure 15 as fulfilling a promise made by the little suspension into measure 2. An affinity of sonority thus connects measures 2, 10, and 15. And if you look ahead to measures 22 and 24, you will hear further echoes of the same sonority.

Now here's a little sonorous detail that turns out to have a much larger significance in the movement as a whole. In measures 2–3, the second violins descend E-D-C-B-A and the cellos and (until the last note) the violas accompany the line in parallel thirds: C-B-A-G-F♯. Now look at the bassoons in measures 6–7: they're playing a figure that connects the first two phrases. They have E-D-C-B on top accompanied in parallel thirds by C-B-A-G. This

EXAMPLE 11.1 (*Continued*)

EXAMPLE 11.1 (*Continued*)

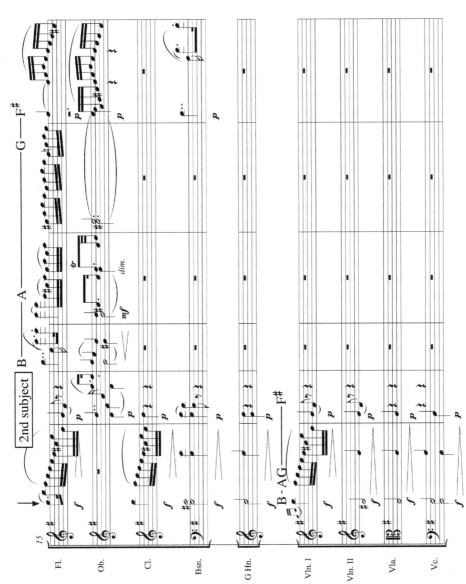

EXAMPLE 11.1 (*Continued*)

unassuming little bassoon duet, with its source in measures 2–3, has important implications for the movement as a whole, although it will take me a while to fully tease them out.

Now let's look at the music starting in measure 9. In many editions, there's a *crescendo* in measure 9, leading to a *sforzando* on the downbeat of measure 10, followed by a *descrescendo*. None of these markings is actually Haydn's, but the *piano* on the downbeat of measure 11 is by Haydn. The editors probably wondered why Haydn bothered to write a *piano* there when the last dynamic he wrote, back in measure 4, was also *piano*. They doubtless concluded that Haydn would have expected the performers to get louder leading into measure 10, and that Haydn's *piano* marking in measure 11 would have been his response to that expectation. So the editors are probably correct as a matter of performance practice, even if their markings are inauthentic.

EXAMPLE 11.1 (*Continued*)

I think of the music from the beginning of measure 9 through the second beat of measure 11 as prolongation of II. The melody has a strongly A-minorish feel (play the first violin part and notice how the melodic line is permeated by the chord of A minor) and the II chords are quite prominent. As a result, the G-major chord on the third beat of measure 10 is understood as the product of voice leading within the prolongation of II, rather than as a true tonic. There's thus an interesting connection with measures 1–2. There, we had an A-minor chord that was part of a larger prolongation of G. Here, in measure 10, we have a G-major chord that is part of a prolongation of A—a reversal of their previous roles. In other words, the A-minor $^6_3$ chord at the beginning of measure 9 continues until the same A-minor $^6_3$ chord (now with the bass an octave lower) in measure 11. That II⁶ chord then goes through a dominant-seventh chord to the tonic. There is a structural connection from the opening tonic in measure 1 to the tonic at the end of the second phrase in measure 12, but the G-major chord in measure 10 is not part of that larger continuity.

Here's a sketch of measures 1–12 [Example 11.2]. I've compressed both the diatonic voice exchange in measures 1–2 and the chromaticized voice exchange in measures 7–8 into the beginning of the reduction. In measure 9, the upper voice moves from B (within tonic) to A (within the II harmony). Then there is a beautiful little flourish in A minor up to the high E, and the melody then descends by step: E-D-C-B. Within that span, D is a

EXAMPLE 11.2 *Haydn, Symphony, Adagio, mm. 1–12, analytical sketch.*

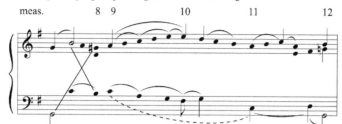

passing tone, and it's supported by G major; the G-major chord thus does not have tonic function, but rather has the function of supporting a passing tone.

That melodic descent, E-D-C-B, bears a motivic resemblance to things we've heard earlier. First, there are those inner voices in measures 2–4 (there, the descent is through a fifth), and second there is the bassoon duet in measures 6–7. That same descent has implications throughout the movement, but I'll have to get into the coda before I can make a really persuasive argument. As we'll see, Haydn takes the little link between the antecedent and consequent phrases, creates slightly concealed statements of it within both the antecedent and consequent phrases, and then proceeds to build something quite remarkable out of it.

Have you noticed how continuous and unbroken the melody is? Other than the brief silences in measures 4 and 6, everything is continuous until we get to the second subject (m. 16). And even after the second subject begins, just as the violins are finishing their phrase, the oboe comes in (m. 16), and then the flute duetting with it (m. 17), continuing without break until the cadence in measure 27 at the end of the section. What Haydn does here is really incredibly beautiful, and it's as endless a melody as anything Wagner ever wrote.

The E♯ in the oboe part in measure 25 is not shown in the better, more authentic editions of this symphony, but is possibly nonetheless correct (compare the second violin part in measure 69). There are multiple sources for the symphonies Haydn composed for London. First, there are Haydn's autographs. Second, there are several sets of manuscript copies that were made under his supervision and sometimes with his corrections. So, as with Chopin, there are variant readings, all of which can lay some claim to authenticity.

Now I want to get back to that descending fourth, E-D-C-B, and suggest that another descending fourth, B-A-G-F♯, also has an important motivic role. You can hear it in the first violins in measures 2–3. The F♯ on the second beat of measure 3 does not sound like a stopping place at all, and one would not be inclined to think of it as the endpoint of a motive. But the way Haydn treats it as the movement goes on suggests very strongly not only that that's exactly what's happening, but also that he was quite consciously aware that it was happening. In measure 15, as we approach the beginning of the second subject, the first violins have the same B-A-G-F♯ motive, now spread over two registers.

In traditional form terminology, this movement would have been described as a monothematic sonata form, where the second theme was essentially a transposition and reorchestration of the first theme. Haydn has many other claims to fame, but traditionally one of them is as an exemplar of monothematic sonata movements. It's a quite bad term in my opinion, because it suggests that there's only one theme, and that's not necessarily the case. What usually happens in sonata movements labeled as monothematic is that the beginning of the second part of the exposition is derived from the first part of the exposition, but the derivation doesn't necessarily continue even for one complete phrase, much less for the entire rest of the exposition. There may well be other subordinate themes, closing themes, and additional material of all kinds. In this particular apparently monothematic movement, there is not in fact a great wealth of thematic material. That's usually the case in slow movements, where composers are naturally inclined to be a bit more economical in the number of notes they use, because of the slow tempo. But even here, apart from the brief statements of the first theme in the oboes (mm. 16–17) and bassoon (mm. 20–21), it's pretty much all fresh material.

At the beginning of the second subject (m. 16), the oboe has the theme, and then the flute enters on B (m. 17). As the flute part continues, it descends through that familiar fourth: B-A-G-F♯ (arriving on F♯ in m. 20). Of course, this recalls the same descending fourth in measures 2–3, but now in a totally different tonal context. At the beginning, the B was not only part of the tonic harmony but was also the structural beginning of the *Urlinie*. The A that followed it was a passing tone within a prolonged G-major tonic chord. In measures 17–20, in contrast, the B is a neighbor of the A, and the element that belongs to the local tonic harmony is the third A-G-F♯. At the beginning, the inner articulation of that fourth was as a third (B-A-G) plus a second (G-F♯); in measures 17–20, the inner articulation is as a second (B-A) plus a third (A-G-F♯). The third, A-G-F♯, belongs together because it belongs to the prolonged D-major chord; the B is an upper neighbor. So it's the same motivic idea, B-A-G-F♯, but articulated in two different ways, reflecting the different tonal situation.

As we discussed in a previous class, people argue about whether or not to consider these two different melodic statements as representing the same motive. For some people, there cannot be a real melodic relationship when the functions of the notes are different. People sometimes insist that if there is not complete congruence in the way each of the notes functions with regard to the others, then it is not really a significant motivic relationship. For me, the statements of B-A-G-F♯ in measures 2–3, 15–16, and 17–20 really do have something in common, something worth calling attention to.

Now let's talk about the large-scale motion of the top voice. B is the first tone of the *Urlinie* (its *Kopfton*, or "head tone"). It's supported by tonic harmony through the first subject. When the second subject begins, and we get to the prolonged dominant harmony, the *Urlinie* B moves down to A. The A comes in first in an anticipatory way (m. 15) within the dominant of the dominant, and then definitively within the second subject itself (m. 18). From there, the A descends to G (end of m. 19) and F♯ (m. 20) [Example 11.3].

EXAMPLE 11.3 *Haydn, Symphony, Adagio, mm. 17–27, analytical sketch of the upper voice.*

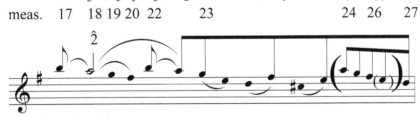

Then back up to B (as neighbor note) and again to A (m. 22), and descending again, via some rather complex unfolded thirds, to G, F♯, and E. We're headed toward D in the upper voice, and at this point (end of m. 23), we're within greeting distance of it, but Haydn doesn't want to end things quite yet.

What happens next (mm. 24–26) is a kind of interpolation, or parenthetical comment, delaying the arrival of the expected D, which comes on the downbeat of measure 27. We could have gone directly from the end of measure 23 to the beginning of measure 27, but the three interpolated measures create an intensification of the eventual resolution. But we could also feel, even within that interpolation, that the *Urlinie* is present in a hidden way: from A in the flute (m. 24) to G-F♯ in the oboe (mm. 25–26), then, at the end of measure 26, C♯ substitutes for E in the flute, and finally to D at the beginning of measure 27. So we get a second statement of A-G-F♯-E-D buried within the interpolation.

The arrival on D in measure 27 completes the second theme, which prolongs scale-degree $\hat{2}$ (A) with a descending fifth-progression (A-G-F♯-E-D). That descending fifth-progression represents $\hat{5}$-$\hat{4}$-$\hat{3}$-$\hat{2}$-$\hat{1}$ in the dominant, D-major, the key area of the second theme. The arrival on D thus marks the end of the second theme and the beginning of the closing theme, or codetta. It's typical of Haydn to have something very sophisticated and somewhat difficult to follow in the second theme, and then to lead into something very simple and folk-like in the closing theme or codetta.

Note that there are two descending fifth-progressions in the upper voice, one belonging to the second theme, and the other to the closing theme. The first one finishes in measure 27, the second one finishes in measure 33, and both are supported by perfect authentic cadences in the dominant key. There is a kind of overlap between these themes, in that the final melodic tonic of the second theme becomes an inner-voice tone, covered by the beginning of the closing theme. Which of these themes is on a higher structural level? How we answer that question has important bearing on our interpretation of the *Urlinie*, for the resolution of the top-voice structure takes place when these two themes are brought back in the recapitulation. Therefore I would rather wait and address this issue more fully when we discuss the recap. At present, I'll only remind you that there are two possible readings: if you read the main descent as the one ending in measure 27 with the closing theme, D becomes the local top-voice tone, and the A of measure 31 functions as part of the prolongation of the D; if you read the main descent as the one ending in measure 33, then the A of measure 31 is retained as a main tone until the descent that takes the line down to D in measure 33. Also, bear in mind that the second theme continues to its end in the light, soloistic textures with which the exposition begins. The closing theme, on the other hand, is a forceful *tutti* perhaps more suitable for a point of formal articulation. This might already suggest that the second descent is the structural one.

That brings us to the development section, which starts in measure 35. Before we get into the details, I want you to think a bit about the overall key scheme in this symphony. The key of the symphony as a whole is E♭ major, and this slow movement is in G major. That sort of remote key relationship involving the slow movement in a multi-movement work occurs from time to time with Haydn. Mozart, in contrast, would never—and I really mean never—do something of that kind. And, in Haydn, there's often some sort of cross reference between the movements, related to the relatively remote key relationship.

If you look at the first movement of the symphony, you'll see that the slow introduction goes to a G-major chord, which functions as an altered III in E♭ (mm. 14–17) [Example 11.4]. So, in the first movement, G is thus prefigured within E♭. In the slow movement, in G major, there are then echoes of E♭, especially in the development section, as we will soon see.

There's something similar but even more dramatic in Haydn's String Quartet Op. 74, No. 3 ("The Rider") [Example 11.5]. The key of the quartet is G minor, but the second movement is in E major. In measure 8, there is a big augmented-sixth chord leading to the dominant of B major. In the context of this movement, the augmented-sixth chord arises from a chromaticized voice exchange with the opening tonic: G♯ over E (m. 1) becomes E♯ over G (m. 8). But in the context of the quartet as a whole, this augmented-sixth chord built on G is a memory of the G-minor tonic of the quartet and the key of G major to which it

EXAMPLE 11.4 *Haydn, Symphony No. 99, first movement, slow introduction (Adagio), mm. 1–18, annotated score.*

turns at the end of the first movement and at the end of the quartet as a whole. This sort of thing might not be so unusual if we were looking at something written by Brahms in, say, 1862, but in an eighteenth-century piece, it's pretty remarkable.

One more preliminary observation before we get into the development section. If you look at the instrumentation, you'll notice that there are timpani in G and C, instead of G and D, which would virtually always be the case in a piece in G major. It suggests an unusually important role for the C chord in the development section. We haven't heard the timpani in the exposition, so we can't be sure of the reason, but perhaps we'll find out in the development.

Let's start at the end of the development section, and with the fact that it ends on a B-major chord (mm. 52–53). You might think of this as the dominant of E minor (V/VI). And although E minor does not play a particularly significant role in the piece as a whole, it is certainly the local key of the ending of the development section, beginning with the E-minor $^6_3$ chord in measure 50. What is more, it is generally acknowledged that in major-key sonata forms earlier in the eighteenth century, the most usual place to move to in the development section would, in fact, be to VI. So, for a sonata form in G major, like this one, E minor would be a very plausible and frequent goal of the development section, which could then lead very directly to a D, with the bass descending directly from E to D as V/V or rising from E to F♯ (as V$^6_5$ of V)—there are lots of different possibilities.

EXAMPLE 11.5 *Haydn, String Quartet, Op. 74, No. 3 ("The Rider"), second movement, mm. 1–10, annotated score.*

Some composers may have felt that they didn't want to be going to VI all the time. Instead, they might pretend to go there by getting to its dominant (V/VI), but then not actually make good on the seeming promise, and just go directly from there to the tonic. Given the sorts of harmonic expectations that might be aroused during performance, it might be plausible to think of a development section like this one as ending on V/VI, implying (but not granting) E minor.

But I don't think that's the best way of thinking about this. Notice that the E minor is never anchored to the larger harmony by a cadence confirming the key, nor does the E-minor chord enter into large-scale voice-leading motions. The fact is that there is a whole family of sonata movements by Mozart, Haydn, and Beethoven where, if we think in Schenker's terms, the bass of the development section basically arpeggiates the tonic chord downward: from V (at the end of the exposition) to III (at the end of the development) to I (at the beginning of the recapitulation). The downward arpeggiation in the bass line provides the large-scale structure that connects the B chord to the *Ursatz*. In that sense, I would rather think of the B major chord in measures 52–53 as III$^{\sharp3}$ rather than V/VI. One might think that the suggestion of E minor has somewhat the nature of a red herring in a mystery novel.

This approach will not allow you to hold to the usual view of a development section as a prolongation of the dominant, because a development that leads to III$^{\sharp3}$, and from there directly to I, does not, in fact, prolong the dominant. Typically, a development like that touches on several harmonies, but never entirely stabilizes any one of them. What is being prolonged is not any single harmony, but rather a motion from harmony to harmony, namely from dominant, through III⁽³, to tonic [Example 11.6].

EXAMPLE 11.6 *Haydn, Symphony, Adagio, tonal overview.*

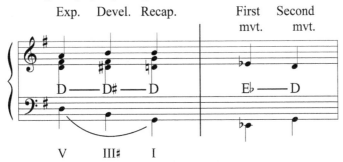

In addition, this approach forces you to come to terms with chromaticism at a very deep level of structure. In the progression V-III⁽³-I, there is a chromatic half-step (augmented prime) between D♯ and D, which results from going directly from a B-major chord to a G-major chord. That might well be related to the fact that in going from the first movement of this symphony to the second movement, we are going from an E♭-major to a G-major chord. That progression brings in the minor second, or diatonic half step (E♭-D), which is echoed in the chromatic half step (D♯-D) we get within the second movement in going from B major directly to G major.

Working backward in the development section, look at the moment where the timpani come in for the first time (m. 40). Up until that point, Haydn has composed the movement as though it were a piece of chamber music. Until we reach the codetta, we very seldom have more than a few instruments playing at a time, and there is nothing in the music to warn us that a big *tutti* passage, with trumpets and timpani, is about to arrive, as it does here. The development section begins as if in D minor, and then leads toward C major—we get to the dominant of C major in measure 42 and then have a thematic statement in C major, beginning in measure 43. Within that progression, the D-minor harmony is II⁶ and the C⁷ chord in measure 40 is an applied dominant of the subdominant F, on the way to an arrival in C major.

The F toward which this applied dominant seems to point is not itself part of the background structure of the movement. Rather, it is the C⁷ itself that is the important thing. That's because there is a direct association between this C⁷ (m. 40) and the augmented-sixth chord on C in measure 51, right before the arrival on B major: C-E-G-B♭ becomes C-E-G-A♯. As an applied dominant to a chord (the F chord of m. 41) that is itself not part of a large-scale structural framework, the C⁷ of measure 40 would seem to be a most unlikely candidate for such a dramatic compositional gesture. It is its enharmonic connection to the later augmented sixth that explains the great emphasis Haydn lays on the C⁷.

I mentioned earlier that the unusual tuning of the timpani in this movement might suggest that C will play a pivotal role later, and it certainly does so. To appreciate how this works, let's look at the bass line over the course of the whole development section [Example 11.7]. In measures 35–43, the bass line goes as follows: F (m. 35)-E (mm. 39–40, as a neighbor to F)-F (m. 41)-F♯ (m. 41, as a chromatic passing note)-G (m. 42)-C (m. 43).

EXAMPLE 11.7 *Haydn, Symphony, Adagio, development section (mm. 35–52), analytical sketch of the bass line.*

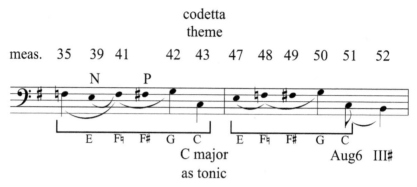

In measure 43, we have the beginning of the codetta theme in C major. In measure 47, the bass starts to move again, and watch carefully the path it takes. First we have E in measure 47. We might have expected a first inversion of the C-major chord there, but instead we get an applied diminished-seventh chord, clearly derived from D minor (C-E-G has become C♯-E-G-B♭). Then the bass moves up to F (m. 48, as part of a D-minor chord), then F♯ (m. 49, as part of an applied dominant leading to E minor), then to G (m. 50, within an E-minor chord), and finally to C (m. 51).

In the two halves of the development section, then, the bass line is thus pretty much note-for-note the same: E-F-F♯-G-C. But the second arrival on C is quite different from the first. The first time through, we emerged (m. 43) on a thematic statement in C major. The second time through, instead of leading to C major as a consonant goal, we arrive (m. 51) on an augmented-sixth chord that takes us to B (III♯³). We still get a resolution to C, but now with no tonic potential.

In going from a C-major triad, like the one in measure 43, to an augmented-sixth chord on C, like the one in measure 51, there are various things a composer can do. Perhaps the simplest is to move to an E-minor chord that supports a passing note B. When the B continues down to A♯, we have our augmented sixth over C [Example 11.8].

EXAMPLE 11.8 *Haydn, Symphony, Adagio, mm. 43–52, harmonic reduction.*

But that basic outline can be fleshed out and filled in in various ways. The span between C and E in the bass can be filled in with a passing $^6_4$ chord (Haydn actually uses a V in root position here in m. 46). The E (m. 47) is harmonized with an applied diminished-seventh chord leading to D minor, with F in the bass (m. 48). The same thing then happens sequentially a step higher when an applied diminished-seventh chord on F♯ leads to E minor, with G in the bass. Then comes our augmented-sixth chord and its resolution to B major.

In its broadest outline, we can see the exposition as the usual $\hat{3}$-$\hat{2}$ in the top voice supported by I-V in the bass, with the $\hat{2}$ elaborated by a descending fifth (which would be $\hat{5}$-$\hat{4}$-$\hat{3}$-$\hat{2}$-$\hat{1}$ in the key of the dominant) [Example 11.9].

EXAMPLE 11.9 *Haydn, Symphony, Adagio, analytical sketch in broad outline.*

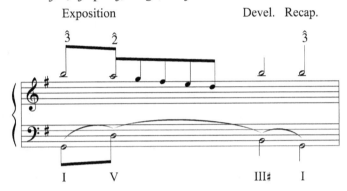

The goal of the development section is III♯^{3}, and then the recapitulation begins with $\hat{3}$ over tonic harmony.

At a level a bit closer to the surface, we get to the III♯^{3} by way of an augmented-sixth chord (m. 51) [Example 11.10].

EXAMPLE 11.10 *Haydn, Symphony, Adagio, development section, synoptic analytical sketch.*

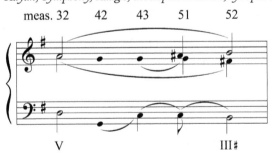

Continuing to work backward, we get to the augmented-sixth chord from a tonicized C-major chord (m. 43). To break up the parallels involved in going directly from D major (end of the exposition) to C major (m. 43), we interpose V of C, with G on top. The G is then retained as an inner voice when the true top voice ascends from A to A♯ (over the augmented-sixth chord) to B (over III♯^{3}).

Now let's talk a bit about the recapitulation. Right at the beginning there's a telling detail in the passing chromatic notes added to the recapitulation of the first theme. I'm referring especially to the passing B♭ at the end of measure 55, and again at the end of measure 57. It beautifully recalls both the C⁷ chord in measure 40 (with B♭ on top) and also the augmented-sixth chord on C in measure 51 (with B♭ respelled as A♯ on top). From a formal point of view, Haydn conflates the consequent phrase of the first theme with the second theme. (The conflation is possible only because the first four bars of the two themes are so similar.)

In the exposition, the first theme is composed as an antecedent with an expanded consequent that morphs into a transition to the second theme. As I noted previously, Schenker sometimes analyzes this situation as an antecedent with modulating consequent (in *Tonwille* [Schenker 2004], he calls it a "consequent and modulation"). Since the beginning of the second theme is closely modeled on the beginning of the first theme, Haydn can bring in the second theme early in the recap, in place of what had been the consequent phrase in the exposition. It is quite wonderful to see in Haydn (as in Mozart and Beethoven) a special sensitivity to duration in his compositions. By that, I am referring to a feeling of where it's necessary to cut things short, and where it's appropriate to inflate things and make them longer. In this case, Haydn is going to broaden the pace at the end of the recapitulation and into the coda, so his decision to shorten the first theme at the beginning of the recapitulation seems to me a very appropriate response to the necessities of the piece as a whole.

Let's see what happens to the *Urlinie* during the second theme. Remember that A was the main upper-voice tone in the second theme in the exposition. Although A is the overall scale-degree $\hat{2}$, it was scale-degree $\hat{5}$ in the local tonic, which was D major, and a descending fifth, $\hat{5}$-$\hat{4}$-$\hat{3}$-$\hat{2}$-$\hat{1}$, spanned the second theme in the exposition. As result, we can expect D, as scale-degree $\hat{5}$ in G major, to play an extremely important role in the second theme in the recapitulation.

Just as in the first movement of Beethoven's String Quartet, Op. 18, No. 6, which we discussed a few weeks ago, the top voice in the recapitulation, instead of being simply $\hat{3}$-$\hat{2}$-$\hat{1}$, will become $\hat{5}$-$\hat{4}$-$\hat{3}$-$\hat{2}$-$\hat{1}$. You can see that quite clearly in the second theme, which starts in measure 60. In measure 61, the first violins give us E as a neighbor note to D. Then we have the descent from $\hat{5}$: D (m. 62)-C (m. 63)-B (m. 64)-A (m. 67). There we get the same parenthetical insertion we had in the exposition, before the line closes on G (m. 71). At that point, we have our closing theme, or codetta theme.

You'll remember from the exposition that both the second theme and the closing theme have top voices that descend a fifth to the tonic note. In discussing the exposition, I raised, without answering, the question of priority: which of the fifth progressions is the structural one? The situation in the recap is a bit more complicated, for now we have three descents (fifth-progressions) instead of two. The first descent belongs to the second theme, while both the others belong to the closing theme.

Both Schenkerians and theorists of sonata form seem mostly to agree that the first strong cadence in the secondary material of the exposition or recap will normally take priority, relegating everything that follows to the status of coda material. That would suggest that the structural close of the movement would occur with the close of the second theme in measure 71. Though this may well be true as a generality, with regard to this movement, it seems to me a complete impossibility.

In the closing theme, we have two descending thirds (B-A-G and C-B-A) as part of a larger rising third from B (m. 71) through C (m. 73) to D (m. 75). From the D in measure 75, we have a descending fifth, D-C-B-A-G, leading to the apparent end of the recapitulation. That strong descent into measure 77 raises an interesting question about the whole idea of ending something and of achieving closure. According to the norms of Schenkerian theory, measure 77 marks the place where scale-degree $\hat{1}$ arrives in the *Urlinie* and consequently where the *Ursatz* is finished. At the analogous spot in the exposition (m. 33), we just had two more measures to confirm the local tonic, ending on a big *tutti* chord. Something similar is what we would expect in the recapitulation: a brief passage of confirmation culminating in a celebratory tonic chord.

But at the very moment where we expect things to close off and conclude, instead, they start to open up and we have a new beginning of something. And that might make us reconsider our idea that the *Urlinie* has actually closed with scale-degree 1̂ in measure 77. According to the norms of sonata form, the coda lies outside the structure, outside the frame. But perhaps the frame itself has widened here and the structure is not yet complete? (This is an issue we discussed previously with reference to Mozart's Violin Sonata, K. 481). To make a decision, we will have to look closely at the coda, where it is clear that something momentous is happening [Example 11.11].

The coda begins with an ascent through an octave and a fifth to the high D on the downbeat of measure 81. That is followed by a descent to F♯ (m. 82), a motion into the inner

EXAMPLE 11.11 *Haydn, Symphony, Adagio, coda, annotated score.*

EXAMPLE 11.11 (*Continued*)

voice. From there, we have repeated statements, in both the top voice and the bass, of a descending diminished fourth: Bb-A-G-F#. This passage is a wonderful apotheosis of the descending fourth-motive B-A-G-F# from the exposition. The other fourth-motive from the exposition—E-D-C-B—receives an equally splendid transformation as the top voice of the passage leading to the return of the codetta (m. 89).

I think of this passage (mm. 85–88) as the climax of the movement, and a lot of the effect has to do with the melodic parallelisms I have been talking about. Strictly speaking, I cannot prove to you that the parallelisms I have pointed out are purposeful, but for myself, I cannot believe that Haydn wasn't conscious of them. It's not that I don't recognize the great role that unconscious thinking can have in musical composition. But these relationships, I think, are just too detailed and too specific to be anything but a result of conscious thought. So, in spite of the fact that the various statements of that figure are not always the same in their inner meaning, nevertheless the descending fourth seems to me to be vital to the life of this piece.

EXAMPLE 11.11 (*Continued*)

EXAMPLE 11.11 (*Continued*)

EXAMPLE 11.11 *(Continued)*

EXAMPLE 11.11 (*Continued*)

EXAMPLE 11.11 (*Continued*)

This climactic passage (mm. 85–88) can be thought of as a kind of cadenza for the whole orchestra. I don't mean cadenza in the voice-leading sense—it's not inside the resolution of a $^6_4$ chord or anything like that—but perhaps it's something like an *Eingang* or lead-in, using an extended dominant-seventh chord to lead to the final statement of the codetta theme. That final statement, beginning in measure 89, has a wonderful, happy sound, with strummed *pizzicato* chords, a throbbing accompaniment, and a melody that floats above. This time, there is no doubt that we have fully achieved the conclusion and the sense of closure that eluded us back in measure 77.

Beethoven, Piano Sonata, Op. 53 ("Waldstein"), first movement

We'll spend all of our time today with the first movement of Beethoven's "Waldstein" sonata. [Editor's Note: Only the exposition of the movement is reprinted here.]

As YOU ALL KNOW, THE FIRST MOVEMENT OF BEETHOVEN'S "WALDSTEIN" Sonata has an unusual tonal plan, namely, it gravitates to III in the second part of the exposition, as though it were in a minor key. The only earlier instance of such a thing in a Beethoven piano sonata is Op. 31, No. 1. The "Waldstein" is in C major and its second theme is in E major; Op. 31, No. 1, is in G major and its second theme is in B major. There are later pieces by Beethoven that do the same thing—the "Leonora" Overtures No. 2 and No. 3, for example—but I don't know of any earlier ones.

Beyond their shared tonal plan, the "Waldstein" and Op. 31, No. 1, have another unusual feature in common: they both make prominent use in the first theme of the harmony ♭VII (B♭ major in the "Waldstein" in measure 5 and F major in Op. 31, No. 1 in measure 11). Tovey mentions this aspect in his companion to the Beethoven sonatas [Tovey 1931], a book that is definitely worth consulting. It's not an approach to analysis that I would follow myself, but he was an amazingly gifted and knowledgeable musician, and the questions he raises are often very instructive and helpful. He seems to be losing popularity, even in Britain, which is a pity, because he's really very good. The question is, why should these two things—the use of ♭VII at the beginning of a movement, and the use of III♯ (that is, III with a sharp third) almost at the end of the first part of the exposition—exist in such different works? Is there some kind of connection between these two seemingly unrelated things? This is a question that we will ask ourselves as we go along.

As I'm sure you know, Beethoven made use of other unconventional second-theme key areas, especially in his later works. VI is one such unconventional destination, and he uses it as early as the String Quintet, Op. 29, a very beautiful and strangely under-performed piece. He modulates to VI in other pieces, including the first movement of the "Archduke" Trio (first theme in B♭ major; second theme in G major) and most famously in the first movement of the Ninth Symphony (first theme in D minor; second theme in B♭ major).

In *Free Composition* [Schenker 1979], Schenker discusses sonata form at some length, but necessarily incompletely. That's the one place where Ernst Oster, the translator and editor of the English edition of *Free Composition*, did more than just translate and add an occasional footnote. Instead, he provides a sustained and extremely valuable piece of writing on sonata form from Schenker's point of view. Among many things, Oster points out that although composers later in the nineteenth century were to follow Beethoven in many of these unusual tonal plans in sonata expositions, there was one earlier composer who anticipates Beethoven's practice: in the music of Domenico Scarlatti, the first reprise (i.e., the exposition) will sometimes go to VI or III.

Now let's begin to work through the first movement of the "Waldstein" Sonata, starting with the very first note, that low C, sounded all alone [Example 12.1]. It seems significant to me that the piece begins with the tonic note alone, set apart from the chords that follow. When the theme is repeated with the tremolos (m. 14), the downbeat chord is again texturally distinct from its continuation. That's also the case in the first ending of the exposition

EXAMPLE 12.1 *Beethoven, Piano Sonata in C major, Op. 53 ("Waldstein"), first movement, exposition (mm. 1–85), annotated score.*

EXAMPLE 12.1 (*Continued*)

repeat (m. 86), when the theme comes in F major toward the beginning of the development (m. 90), at the beginning of the recapitulation (m.156), and at the restatement of the first theme (m. 174). In every case, the first beat is set apart for special emphasis.

Many pianists ignorantly play the beginning of this theme as a kind of rumble, without a defined rhythm. If they want to have a rumble *following* the downbeat, they're welcome to it. Actually, I wouldn't try to articulate those repeated chords terribly much myself, but I would want to have a definite beginning. That single bass note tells us where a hypermeasure begins. It tells us that measure 1 is not a kind of upbeat to measure 3, but a true beginning and a true downbeat.

This has a bearing also on how one hears the harmony. There are analyses out there that claim that the piece really begins in G major, with a IV-V-I progression (the opening C-major harmony is IV in G major). I don't deny that implication, if one hears the three chords in isolation, but more significantly, the opening progression takes place within a larger tonic framework. In that sense, the opening tonic note provides a strong beginning accent that helps to establish and define the key and to lend a particular shape to the phrase.

EXAMPLE 12.1 (*Continued*)

The tonic harmony is established in measure 1, but the top voice gravitates to G as the main tone, not arriving until measure 3. There is thus a kind of opposition between the rhythm of the bass, which is first-measure-oriented, and the rhythm of the upper voice, which, within these four-measure groups, is third-measure-oriented. That opposition between bass and upper voice gives this theme a special rhythmic character.

After the opening tonic, the bass line begins to descend chromatically: C-B-B♭-A-A♭-G (mm. 1–9). Within that descent, the B♭ (m. 5) strikes me as the most shocking, unexpected note. It is harmonized with ♭VII (m. 5) which leads eventually to V⁷ (m. 9). This represents a reasonably common situation in tonal music, where VII functions as an upper-third of the dominant.

There are three main ways this happens in major keys [Example 12.2]. First and least important, a diminished triad (B-D-F in the key of C major) can be used as an entrée into the dominant-seventh chord (G-B-D-F), with all three notes of the diminished triad retained within V⁷. Second, there is a chromatic version in which the third and fifth of that diminished triad (sometimes only the fifth) are raised, giving us a major or minor chord (B-D♯-F♯ or B-D♮-F♯)—Schubert's music is full of this. In this case, the B is still functioning

EXAMPLE 12.1 (*Continued*)

as the upper third of a prolonged dominant-seventh chord, but one or two chromatic notes (F♯ or D♯ and F♯) have been introduced. Third, we can do what Beethoven does here, building a major chord on the lowered form of scale-degree $\hat{7}$ (B♭-D-F), giving a color of minor. When that chord moves to V⁷, the D and F can just be held (as they were when the diminished triad, B-D-F, moved to V⁷). I want to call your particular attention to a chromatic adjustment that is awakened when ♭VII goes to V, namely, that B♭ moves to B♮. B♭-B♮ is a motive we're going to encounter at many places in this music.

In fact, you can hear it in the way Beethoven gets to the key of E major for the second part of his exposition. Follow the upper voice from the restatement of the first theme (m. 14) to the arrival on the dominant of E major (m 23). First, we get E-F♯-G (mm. 14–16), with G confirmed in the upper octave (m. 17). Then G♯ (m. 19) brings the line up to A (m. 20), confirmed in the upper octave (m. 21). From there, the line ascends through A♯ (m. 22) to B (m. 23), arriving on B as the harmony gets to the dominant of E major, with both the upper-voice tone and the harmony sustained for quite a while. That climactic A♯-B has the same sound as the B♭-B we spoke of a moment ago, but in a different context and with a totally different meaning, with one on the sharp side of things and the other on the flat side. Still, that similarity in sound creates a bond between the first theme and the bridge to the second theme.

Something very similar happens in Op. 31, No. 1 [Example 12.3].

EXAMPLE 12.1 (*Continued*)

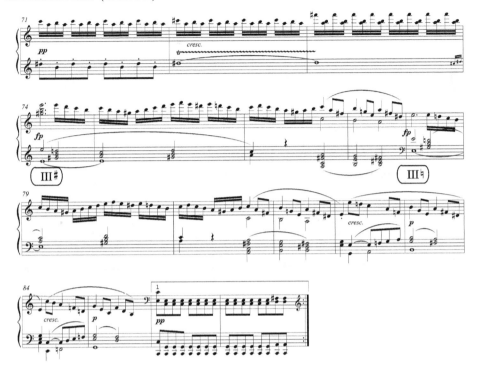

EXAMPLE 12.2 *Three uses of VII as upper third to V.*

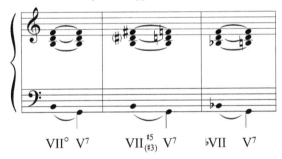

In the first theme, the harmony moves to ♭VII (m. 12), which contains F♮. When ♭VII moves to V (m. 25), the F♮ is adjusted to F♯. In the bridge to the second theme, which is going to occur in III♯, as we noted previously, E♯ comes in as part of an augmented-sixth chord, leading to F♯ within the dominant of B major (mm. 55–56 and 61–62). So F♮-F♯ in one context resonates with E♯-F♯ in another. These two sonatas, although they mostly sound quite unrelated to each other, nonetheless have these two striking features in common: modulation to III♯ for the second theme and ♭$\hat{7}$ giving way to ♮$\hat{7}$ as ♭VII is absorbed into V⁷.

There are certain situations in major keys where composers prefer to use III♯ instead of the diatonic form of III. It happens especially when you have a bass that arpeggiates downward: $\hat{5}$-$\hat{3}$-$\hat{1}$. In the development section of the first movement of the "Spring" Sonata,

EXAMPLE 12.3 *Beethoven, Piano Sonata in G major, Op. 31, No. 1, first movement, mm. 1–26 and 53–67, annotated score.*

Op. 24, for example, as we discussed, Beethoven moves from C major (the dominant) through A major (III♯) to F major (the tonic) when the recapitulation begins. A minor (the diatonic form of III) would have sounded relatively anemic in comparison to the chromaticized variant of it. The one case that I can think of where Beethoven does go prominently to III as a minor chord is the Finale of the Seventh Symphony: the piece is in A major and the modulation is to C♯ minor. But that's done in a very different way, and the whole context is quite different.

Returning to the "Waldstein" Sonata, note that when we get to the closing area at the end of the exposition, the chromatic gives way to the diatonic. We had E major for the second theme, but as the exposition draws to a close, we get E minor instead (m. 78). This makes an easier transition both back to the tonic when the exposition is repeated and forward to F major, the main key at the beginning of the development section.

All I'm going to say about the development section for the moment is that we get a very powerful dominant beginning at measure 136 building up to a huge climax (perhaps unprecedented in solo piano writing) and bringing us to the recapitulation (m. 156). The first twelve measures of the recapitulation are the same as the exposition, but then in measure 168 there is a change. It's interesting to note that this change is not designed to facilitate a modulation, because in fact the passage ends up back on the tonic (m. 174). What happens at the fermata chord (m. 168) and the measures immediately following is something we'll come back to in a moment.

For now, however, I want to jump ahead and see what happens when the second theme begins (m. 196). At the same point where the harmony went to E major (III$^{\sharp}$) in the exposition, it goes to A major (VI$^{\sharp}$) in the recapitulation. But instead of letting that A major last for any considerable amount of time, after only four measures, Beethoven composes a phrase that begins in A minor (m. 200), and leads almost immediately back to C major (m. 203). Here again there are similarities to Op. 31, No. 1, which has a shift in the exposition from B major to B minor and then, in the recapitulation, a motion to E as VI of G major, just as A in the "Waldstein" is VI of C major.

One obvious question is why Beethoven doesn't just stay in the tonic, C, for the second theme in the recapitulation. One answer that many people give—a perfectly good answer, in fact—is that staying in the tonic key wouldn't permit him to maintain a reasonable level of tension. There's also an analogy to what usually happens in a sonata form, namely, that the second theme in the dominant in the exposition is transposed down a fifth in the recapitulation. Here, from E major in the exposition to A major in the recapitulation is also motion down a fifth.

There's an additional factor that may be at least as important as these, having to do with chromatic inflections. In the exposition, moving from C major to E major entails a chromatic progression from G to G$\sharp$. In the recapitulation, going from C major to A major also produces a chromatic progression, in this case C to C$\sharp$. There's a very audible kind of analogy there. We've mostly been concentrating on harmony, and I do want to talk about the large-scale melodic line. But before we do, I want to mention an interesting aspect of the range of the piece, one that actually bears on the large-scale melodic line. This sonata movement is the first one that Beethoven wrote with a note higher than the F that lies two octaves and a fourth above middle C. The standard Viennese piano (and all of Mozart's piano music) fits into five octaves, with that F as the highest note. Apart from one anomalous F$\sharp$ in the first movement of the Piano Sonata, Op. 14, No. 1 (m. 41), which may have been added by the publisher, Beethoven never breaches that upper limit until the "Waldstein" Sonata. By that time, he might have expected people to have purchased newer instruments with an extended range.

It's noteworthy that Beethoven is very careful in establishing a new field of musical space. The first time you see a higher note is the F$\sharp$ in measure 73, part of the giant cadence that concludes the second theme (closing material follows). Later in the movement, he goes even higher, finally reaching up to the high A at the analogous spot in the recapitulation (m. 232). By the way, although this is the first time Beethoven wrote these notes in a piano sonata, he already included them in, for example, the C-minor Piano Concerto,

Op. 37. People who played the concerto would have been expected to play it on one of the newer instruments with a wider range, but the piano was very much a domestic, house instrument, and people didn't get rid of them every two or three years, as they do nowadays with computers.

Given that these higher notes were now available, it is curious that it's the F that is so heavily foregrounded here (I'm using that term in its literary-critical rather than its Schenkerian sense). The emphasis begins early in the piece, with repeated statements of it in measures 9–11. The F receives even heavier emphasis in the somewhat-related music that leads up to the recapitulation (mm. 152–155). And then near the end of the coda, right before the second theme is brought back in its entirety—the first time we hear it all in C major—the note is heard under a fermata (m. 281). And right at the end of the piece, in the section I think of as a "coda to the coda" (mm. 293–301), there's yet another heavily emphasized high F (mm. 297–298). I'm not trying to suggest that Beethoven is showing off the F just because it is the highest note on the piano that people used to have—that would be silly. Rather, the F has an important role to play in the large-scale melodic line, as we will see.

Now let's go back to the beginning of the movement and think especially about the large-scale upper voice. One of the first decisions you have to make is whether to read the top voice from G ($\hat{5}$) or from E ($\hat{3}$). My own preference is G ($\hat{5}$), and that's partly because choosing E ($\hat{3}$) would lend a rather static character to one's conception of the piece: the first theme would have E (in C major), and the second theme would still be more or less on E (now in E major). It's a little bit analogous to what sometimes happens not just in sonatas, but in lots of different kinds of pieces, when the harmony goes from tonic to dominant. Scale-degree $\hat{5}$ is a common tone—it's present both in tonic and dominant. So there's the possibility, again, of an overly static character, with $\hat{5}$ simply retained as the harmony changes. Generally, one would prefer an upper voice that doesn't just stay in one place, and that's why I prefer to read the first movement of the "Waldstein" from G—in the second theme, in E major, the upper voice will descend G♯-F♯-E. There was an important Schenkerian named Saul Novack who read the first movement of the "Waldstein" from E, so people can disagree about these things. Schenker himself did not publish a graphic analysis of the "Waldstein," but he did write about the first movement in *Free Composition*, and he quite clearly takes it from $\hat{5}$, not from $\hat{3}$.

There's a real question, and not an easy question to formulate, let alone to answer, about the extent to which one should try to make an individual piece conform to what one regards as norms, and to what extent one should say, "well, this piece really doesn't conform to these norms, at least not in these respects, and we should try to find a way of dealing with the piece apart from its resemblance to what we would expect in such a piece." This question confronts us in dealing with anomalous features of the top voice. The top voice begins E-F♯-G (with the G repeated two octaves higher) and then D-E-F (with the F repeated two and then three octaves higher) [Example 12.4]. We could read the F in measures 9–11 as resolving first to E♭ (m. 12) and then to an implied D (m. 13). But that D is so evanescent—it disappears into a kind of black hole—that I'm inclined instead to read F as retained as top voice note, not moving to E until the first theme begins again (m. 14).

The bridge section begins in measure 14 and reestablishes the main upper voice tone G in measure 16. From there, the line ascends—G-G♯-A-A♯-B—arriving on B over the dominant of E major (m. 23) [Example 12.5].

EXAMPLE 12.4 *Beethoven, "Waldstein" Sonata, first theme, mm. 1–16, analytical graph in two levels.*

a)

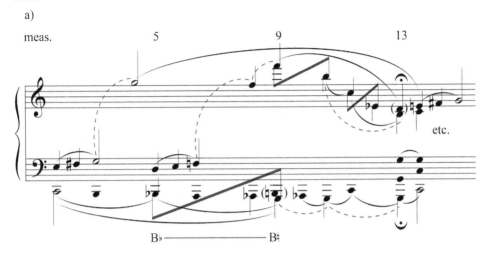

b)

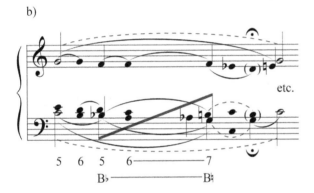

As we discussed a moment ago, the A♯-B at the top of the ascent relates back to the B♭-B within the first theme. In fact, the network of chromatics extends to the sixteenth-notes at the end of measure 24 [Example 12.6]. From the high B (m. 23), the top voice then descends through A (mm. 34–35) to G♯, which is the main upper-voice tone in the second theme [Example 12.7]. At the highest level, then, the top voice moves from G over C major in the first theme to G♯ over E major in the second theme.

Looking at the second theme in a bit more detail, we might ask where we get the strongest feeling of motion to E in the top voice: is it in measure 42, measure 50, or measure 74? I would take the two statements of the second theme (mm. 35–42 and 43–50) as involving subsidiary descents G♯-F♯-E, with the big motion to E coming, via that novel high F♯, just before the closing material comes in (m. 74). Certainly if I were playing this I would aim for that high F♯ in measure 73 as a sort of transcendent moment [Example 12.8].

Either way, however, this movement stands in contradiction to what Schenker called, in German, *Diatonie*. There's no exact English equivalent of this term. In his translation of *Free Composition* [Schenker 1979], Oster just changed the spelling slightly—"diatony"—putting a "y" at the end of it. It doesn't mean simply "the absence

EXAMPLE 12.5 *Beethoven, "Waldstein" Sonata, bridge section, mm. 14–23, analytical graph in two levels.*

a)

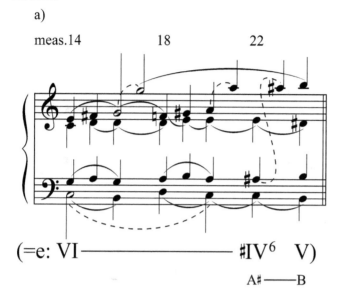

meas.14   18   22

(=e: VI ——————————— ♯IV⁶ V)
                                    A♯ —— B

b)

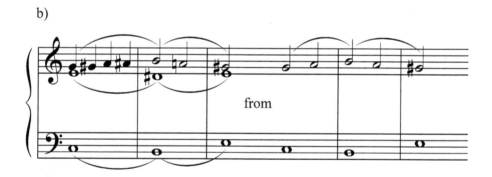

from

of chromatic things," but it does mean "showing how the different notes of the diatonic scale relate ultimately to the tonic triad, and to the tonic note itself." For Schenker, that kind of "diatony" is fundamental to the *Ursatz*. But Schenker was very frequently willing to transgress his own theories, and in the "Waldstein" he considered the structural line to be G-G♯-F♯-E, as part of the *Urlinie*. In that sense, actually, the F♯ rather than the G♯ is the really dangerous element. The G♯ can always be thought of as a chromatic alteration of G, returning to G in the closing material. But the F♯ is not just a variant of F♮; rather, it's a contradiction of F♮.

One of the distinguishing aspects of Schenkerian analysis is the way in which the individual features of the piece exist in a kind of dialogue with the norms of the tonal system, very often pretending to disobey them while, on a deeper level, actually conforming to them. But that's not what's happening here. In the presence of G♯ and especially F♯ in the *Urlinie*, we find a dialogue between the individual and the norm that is strikingly uncompromising. The

EXAMPLE 12.6 *Beethoven, "Waldstein" Sonata, network of chromatics.*

EXAMPLE 12.7 *Beethoven, "Waldstein" Sonata, second theme, mm. 35–74, two analytical graphs.*

* N.B.: m. 50 is the cadential point of the varied repetition of the theme.

EXAMPLE 12.8 *Beethoven, "Waldstein" Sonata, second theme, two interpretations.*

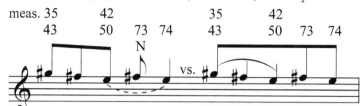

very lack of unanimity between them is something that can play out in various ways later on in the movement.

I want to jump ahead now to the development section. The main harmonic area in the development section, between the III at the end of the exposition and the V which is the goal of the development section, is IV (F major, m. 90). Between that IV and the eventual V, there's a modulation to C major (m. 112), but that doesn't function as a tonic in a deep sense at all, but is in a very general way, a means of getting from IV to V [Example 12.9].

Within this first phase of the development section, in the motion from IV to the apparent tonicization of C major, there's an interesting textual problem. I'm referring to the bass note on the first and second beats of measure 105: some editions have it as F♭ and some as F♮. The F♮ is correct, and here's the story. Beethoven's own autograph manuscript actually has F♭. In the first edition, however, the flat sign is gone, and it's F♮. When Schenker was working on his edition of the Beethoven sonatas, he tried to look at all the autographs he could, but the "Waldstein" autograph was in England and not accessible to him. As a result, he just followed the first edition and showed the note as F♮. When the autograph became generally available, people saw the flat and thought, "We have to restore the F♭, which was obviously Beethoven's original idea." As a result, the earliest Henle edition of the complete sonatas, for example, which is probably still in circulation fairly widely, even though it's been superseded, had the F♭.

But then people started looking really closely at copies of the first edition, and they noticed a ghost of a flat sign, visible more in some printings than in others. Apparently, the engraver of the printed music, following Beethoven's autograph, had engraved the flat sign, but when Beethoven was proofreading, he changed his mind and had the engraver scratch it out from the copper plate. The scratch-out was imperfect, however, so especially on some of the later impressions made from the plate, you can see remnants of it. Now there's no way that the printers themselves would have made that change without Beethoven's authorization. So every good edition now has the F♮. If Beethoven had stuck with his first idea, F♭, it would have created a brief tonicization of the C♭ chord in the second half of measure 105. Evidently Beethoven decided he preferred something a little more contrapuntal and a little less harmonically oriented.

Looking at the development section as a whole, the music moves from F major (m. 90), to F minor (m. 104, still prolonging F), to C major (m. 112, supporting the passing tone E in the upper voice), inflected to C minor (m. 132), to G (m. 136, the big dominant goal of the development section). That G supports D as a top-voice tone. The D goes up to F (m. 152), which resolves to E as the recapitulation begins (m. 156). From that E, which becomes an inner voice tone, the upper voice ascends immediately to G as *Kopfton* (m. 158).

Backing up a bit, and looking at how the music goes from the exposition into the development, we can see E moving to F in the top voice and, at the same time, E moving to F a couple of octaves lower in the bass [Example 12.10].

EXAMPLE 12.9 *Beethoven, "Waldstein" Sonata, development, mm. 86–156, analytical graph.*

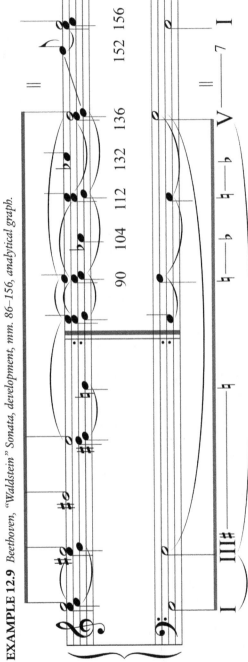

EXAMPLE 12.10 *Beethoven, "Waldstein" Sonata, moving from exposition to development, analytical summary.*

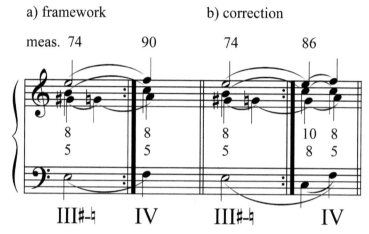

I've previously told you not to worry about apparently faulty parallel octaves like this. There is a lot of misinformation going around on this topic, to the effect that you must never have any faulty parallel octaves or fifths in the middleground. Schenker never said any such thing. What he said was that if there are parallel octaves or fifths, it is the task of the foreground, or perhaps later levels of middleground, to break them up. So instead of having 5-5-5, one might have 5-6-5-6-5-6. Or, instead of 8-8, one might have 8-10-8. 8-10-8 is a particularly common intervallic pattern, and it's what we have here. Going from the E major or E minor of the closing area in the exposition, we go to F major by way of C, its dominant. The resulting tenth, C-E, breaks up the parallel octaves, E-E to F-F.

The idea of something happening at one level in response to something that happens at another is related to the idea that music can also, in a diachronic way, relate to itself and to its past history, and perhaps make good on some promises that were made earlier but not yet kept. We've already noted that in the exposition, the F♯ in the *Urlinie* in a sense supplants the expected, normal F♮ (♯4̂ instead of ♮4̂) [Example 12.11].

In the second theme area of the recapitulation, there is not so much the "wrong" form of scale-degree 4̂ as the notable absence of scale-degree 4̂ in what is supposed to be the final descent of the upper voice. The recapitulation begins in C major, of course, and the second theme comes in A major (m. 196), turning to A minor (m. 200) and then back to C major (m. 204). That progression brought with it an upper-voice motion from C (in the C major of the first theme) to C♯ (in the A major of the second theme), and then back to C♮ (when the second theme turns to A minor, and then goes back again to the tonic, C major). That progression, C-C♯-C, is not in the area of the *Urlinie*, as the analogous motion in the exposition, G-G♯, was. The *Urlinie* is still presumably a 5-line moving from G, and so I analyze the top voice of the second theme in the recapitulation as an inner voice. That melodic C goes up to E when we get to the statement of the second theme in C major (m. 204). Back in the exposition, the second theme (in E major) descended 3̂-2̂-1̂ (G♯-F♯-E). So here in the recapitulation, the second theme (finally in C major) also descends 3̂-2̂-1̂ (now E-D-C). But scale-degree 4̂ is missing. That is, the first theme gives us G and the second theme gives us E-D-C, but that E is not connected to the G with any comparably important F. I call that one of the structural anomalies of this movement.

EXAMPLE 12.11 *Beethoven, "Waldstein" Sonata, exposition and recapitulation, analytical graphs.*

a) Exposition: N.B. #4̂

b) Recapitulation: N.B. no 4̂ (gapped line)

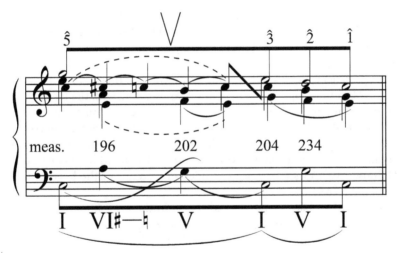

These anomalies are in a sense "corrected" in the coda [Exampe 12.12]. In measure 276, we get a high A (the highest note in this piece, and the highest note in any of Beethoven's piano sonatas up to this point). That A brings us to the F in the same register in measure 282 (marked *sforzando* and under a fermata), then repeated an octave lower in measure 283 (again *sforzando* and under a fermata). The F resolves to E in measure 284, and we get, for the first time in the piece, a complete, intact statement of the second theme in C major. In the recapitulation, the second theme came in different keys (first A major, then A minor, then C major) and without any proper upper-voice F. Here, in the coda, we get an intact statement of the second theme in C major and we get an appropriately emphasized F. There is, therefore, a kind of correction in the coda of an anomaly in the recapitulation.

EXAMPLE 12.12 *Beethoven, "Waldstein" Sonata, coda, mm. 259–end, analytical graph.*

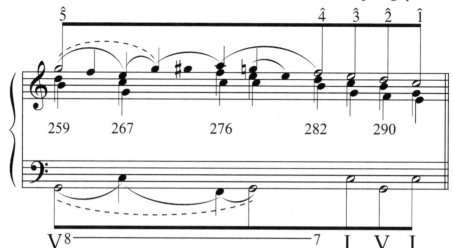

You find a similar sort of thing in another very important piece, written not long after the "Waldstein," namely, the first movement of the Piano Sonata, Op. 57 ("Appassionata"). In that movement, the 5̂-4̂-3̂-2̂-1̂ is weakly presented in the recapitulation, but very strongly presented in the coda. So one of the things that, perhaps, Beethoven was trying to do was to bring a kind of inner dynamic to the resolution of the *Urlinie*, making it rather needing of improvement at first, and then, toward the very end of the movement, bringing it into a more satisfactory form.

But that presents us with a difficult question: which of these two is the main descent of the *Urlinie*? Is it the gapped descent in the recapitulation, with the F missing, in which case the coda would be understood as just a prolongation of tonic, with scale-degree 1̂ already established in the top voice? Or is it the complete descent in the coda, in which case we would judge that the recapitulation had failed to establish scale-degree 1̂, precisely because of the gap in the top voice where 4̂ (F) would have been expected and needed? Those two views give you very different readings of the large-scale form and structure of the piece.

Now I want to go back to the second theme in the exposition and another sort of anomaly that is corrected later [Example 12.13]. Starting in measure 35, the upper voice descends through a perfect fifth G♯-F♯-E-D♯-C♯, but the lowest note (C♯) is not part of the chord that's being prolonged (E major). (This might remind you of a similar situation we discussed in Lesson 7. There, the melody at measure 43 descended through a perfect fifth F-E♭-D♭-C-B♭, but the final note of the descending line, B♭, did not fit comfortably in the prevailing harmony, which was D♭ major).

Let's see how that melody is coordinated with the bass. Starting in measure 35, the bass moves down a seventh as a way of expanding the second from E to F♯. That E-F♯ is part of a larger ascending fifth: E-F♯-G♯-A-B. At the same time, in the top voice, the B, which is part of the E-major chord, moves down together with the left hand. But it gets only as far as the C♯. At that point, it connects with the B of the inner voice and we get an ascending sixth-progression: B-C♯-D♯-E-F♯-G♯. It's as though the descending fifth was a frustrated, incomplete sixth. When the music repeats, starting in measure 39, we actually do get the descending sixth, G♯-F♯-E-D♯-C♯-B, in place of the fifth we had before. The sixth fits perfectly into the prolonged E-major chord, perhaps fulfilling in that way an earlier promise. There's a

EXAMPLE 12.13 *Beethoven, "Waldstein" Sonata, mm. 35–42, analytical sketch.*

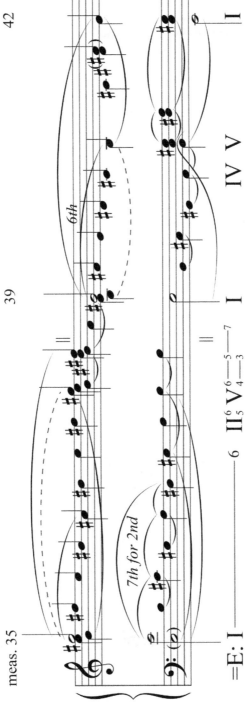

sort of analogy to interruption: we're descending from G♯ to B, but the first time we get only as far as C♯; then we begin again, and this time get all the way down to B, thus integrating the progression into the harmony.

I want to point out a marvelous rhythmic phenomenon in the closing section of the exposition. Starting in measure 50, we get three statements of a two-measure idea (mm. 50–51, 52–53, and 54–55). Then we have two statements of a one-measure idea (mm. 56 and 57), one measure where the idea lasts for one-half of a measure (m. 58), one measure where the idea lasts for one-quarter of a measure (m. 59), and finally a measure where the idea has shrunk to one-eighth of a measure (m. 60). At this point, we've gotten pretty much to the tremolo form of the texture of the first theme in its second statement (m. 14). By successively reducing and constantly foreshortening the area governed by this diminution, Beethoven makes the music more and more urgent. I can't think of any other composer who did things like that in working with rhythm. You can't say this is a phenomenon of pure rhythm, because without the tonal aspect, the rhythm wouldn't make sense. But it's as close to pure rhythm as it gets.

Now I would like to backtrack a bit and discuss with you again the chromatic consequences of Beethoven's going to B♭ in measure 5 in his bass line as part of the chromatic descent C-B-B♭-A-A♭-G [Example 12.14].

EXAMPLE 12.14 *Beethoven, "Waldstein" Sonata, chromatic issues.*

Certainly the B♭ is the most arresting, the most surprising, the most rhythmically foregrounded tone in that series. As you'll recall, when the bass arrives on G, and we reach dominant harmony at the end of the phrase, the B♭ (m. 5) gives way to B♮ (m. 9). The connection between B♭ and B♮ is something that leaves footprints in other parts of the movement.

In the second statement of the theme starting in measure 14, the upper voice reduces to the chromatic line, G-G♯-A-A♯-B. That is quite audibly related to the chromatic descent of the first phrase in the bass. In fact, it's a retrograde of the last five notes in the chromatic descent that starts in measure 1: C-B-B♭-A-A♭-G becomes G-G♯-A-A♯-B.

As the bridge section continues, we have sixteenth-note figuration leading up to a high B as a goal tone (mm. 24–25). You'll notice that the last notes leading up to and including the B are G-G♯-A-A♯-B. So a kind of of dramatization of the chromatic clash between the B♭ and the B♮ in the first nine measures is incorporated into this bridge passage.

F major is the main key area of the opening phase of the development section [Example 12.15]. By measure 104, we arrive in F minor, which is still obviously structurally connected to and still part of the composing out of the F chord. A descending bass line follows, taking us first down an octave (m. 110), and then all the way down to cello C in measure 112.

Now let's go into the second part of the development section, which we haven't discussed previously [Example 12.16]. We start in measure 112 on a C-major chord. Four measures later (m. 116), we're on F, and four measures after that (m. 120), we get to B♭. At that point, things change. We remain longer on the B♭ than the previous harmonies, and it changes enharmonically to A♯ (m. 126) before moving to B with a B-minor chord above it (m. 128). From there we go through C minor, with a Neapolitan sixth chord and a passing diminished-seventh chord, to the G chord in measure 136, which is the goal of the development section. This is the point where we reach the structural dominant on the highest level for the first time in the movement (because the second theme in the exposition is on III instead of V).

So we've gone from I to III in the exposition and from IV to V in the development. The IV is thus functioning as a very high-level passing bass tone between the III and the V. That's very much what we would find in a minor-mode sonata of Beethoven's time or earlier, and as we discussed last time, it's not the first time Beethoven does this in a major key. In Op. 31, No. 1, he already had a very similar harmonic scheme.

What I want to point out to you today is something a little off to the side, but very fascinating. Look at the bass line from measure 120 to measure 128. The B♭ is respelled as A♯, which rises to B. This is yet another juxtaposition of B♭ and B, a motivic idea that has its roots in the first theme, with echoes in the bridge section, as we discussed a moment ago.

Now let's look at the recapitulation, and I want to focus on the moment where the first theme music from the exposition changes, and does so in a momentous way. I'm referring to the surprising A♭ in measure 168 and the five measures that follow, which take us to E♭ major and then back to C major for the second statement of the first theme [Example 12.17]. Notice that this alteration in the first theme was in no way necessitated by the eventual modulation to A major, because this new music ends up right back on the tonic (m. 174). When talking about *musica ficta*, medieval theorists said that it could arise for two different reasons: *causa necessitatis* (caused by necessity), and *causa pulchritudinis* (caused by beauty). There's no question that what happens in measures 168–173 is caused by beauty, not by some practical necessity of getting to where he wants to go.

So let's think a bit about what this new, inserted music is doing from the point of view of large-scale voice leading. At the beginning of the recapitulation, we have the *Kopfton* G

EXAMPLE 12.15 *Beethoven, "Waldstein" Sonata, opening phase of the development section (mm. 90–112), analytical graph.*

EXAMPLE 12.16 *Beethoven, "Waldstein" Sonata, second phase of the development section (mm. 112–141), analytical graph.*

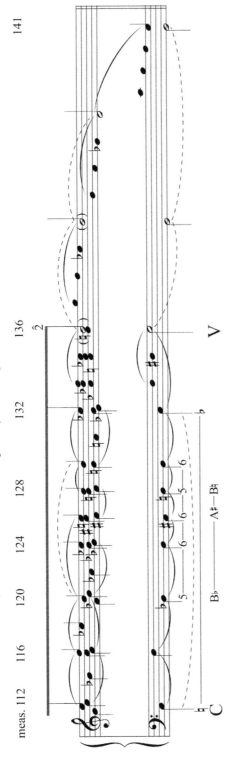

Detail of measures 112 to 128:

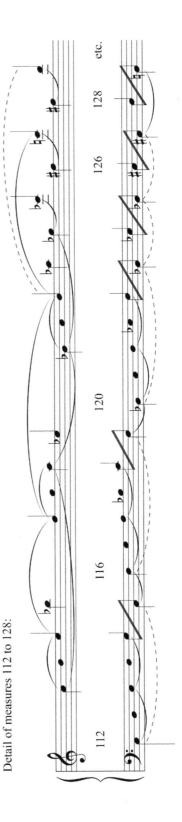

EXAMPLE 12.17 Beethoven, "Waldstein" Sonata, recapitulation: first theme and bridge (mm. 156–192), analytical graph.

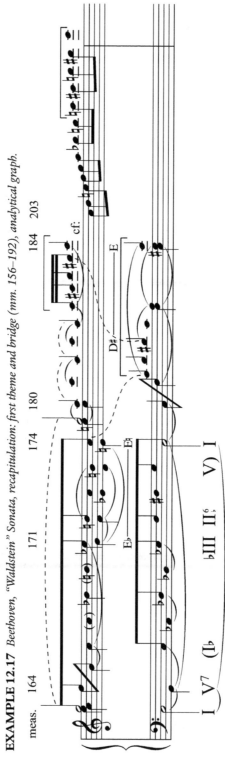

over the tonic, C major. In measure 164, the upper voice moves down to F over V⁷, and the F is strongly emphasized in measures 164–166. Where does that F resolve? I would say that the resolution does not take place until we get the E♭ in measure 171, which arises out of the inner voice. The E♭ then becomes part of a descending fifth from G that continues to measure 174.

The E♭ does something else also. It permits Beethoven to make an enharmonic relationship with D♯, and that D♯ can get him to E, which will be part of the dominant of A major and will help him to ease the modulation. And that's just what happens in the counterstatement of the first theme. Starting in measure 182, we get a rising chromatic line, C-D-D♯-E (you can see it in the top of the sixteenth-note figuration in the left hand), bringing us to the dominant of A major.

There's a subtle reference to that chromatic line in the second theme. It starts in measure 196 in A major, then shifts to A minor (m. 200) and then to C major (m. 203). At that point, rising triplets lead to a varied repeat of the second theme. Look at the end of those triplets in measure 203: C-C♯-D-D♯-E. All of this is composed with such incredible attention to detail, and it's all the more incredible because the basic feeling of this movement is one of constant sweep forward. It wouldn't seem to have the sort of contemplative character that one might normally associate with that sort of composition, but the subtlety and the detail are certainly there. It is quite amazing.

Now I want to zoom out and talk about some larger issues, not necessarily at a background level, but getting closer to the background. In the exposition, the *Urlinie* is G for the opening tonic, going to G♯ for III with a raised third, and then descending G♯-F♯-E [Example 12.18].

EXAMPLE 12.18 *Beethoven, "Waldstein" Sonata, exposition, summary analytical graph.*

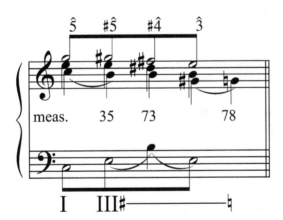

At some higher level, we could reduce the G♯ out of it without doing violence to logic, because the G♯ can be thought of as just a chromatic alteration of the G♮, and indeed it resolves back into the G♮ in the latter part of the closing section of the exposition, when the music turns from E major to E minor. But the F♯ is something that we absolutely cannot explain away. There is no way of turning that into an F♮. So there is, in this, a violation of what Schenker called *Diatonie*, that is, the kind of diatonic order in which each of the tones is related in a unique way either directly to the tonic or through another tone that is directly related to the tonic. The exposition offers us no satisfactory diatonic explanation for that F♯, which thus stands in contradiction to some of the basic ideas of Schenker's approach. Despite this, however, it's quite clear that Schenker took the upper voice in the exposition as G-G♯-F♯-E (he didn't graph the piece in *Free Composition*, but he described it there). In the development section, we eventually get to D over the dominant. That would suggest the typical configuration of interruption, except that we have, from the beginning of the movement, a very eccentric top voice of $\hat{5}$-♯$\hat{4}$-$\hat{3}$-$\hat{2}$.

This is a piece in which the diatonic form of scale-degree $\hat{4}$ (F♮) plays a very important role, initially by its very absence. That is rectified, to some extent, in the development section, where the F does enter into the top voice, but we get very far into the piece without having F on a primary level. Normally, the recapitulation would be a place where scale-degree $\hat{4}$ could be quite nicely integrated into the top voice. Scale-degree $\hat{3}$ comes in with the second theme in C major, and you would expect to have the structural $\hat{4}$ before it. But Beethoven's decision to begin the second theme in A major makes it impossible to do that [Example 12.19].

At the beginning of the recapitulation (m. 156), we have scale-degree $\hat{5}$ in the upper voice. The main melodic activity that follows takes place in an inner voice, arising from an inner-voice C in measure 180. We seem to be stranded on the inner voice at this point, and the line from the G has actually kind of disappeared, like a stream that goes underground for a while. But this stream has apparently run out of water, because when we get to the E in measure 204, where the second theme comes in C major, you can see that there's no F before it at all. So whereas the exposition has one sort of problem with scale-degree 4, namely that it's been replaced by ♯$\hat{4}$, the recapitulation has a different problem with it, namely, that it doesn't happen at all, and the line skips down from G to E-D-C [Example 12.20].

Fortunately, we still have the coda to reckon with. It's a very big coda, which is usually the case in the music of Beethoven's so-called heroic period [Example 12.21]. The resolution of the *Urlinie* really takes place here, in the coda, not in the recapitulation. As I mentioned last week, Beethoven does something related in the first movement of the "Appassionata" Sonata, Op. 57. In that piece, one can find a scale-degree $\hat{4}$ in the recapitulation, but it is so dwarfed by what happens in the coda that I think one ought to view the descent as taking place there. Similarly with the Adagio movement of our Mozart Violin Sonata, K. 481, there is a strong possibility of taking the resolution of the *Ursatz* in the coda, not because of any missing top-voice tone or anything of that sort, but just because of the emphases built into the composition. And in the "Waldstein," as I've indicated, I think there's no way to read it in Schenkerian terms other than having the coda house the resolution of the *Urlinie*.

One might ask: why can one not infer an implied *Urlinie* in measure 202? That could eliminate the skipped top-voice line and produce a normal, stepwise *Urlinie*. Well, one could, but should one? And I would maintain that one should not. In this movement, as we have seen, Beethoven tells a story around F and its resolution to E, a story that begins in measure 8 with the climactic F³ over V⁷ and that finishes only near the very end of the movement, in measures 299–301. The climax of this story is the cadenza-like approach to the second theme when it appears in the tonic key in the coda. How much more artistic to hear this climax in the context of the *Urlinie*

EXAMPLE 12.19 Beethoven, "Waldstein" Sonata, recapitulation (mm. 156–end), analytical graph.

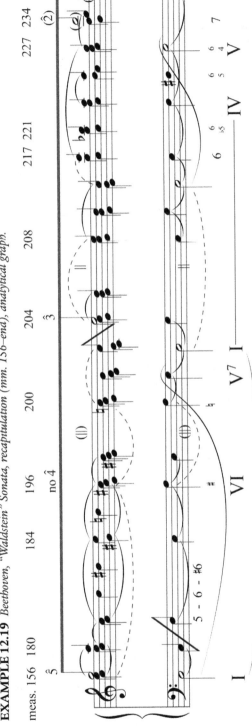

EXAMPLE 12.20 *Beethoven, "Waldstein" Sonata, recapitulation, summary analytical graph.*

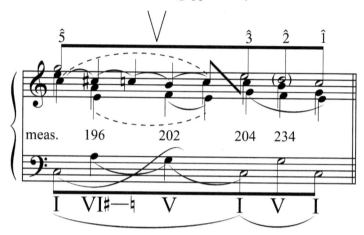

Recapitulation: N.B. no $\hat{4}$ (gapped line)

descent than as a weakly motivated foreground repetition—particularly since nothing in the neighborhood of measure 202 strongly offers a local reason for making such an inference.

The final arrival of scale-degree $\hat{1}$ of the *Urlinie* takes place on the downbeat of measure 294. Following that, the last eight measures of the piece can be thought of as a coda of the coda. The bass descends C-B-B♭-A-A♭-G, just as in the beginning of the movement, but now with a very different meaning. The B♭ is harmonized not with ♭VII but rather as an applied dominant to IV. The top voice goes to G in measure 296, which is then transferred up a seventh to F (m. 297). This is not the first time we've encountered a motion of an ascending seventh (in this case divided into two fourths) representing an underlying descending second (G-F). The motion F-E-D in measures 297–98 I would take as a motion into the inner voice rather than representing an upper-voice arrival on scale-degree $\hat{2}$. To my ear, the high F in measures 297–298 resolves to E in measure 300, on the downbeat. The three big chords at the end are a triumphant rising substitution for $\hat{3}$-$\hat{2}$-$\hat{1}$, the descending third presented as a rising sixth, and with the D (scale-degree $\hat{2}$) present in the dominant harmony, but not actually part of the melodic line at all.

You might wonder why it's not possible to have an *Urlinie* with a gap in it. In fact, there are pieces that go $\hat{5}$-$\hat{3}$-$\hat{2}$-$\hat{1}$, but those are usually considered 3-line pieces with a cover tone. As William Pastille points out in a very interesting article [Pastille 1990], the stepwise nature of the *Urlinie* grows out of Schenker's idea of *Fließender Gesang*,"flowing song" or "melodic fluency," as it's more elegantly translated, resulting from the primarily stepwise motion found in species counterpoint. The fact is that the norm for melodic motion is motion by small melodic intervals, and this is apparently true not only of Western art music, but of lots of other music, too. The *Ursatz* is a kind of manifestation of basic principles of tonal motion, one of which is the idea of stepwise motion in the leading melodic part (the *Urlinie*).

People will also ask, if you have a piece with a very broad initial ascent, where the *Anstieg* may take up as much or perhaps more room in the piece then the descent, why

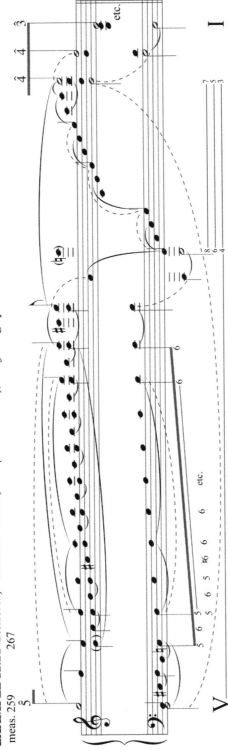

EXAMPLE 12.21 Beethoven, "Waldstein" Sonata, coda (mm. 259–end), analytical graph.

not say that the *Urlinie* goes first up and then down? But the *Urlinie* is not just an image of the structure of an individual piece, but of the broader principles of tonality as embodied in that piece. One of those principles, I think, is the prevalence of stepwise motion in melodic parts, and another is the greater weight assigned to descending as opposed to ascending lines.

Postlude

Q and A

[Editor's Note: In the final hour of the twelve three-hour sessions that comprised this seminar, Schachter responded to questions submitted in writing by students in the class. Their written questions, and his informal responses, follow.]

What would you like to be best known for having done, and what sort of larger influence do you hope to have achieved?

I'd like to be known for writing technically about music in decent English. That is something I have always tried to do, and I hope I have succeeded to some extent. Part of my work has been writing textbooks. I hope people will take that seriously, because I see that less and less time is given in music curricula, even for music majors, for serious work manipulating tones and dealing with them. I would certainly hope that future generations will not continue that trend, but try to reverse it.

How can an active performer balance out the time demands of analysis with other aspects of performance? And, more generally, could you comment on the relationship between performance and analysis?

These are issues that people have to work out for themselves. Analysis is time-consuming; there's no doubt about it. But there are certain things that one can do to make the process easier, including something as simple as having a photocopy of the score in which you write things that seem to you to be important, dealing with aspects of both performance and analysis. There would be nothing wrong with writing "scale-degree $\hat{3}$" above a certain note, or "V" somewhere on the score.

I don't think it's possible, let alone necessary, for a performer who has a serious career, to spend a lot of time doing analysis, so you do what you can, and the more of it you do, the more efficient you get at it. Performance should not turn into a lecture, where you point to this feature, that feature, and the other feature. Analytical things should become assimilated to your fluency with the music in a way where you are possibly not even consciously aware that you're dealing with the analysis in playing.

I would make the following comparison: a visual artist painting the human face is not going to show directly the bone structure of that face, but if he or she understands anatomy, knows what the bone structure is, it's going to make the visible surface different. To a considerable extent, I think, a lot of the analysis that one does helps to give a kind of shape to what one is doing.

Some sorts of analytical knowledge can have a direct bearing on performance. For example, if you notice that there are two dominant chords in some phrase, both of which go to tonic, and you ask if they are on an equal level or if one is subordinate to another, the answer might impinge very closely, and in a very positive way, on a performance. On the other hand, if you notice, for example, something about the proportional relationship of the different sections to each other, you might find something valid analytically, but I don't know what you do about showing that in performance. Relationships like that are there in the music, but no listener can be expected to try to count measures as they're listening, and no performer can make them do so. So I think there can be lots of things that analysts might be interested in that are not transferable directly into performance.

Knowledge of what William Rothstein calls the "imaginary continuo"—which shows where the dissonant notes are and where they are going—can have a lot of bearing on performance. Motivic relationships can also have a bearing. You're not going to want to hammer out the motives, but knowledge of them might affect your playing. To take a familiar example, one that originated with Jonas and which you can find at the beginning of Aldwell's and my harmony text, there's a descent A-G-F-E presented directly and then greatly expanded at the beginning of Mozart's Piano Sonata, K. 545. Somehow, if you know about that, you will, in one way or another, do it differently. And maybe different people will do it differently. Being aware of things like that can be very helpful in performance.

What do you think is the largest unsolved question in music theory, music analysis, and musicology?

For me, the largest unsolved problem is the problem of quality. That is, what makes a piece of music a good piece, or a great piece, or a poor piece? That's something that touches the work of theorists and analysts and musicologists, and is probably not a question that's answerable, at least not in a general way. There's a funny story told by Milton Babbitt—a person of incredible intelligence and devastating wit—about an encounter he had with Ernst Oster. Oster was saying to him how difficult Brahms's music is and how hard to understand, and Babbitt replied, "How do you know it's good if you can't analyze it?" [Babbitt 2003a]. One is never going to answer that question completely, but that doesn't mean that analysis and quality don't have anything to do with each other.

Certainly, when you analyze a piece, you want to love the piece more as a result of that analysis. On the other hand, the things that one loves about analyzing it are not necessarily the things that one would bring to a performance of it, or that someone who's not analytic would appreciate. Alban Berg has an analysis of "Träumerei," that beautiful little Schumann piece. I think it's an awful analysis, to tell you the truth, but I think the piece meant more to him as a result of his having done it. We are all convinced, I think, that the music we're dealing with has value. But to try to demonstrate that in any sort of definite way seems to me, so far, an unsolved problem.

When we evaluate the quality of a piece, we almost inevitably put it in dialogue with other comparable pieces. Of course, if we only had one Beethoven sonata in the world, it would be very difficult to evaluate it. When we were going through the "Waldstein," for example, a lot of our discussion was in terms of "this is unusual," "one doesn't do this very often," and the like. But there are other pieces, great pieces, that seem to stand entirely on their own. The C-major Prelude in the first book of the *Well-Tempered Clavier*, for example: nobody in the whole history of the world could have written that but Bach. It doesn't seem to be in dialogue with other pieces or with some kind of genre at all. What's unusual about it is not the way it deals with the articulated harmony or its texture, but rather what its notes are doing. These are difficult questions!

Could you say something about applying Schenkerian analysis to music outside the common-practice period?

Well, it's been done, and it is still being done. My teacher, Felix Salzer, was the first one to be published doing that. And I think that a lot of the extended tonal repertoire, and possibly some of the early atonal repertoire, does lend itself to at least a modified Schenkerian approach. In the last chapter of *Counterpoint in Composition*, Salzer analyzes a short piece by Scriabin. Joseph Straus has pointed out that when music makes no distinction between consonance and dissonance, it's very hard to say what is structural and what is prolonged [Straus 1987]. On the other hand, one can set up certain contexts, inside the piece itself, which may substitute for those that are given by the language in general. On that basis, I think it is possible to apply Schenkerian analysis outside of the canon. In some cases it may not reveal much at all, and in other cases it might be very helpful. Salzer was heavily criticized, both within the Schenkerian community and outside of it, for his work along these lines, but I think there was more value in what he did than was acknowledged, and I think that's coming to be recognized now.

Motives in Schenkerian analysis seem mostly to manifest, on whatever level, as purely melodic constructs (a descending fourth, a conflict between A and A♭, etc.). Are there any examples you can think of where something other than pitch (such as rhythm, harmony, instrumentation, or texture) might be understood as motivic, and how might such things be graphically represented?

Yes, there can certainly be other kinds of motives, non-melodic motives. Look, for example at the minuet movement (just the minuet; not the trio) from Mozart's late F-major string quartet, K. 590. It consists of three big phrases, all of them somehow ruled by the number seven. The first big phrase is fourteen measures long, and it's divided into 7 + 7. The second group of fourteen measures doesn't divide into 7 + 7, but it is still fourteen measures long, as is the third big phrase. Something like that can't arise accidentally. It's definitely something that Mozart had in mind, and I would call it a sort of motivic duration.

In the first movement of Beethoven's "Spring" Sonata for Violin and Piano, a piece we have discussed several times, when we get to the beginning of the development section, we have an A-major $^6_3$ chord, and the violin plays octave A's (m. 86). The development then proceeds until we get to another A-major $^6_3$ chord and the violin again plays octave A's (m. 112). There's no question in my mind that that becomes a kind of motivic thing. By the way, I don't think these two moments are part of the same prolongation, but they are both landmarks, and their relationship has to do purely with their sound.

Even a texture can be motivic. Think of the Mendelssohn Violin Concerto, and the astonishing sound at the beginning of the first movement: the upper strings noodling above cellos, basses, and timpani in unison (the cellos and basses playing *pizzicato*) and sustained chords. The same texture comes back when the music makes reference to the first theme, for example, after the statement of the second theme. Many different aspects of music can become motivic in that sense.

Would you comment on the tension one often finds in the Schenkerian literature between those like Matthew Brown, who conceive of Schenkerian analysis as a naturalized theory of functional monotonality and those like Kofi Agawu, who treat Schenkerian analysis as an artistic analytical enterprise? As a bit of conjecture, it seems that, as Schenkerians, we often try to reconcile the artistic dimensions of the Schenkerian enterprise with the desire to "explain" the way a certain repertoire of compositions works. I'm not sure a theory can be both prescriptive and descriptive at the same time.

Schenker, in the opening part of *Free Composition*, says that music, in all of its manifestations—composition, performance, theory, even history—is always art (*Kunst*), and never science (*Wissenschaft*). Now, *Kunst* in German pretty much does means "art," but *Wissenschaft* is not exactly "science". In fact, we don't have a word in English that exactly corresponds, because *Wissenschaft* can refer to scholarly study, or even more generally to the pursuit of knowledge—it does not necessarily refer to the natural sciences. Nonetheless, I think what Schenker was getting at was that music is not a purely intellectual thing. It involves aesthetic reaction, even physical reaction.

Schenker divided his own writings into two categories. First, there are the theoretical ones, where he was dealing with different aspects of the tonal system (as he does, for instance, with consonance and dissonance in the counterpoint book), and where whatever pieces he dealt with were there as illustrations of what he was trying to say in a more general way. *Free Composition* is also a theoretical book in that sense. Second, he has analytical monographs, usually on one piece, or sometimes on a category of pieces like fugues (he has an article on fugue, but it's mainly an analysis of the C-minor fugue from *WTC* I).

If I had to locate my own interests along a spectrum from "a theory of functional monotonality" at one end and an artistic or aesthetic pursuit at the other, I would be closer to the latter. This gets to the question of why we analyze music in the first place. After all, one doesn't analyze everything in the world—one doesn't analyze the particular shades of color on traffic lights (unless one is going to build better traffic lights, I suppose). We analyze music because we respond to it. That's the central thing.

In your opinion, what is the real importance of linear progressions? How do they inform an analysis? More specifically, how do they reveal the inner workings of the piece and, perhaps, contribute to an understanding of the compositional process? Also, how do they inform a performance?

This question takes us back to something we discussed a bit earlier, namely, the stepwise nature of the *Urlinie*, and more generally to the fact that stepwise motion is a norm for melodic construction. That means that if one wants a multilevel approach, or a hierarchical approach, one needs to have stepwise melodic motions at the lower and the higher levels. Linear progressions are important because they are the meeting ground between harmony and melody. Their stepwise nature gives them the possibility of real melodic cohesiveness. At the same time, their harmonic aspect gives them beginning and end points, so that we hear a melodic line with a sense of direction.

To a certain extent, we can't say that the final goal of a linear progression is completely implicit right from the beginning. For example, if you have a rising motion C-D-E, the E could very well be the end point, but it could also be a midpoint within a larger ascent, C-D-E-F-G. At any rate, the relationship, which is essentially a harmonic one, between beginning and end points, gives the possibility of a kind of goal-directedness—we are not just going randomly from one pitch to another.

What linear progressions bring to an analysis is precisely what I've been talking about: the relation between the stepwise melodic element and the harmonic framework that is created. In performance, it is not necessary that the linear progressions always be brought out in an obvious way. But the conclusion of a linear progression, say one that gives expression to an opening tonic chord, could be felt as a kind of landmark. Schenker considered linear progressions probably the most important aspect of his approach. It was the one thing that he thought performers had to learn. He didn't feel that performers were capable, often, of understanding everything that he was doing, but he said at least they should learn the linear progressions, because they allow the music to breathe.

I'm curious to know if there are any particular composers whose work you would consider to lie outside of the Schenkerian domain and where it would be a strain to attempt to apply the Schenkerian approach (although some theorists go ahead and do it anyway). I'm interested in having the sense of where even a vague borderline would lie (or what the criteria would be used to establish such a borderline).

Yes, there is a lot of music that doesn't fall within the purview of Schenker's approaches, but it can be hard to establish any clear boundary. Don't forget that Schenker himself did an analysis of a passage from Stravinsky's Piano Concerto, one that was very much praised by Milton Babbitt as providing the most revealing insight into Stravinsky's music [Babbitt 2003b]. Of course, Schenker analyzed it in order to demonstrate that it was bad music, but he did at least try to show what was going on in the notes.

There's also a question of music contemporary with the core Schenkerian repertoire that would not conform completely to his theoretical ideas. Berlioz would be the first example that comes to mind. Schenker was well aware, at least later in his life, of Berlioz's transgressions, shall we say. It's interesting, however, that in the harmony book, his first major theoretical book, he actually defends Berlioz from Schumann. Schumann had written an enthusiastic review of the *Symphonie Fantastique* in which, however, he criticized Berlioz for an apparently unmotivated jump from a D♭-major chord to a G-minor chord. Schenker defended Berlioz by invoking some kind of peculiar Neapolitan relationship to explain the D♭-major chord. Whether it is harmful or helpful to use Schenker's ideas depends completely on the individual piece or passage. There might be some situations where a modified Schenkerian approach would in fact be very helpful, and others where it would not make much sense at all.

I have encountered many different styles and methods of teaching Schenkerian analysis. Since you have been teaching it for many years, I would be very interested in hearing your thoughts on this subject. I refer particularly to young performers and composers at their beginning stage of analysis. These students usually have a strong background in harmony and counterpoint. However, they sometimes find it hard to understand the relevance of analysis to their performance and compositional activities. I believe that deeper challenges underlie this difficulty. One of these could be the difficulty to explain the abstract ideas of Schenker's theory such as the Ursatz and Urlinie, or the voice-leading procedures at different levels of a composition. How would you suggest clarifying these ideas and relating them to harmony and counterpoint? How would you suggest first introducing Schenkerian analysis to young musicians?

It may be unreasonable to expect young musicians, at the beginning stages of studying analysis, to see immediately its relevance to performance or composition. (By the way, Schenker would not at all claim that his approach has any relevance to composition, because he considered it rather an approach to analyzing compositions). So my first response would be to say just to give them some time.

But it's also a question of how you approach the teaching of analysis. I'm not saying there's one curriculum that would fit everybody's needs, but I would suggest starting with foreground things like chordal reductions and imaginary continuos—I used to call these figured-bass reductions. In the Cadwallader/Gagné book [1998], their continuos, sometimes to my eye and ear, stress the stepwise leading more than they need to. I usually try to stay closer to the melodic contour of the piece, even if it means skipping around in some voices.

I start with a few basic concepts, such as linear progressions, neighbor notes, and arpeggios (broken chords). I certainly would not start by talking about the *Ursatz* or the *Urlinie*—that would come quite a bit later.

It's also important not to react negatively to your students' interpretations, even of fairly basic things. If students say they hear something in a particular way, I'll ask them to explain exactly what they hear and why they hear it that way—I'll take their view seriously. I may say, "I hear it differently for this reason or that reason," but I don't say "Your view is wrong," even if it is. Usually, I'm happy if they have an idea about the piece, even if I don't like that idea. So I'm very lenient.

I'm also very lenient about grades in teaching analysis. In counterpoint, you may be able to deduct a certain number of points for each set of parallel octaves. When you do analysis, however, you are leaving the realm of fact and entering the realm of value, and there's always the possibility of losing students if you are too judgmental and too dismissive of their views. As you go on, you may want to get more rigorous, but it's best not to start out in a rigorous way. You tell the student, "Analysis is an opportunity to contemplate a piece of music for no ulterior motive or reason, but just for the sake of the music itself, trying to see what it does, how it's put together."

As for introducing Schenkerian analysis to young musicians, my main suggestion is not to do it too soon. The main thing is hearing: let them learn how to hear intervals properly, how to hear chords. I don't think it's a good idea to try to analyze a whole piece. Even in the later stages, it's hard for students to come up with a comprehensive analysis of a whole piece. Very often, the analysis has to be an additive process–you add this onto that. You try to see that one idea doesn't contradict another, but that they fit together properly.

Undoubtedly, a grasp of harmony and counterpoint is essential in doing analysis. Nonetheless, in teaching analysis, I would recommend making as much use as you can of motives. A lot of the individuality of a given piece depends on that, so I would look for works to give your students which have very interesting motives, and not necessarily obvious ones. In my own class in analysis, I almost always start with Mozart's D-minor Fantasy, K. 397. It's a magnificent piece, and full of wonderful things. I start by talking about the harmony and counterpoint of the first eleven measures. I point out that you have a tonic triad, then a $\frac{4}{2}$ chord that seems to be a II chord, but it goes to another $\frac{4}{2}$ chord, which is a modified tonic acting as an applied dominant, and so forth. And we work on the voice-leading implications of that. Then I get into the motivic aspect, and point out that the beginning of the top voice of the arpeggios of the opening eleven measures (F-G-A) comes back as the top voice when the Adagio begins (yet another observation that comes from Oswald Jonas).

Much of your work, it seems, has been about elucidating the relationship between music's tonal structure and its "expressive content" (I have in mind here the kind of work you did in "The Triad as Place and Action" [Schachter 1999d] and "Motive and Text in Four Schubert Songs" [Schachter 1999c]). In what ways do you think Schenkerian analysis can inform questions about what is these days often designated with the awkwardly alliterative formulation "musical meaning"? Many scholars who are interested in these kinds of questions tend to concern themselves mainly with the "foreground": with the concrete, local details of the music, such as motives, themes, textures, musical topics (e.g., "chorale," "pastoral"), and local tonal events (e.g., unusual harmonic successions). Large-scale relationships are usually limited to global thematic structures (e.g., those of sonata form); and though tonal relationships are often considered on a large scale, they are not usually conceived within a Schenkerian framework. There seems to be an implied consensus that such features of the music—what we might call its "design"—are usually more relevant to questions of meaning and expression than its tonal structure, that the features of a work's design have a more direct effect on a listener's perception of the music, and thus of its expressive content, than those of its tonal structure. So, can you describe any specific ways that Schenkerian analysis might help us answer questions about expressive meaning? How should we weigh considerations of "design" and "structure" in such questions? Should we prioritize one over the other? Is there a kind of expressive meaning that is intrinsically Schenkerian in nature?*

So, how does tonal structure inform musical meaning, expressive meaning? I would start by calling your attention to a famous passage at the beginning of *Free Composition*, where Schenker talks about how, in its motion toward a goal, music encounters obstacles and difficulties. When we listen to music, we predict that certain things will happen, and when they don't happen as we imagine they will, that can be the source of a kind of dramatic discourse. That is, I think it is very often the obstacle to the goal that creates a sense of musical meaning. And this can happen at different levels.

In the "Waldstein" sonata, the absence of scale-degree $\hat{4}$ is at a very high level. Yet, that absence informs the expressive content at lower levels. On the other hand, there are also situations where a foreground event seems to motivate something much larger—it works in both directions. So in the "Appassionata," for example, the D♭-C, which we get out of the voice leading of the very opening, becomes this huge kind of thing, with all kinds of large-scale implications. You hear something happening at the beginning that then enlarges itself more and more. In that sense, it's the design that influences the structure, rather than the other way around. There's something similar in the relationship between analysis and performance, where I find that performance can influence analysis quite as much as the other way around.

There are lots of pieces that are purely pieces of music, where we are not necessarily required to find some kind of nonmusical meaning. Instead, we can think of their meaning as residing inside the domain of music. I think one ought not to force the search for expression onto the music. Let the meaning come by itself, and it will, if it's really there in the first place.

If you gain knowledge about the tonal structure of a piece of music, you've gained something that's valuable, even if it's not complete. Indeed, there's no such thing as a complete understanding of anything—you can't understand anything in the world unless you understand all of its ramifications, and nobody can ever do that. So be grateful that you understand the harmony and counterpoint—that's not a small accomplishment.

Could you tell us how your career came to take the shape it did? What your early educational experiences were? How you changed your orientation from performance to theory and analysis?

Almost everything that's happened in my life has happened as a result of some kind of accident. I came to Mannes in New York to study piano with a famous piano teacher who, as it turned out, almost ruined me. She was a quite sadistic person, and I was very young and vulnerable at the time. I then switched from studying piano to conducting, which somehow appealed to me, and I did well at it. I thought when I graduated that I would look for a conducting position. But I was asked in my last semester at school whether I would teach a few classes, and I did. And when no conducting job made itself available to me, they asked me to continue my teaching. My original idea was that I would teach at Mannes for a couple of years and then get a conducting position someplace, but I got more and more interested in the theory. It wasn't any single piece of music or single person or anything like that; it just happened kind of by itself, from the opportunity to teach.

Can you please comment on Schenker's ideas of the genius and the masterwork, and his view that analysis involves the relationship between an individual analyst and a single score, compared to the more current view that music is a cultural practice, and that composers and works are best understood in relation to widely shared compositional procedures constrained by stylistic norms?

The fact that you can find passages in Mozart that you also get in Wagenseil means nothing more than the fact that I can say "I got up at 8 o'clock this morning" and you might find Ernest Hemingway saying the same thing. There's more to it than just these little snippets of information. I think that one obviously needs to look at a piece in relation to its cultural context. I'm not at all opposed to that. But I feel that the main thing is engagement with the sounds that constitute the music, and I find too much ideological contextualization can be a barrier to that engagement. Sometimes, contextualization can be an escape from what is in fact a much more difficult task, namely, trying to understand how the music itself works. In life, the task of understanding one other person really well is very often much harder (and perhaps more deeply rewarding) than mastering the rules of behavior that might get you through all kinds of difficult social situations, but without any deep engagement.

As far as the masterwork is concerned, it is I think undeniable that whereas there have been hundreds of great painters and authors in the past 500 years, we really have nothing like that in music. The materials of tonal music are very limited: seven tones, as many triads, a family of intervals, some chromatic alterations, and that's about it. Inevitably, then, there will be common, shared sorts of musical elements. For a piece to really stand out from the common herd, there has to be something very special about it. Why are there so few great composers and so few great pieces? Why is our core repertoire so small? And why has it remained so small even after the successes of the early music movement and even after 100 years of musical modernism? I think Schenker's masterworks and his genius composers may have something to do with the nature of the musical language. Something very special happens in musical composition between around 1600 and around 1920 for which there is no analog in the other arts. Schenker talks about these genius composers because they were geniuses, and there weren't so many like them.

Glossary

Anstieg (initial ascent). A rising linear progression culminating on the initial tone of the *Urlinie*.

Arpeggiation. The most basic way of *prolonging* or *composing-out* a chord. The bass of the *Ursatz*, I-V-I, is regarded by Schenker as an arpeggiation of tonic harmony, with the root of V derived from the fifth of I. Similarly, at later levels, a tonal plan like G major-B minor-D major can be viewed as derived from an arpeggiation of a G-major tonic. In the top voice, a rising arpeggiation of tonic harmony can function like an *Anstieg*, leading up to the initial tone of the *Urlinie*, but through disjunct, rather than stepwise, motion.

Background. The structural region that contains the *Ursatz*.

Bassbrechung (bass arpeggio). See *Ursatz*.

Chromatic voice exchange. See *Voice exchange*.

Composing-out (Auskomponierung). The compositional expansion of chords and of tones or intervals belonging to the expanded chord. The most important way to compose-out a chord is to *horizontalize* one of its component intervals and fill in the space thus gained with *passing tones*. Thus G-F-E-D-C might represent a composing-out of a C-major chord, with G-C as the horizontalized interval and F-E-D as the passing tones filling in the space between them. Other ways to compose-out a chord would include *neighbor notes, transfers of register*, chromatic alteration, and complete or partial repetition. Perhaps because "composing-out" has a clumsy sound in English, the term is often replaced by "prolongation" or "chord prolongation."

Coda. For Schenker, whatever occurs following the establishment of the final I and $\hat{1}$.

Coupling. The connection of two registers through the octave relationship, with the emphasis on "connection."

Cover tone. A non-structural tone placed above the *Urlinie*. In most ways it behaves like an inner-voice tone, but its position above the *Urlinie* usually gives it greater prominence.

Diatonie (diatony). The simple stepwise contents of the *Urlinie* counterpointed by the I-V-I of the bass arpeggio. These basic musical materials give rise to the complexities of the foreground; both the profound connection of diatony and foreground and the possibly great contrast between them are significant.

Diminution. The dividing up of a comparatively slow-moving melodic substructure into a larger number of quicker notes. Schenker uses the term to denote melodic ornamentation at all levels, but most often at the foreground.

Elision. See *Overlap.*

Fernhören (distant hearing). Perceiving connections of various sorts between musical events that are not immediately consecutive.

Das fliegende Ohr (the flying ear). The ability of the great composers to forge connections among elements distant—sometimes very distant—from each other.

Foreground. The structural region closest to the musical surface, a region that contains the immediately perceptible events of the composition.

Horizontalization. The conversion of a vertical, chordal interval into a melodic interval by *unfolding* the two notes in time.

Hypermeter, hypermeasures. A hypermeasure is a group of measures whose metrical organization is that of a single measure writ large. A waltz, for example, will usually proceed in hypermeasures of four bars, with the first bar receiving the metrical (or hypermetrical) accent. "Hypermeasure" points to a specific measure; "hypermeter" refers to the phenomenon in general Neither term is used by Schenker.

Inner voice. See *Motion to or from an inner voice.*

Interruption. A device, both melodic and harmonic, that divides a one-part melodic/harmonic construct (like the *Ursatz*) into two interdependent parts. This happens when the descending top voice ($\hat{3}$-$\hat{2}$-$\hat{1}$ or $\hat{5}$-$\hat{4}$-$\hat{3}$-$\hat{2}$-$\hat{1}$) halts on $\hat{2}$ and the accompanying bass halts on V. Instead of proceeding to a conclusion on $\hat{1}$ and I, the music starts over again, usually with a repetition of the material of the beginning. This second time around, the structure completes itself on $\hat{1}$ and I. The variations and ramifications of this concept are many and far-reaching.

Kopfton (primary tone). The initial tone of a descending *linear progression*. In the *Urlinie*, the initial $\hat{5}$ and $\hat{3}$ function as *Kopftöne* of their respective progressions. At later levels, the primary tone is mentally retained until continued at the same structural level.

Levels. Schenker's term for levels (or structural levels) is *Schichten*, which is more literally translated as "layers" or "strata." In many ways, the structure of tonal music is hierarchical; its elements are ranked as superior or subordinate. Thus, at the beginning of Chopin's E-minor Prelude, the neighbor-note motive of the top voice B-C-B, shows two ranks. The B, which participates in large-scale voice leading, is superior in rank to the C, which connects only to the B, which it decorates. Similarly, in tonal harmony, the progression I-V-I, which can underlie an entire piece, is in principle superior in rank to a prolongation of the opening tonic, such as I-VII⁶-I⁶. Schenker devised ways of ranking tonal events that help the analyst perceive and understand the function of each important element with respect to its immediate connections (*foreground*), to larger events (*middleground*), and ultimately to the structural framework of the piece as a whole (*background*).

Linear progression. See *Zug.*

Middleground. The structural region containing levels intermediate between *background* and *foreground.*

Modal mixture. Juxtaposing elements from the minor mode in a context of major, or major elements in a context of minor.

Motion to or from an inner voice. In the descending linear progression G-F-E-D-C, the fifth G-C represents two "voices" of the horizontalized C-major chord, with G as top voice and C as inner voice. The line of the fifth, then, would be a motion *into* the inner voice of the chord. Similarly, a rising linear progression C-D-E-F-G would be a motion beginning on the inner-voice tone and rising to a culmination on the G, thus a motion *from* the inner voice. Schenker does not use the term "motion from the inner voice." He calls it *Untergreifen* (reaching under).

Neighbor note. At the highest level of middleground, $\hat{6}$ and $\hat{4}$, as upper neighbors to $\hat{5}$ and $\hat{3}$, occur frequently, often in connection with an important IV chord. At this high level, lower neighbors do not occur. These structural neighbor notes often generate motives at lower levels that are also centered on neighbor notes.

Obligatory register (Obligate Lage). Schenker maintained that the top voice and bass are mainly deployed within primary or "home" registers. For the sake of variety they may leave the primary register, but they will typically return to it. Typically, though not inevitably, the first and last tones of the *Urlinie* will occur in the primary register.

Overlap. Schenker uses the term *Umdeutung* (reinterpretation) to point to the overlapping of two groups of measures by reinterpreting the last measure of one group as the first measure of the next. This procedure is often called "elision" because the overlap gives the impression that a measure has been omitted. Here the reinterpretation concerns the *hypermeter*: the fourth or eighth measures (normally weak) are reinterpreted as a first measure (normally strong). Incidentally, an overlap can arise without elision or reinterpretation if the fourth or eighth measures contain a dominant—especially a dominant seventh—whose resolution to tonic occurs in the first measure of the next group.

Passing tone. For Schenker the passing tone is the fundamental type of dissonance; note that it is the first dissonance we encounter in species counterpoint (second species). *Linear progressions*, which constitute the primary examples of directed motion in tonal music, represent expansions of the passing-tone principle.

Prolongation. The elaboration, usually in several stages, of a simple contrapuntal *background* model into a complex and differentiated *foreground*. The "rules" of strict counterpoint, which are followed literally in the model, are modified as the new contents of each *level* create new possibilities and new necessities. Nevertheless, a good and well-educated musical ear can trace connections through the intermediate levels that lead convincingly from model to foreground and from foreground to model. Felix Salzer used the term "prolonged counterpoint" to express how the counterpoint of composition grows out of the strict counterpoint of the simple model. In most present-day usage, the term *prolongation* is also used in place of *composing-out*.

Reaching-over (Übergreifen). The shift of an inner-voice tone above the previously established top-voice tone. Sometimes the tone that reaches over is not literally present but is implied by the harmonic context. The tone that reaches over will be followed by a descending melodic line, usually stepwise. Context will show whether the tone that rises or its descending continuation is the main one.

Reinterpretation. See *Overlap.*

Schichten (levels). See *Levels.*

Structural levels. See *Levels.*

Stufe (scale step). A chord that forms part of a harmonic progression, usually one based on the fifth relationship. Chords whose functions are only contrapuntal—for example, neighbor-note chords—are not *Stufen*. Thus III in a succession I-III-I is not a *Stufe*, but in a succession III-VI-II-V-I, it is one, because of the descending fifth-progression it initiates. Schenker labels with Roman numerals only chords that are *Stufen*.

Teiler (divider). The V that ends the first branch of a progression divided by interruption. Also, a V that closes a segment of music without proceeding to a I, called by Schenker an "applied divider." It is also sometimes called a "back-relating V." The upper third of the tonic is also sometimes used as an applied divider: a "third-divider" or *Terzteiler*.

Transfer of register (Höherlegung or *Tieferlegung).* The placement of a tone an octave (or several octaves) higher or lower than expected.

Übergreifen. See *Reaching-over.*

Umdeutung (reinterpretation). See *Overlap.*

Unfolding (Ausfaltung). The *horizontalization* of a pair of vertical intervals. Thus two voices, G-F-E over C-B-C, might unfold into a single voice, G-C-B-F-E, with the perfect fifth and diminished fifth occurring as horizontal, melodic intervals. When a large-scale pattern of unfolded intervals occurs in the bass, the result may be a succession of *Stufen*, one or more of them tonicized in the *foreground*. The bass pattern C-G-A-D (an unfolded 5-6-5) can generate the *Stufen* I-V-VI-II, and possibly the key succession C-G-a-d.

Untergreifen. See *Motion to or from an inner voice.*

Urlinie (fundamental line). The top voice of the *Ursatz*. A *linear progression* that underlies the upper voice of an entire piece. It is a descending, stepwise, and diatonic line that begins on one of the tones of the tonic triad and finishes on the tonic note. There are only three possible lines that fulfill all of the conditions listed in the last sentence: $\hat{3}$-$\hat{2}$-$\hat{1}$, $\hat{5}$-$\hat{4}\hat{3}$-$\hat{2}$-$\hat{1}$, and $\hat{8}$-$\hat{7}$-$\hat{6}$-$\hat{5}$-$\hat{4}\hat{3}$-$\hat{2}$-$\hat{1}$. The *Urlinie* from $\hat{8}$ occurs very seldom.

Ursatz (fundamental structure). A two-part contrapuntal setting that forms a framework for the piece as a whole. The upper voice is the *Urlinie* in one of its three possible forms. Schenker calls the lower voice the *Bassbrechung* (bass arpeggio); it consists of a motion from I up to V followed by a return down to I. The $\hat{2}$ of the *Urlinie* coincides with the V of the *Bassbrechung*.

Voice exchange. Two voices exchange tones. For example: upper-voice E, lower-voice C becomes upper-voice C, lower-voice E. In this case, the first interval would be a third or tenth; after the voice exchange, the interval will be a sixth. Voice exchanges can be modified in various ways. The most important, because of its long-range possibilities, is the *chromaticized voice exchange*. In our example, an upper-voice E, lower-voice C can exchange to an upper-voice C♯ lower-voice E♭. In this way, our initial tonic can be transformed into an augmented sixth resolving into the V of the dominant key.

Zug (linear progression). A stepwise line that connects two tones that are related harmonically. Most frequently, the relationship between the beginning and the ending tones results from their membership in the same chord. G-F-E-D-C could be a linear progression expressing a *horizontalized* C-major chord in which G would be the top voice and C an inner voice of the harmony. It is usual to specify the interval spanned by a linear progression and sometimes its direction, ascending or descending. Thus G-F-E-D-C would be labeled a *fifth-progression* or a *descending fifth-progression*. Similarly, one might speak of an *Octavzug* (octave progression), a *Quartzug* (fourth progression), or *Terzzug* (third progression).

Works Cited

Aldwell, Edward and Carl Schachter. 1978. *Harmony and Voice Leading*. New York: Harcourt Brace Jovanovich. [As of 2010, this book is in its fourth edition, published by Cengage Learning, and with Allan Cadwallader as a third author.]

Babbitt, Milton. 2003a. "My Vienna Triangle." In *The Collected Essays of Milton Babbitt*, ed. Stephen Peles, Stephen Dembski, Andrew Mead, and Joseph N. Straus, 466–87. Princeton: Princeton University Press.

Babbitt, Milton. 2003b. "Remarks on the Recent Stravinsky." In *The Collected Essays of Milton Babbitt*, ed. Stephen Peles, Stephen Dembski, Andrew Mead, and Joseph N. Straus, 147–71. Princeton: Princeton University Press.

Bach, C. P. E. 1948. *An Essay on the True Art of Playing Keyboard Instruments* [*Versuch über die wahre Art das Clavier zu spielen, 1753, 1762*], trans. William Mitchell. New York: Norton.

Bartha, Dénès. 1969. "Thematic Profile and Character in the Quartet-Finales of Joseph Haydn." *Studia Musicologica* 11: 35–62.

Bartha, Dénès. 1971. "On Beethoven's Thematic Structure." *Musical Quarterly* 56 (1970): 759–78 (reprint, *The Creative World of Beethoven*, ed. P. H. Lang [New York: Norton, 1971], 257–76).

Bartha, Dénès. 1981. "Song Form and the Concept of 'Quatrain.'" In *Haydn Studies: Proceedings of the International Haydn Conference, Washington, DC, 1975*, ed. Jens Peter Larsen, Howard Serwer, and James Webster, 353–55 New York: Norton.

Burkhart, Charles. 1991. "How Rhythm Tells the Story in 'Là ci darem la mano.'" *Theory and Practice* 16: 21–38.

Burstein, L. Poundie. 1988. *The Non-Tonic Opening in Classical and Romantic Music*. Ph.D. dissertation, City University of New York.

Cadwallader, Allan and David Gagné. 1998. *Analysis of Tonal Music: A Schenkerian Approach*, 3rd ed. New York: Oxford University Press.

Caplin, William E. 1998. *Classical Form: A Theory of Formal Functions for the Instrumental Music of Haydn, Mozart, and Beethoven*. New York: Oxford University Press.

Cone, Edward T. 1968. *Musical Form and Musical Performance*. New York: Norton.

Cooper, Grosvenor and Leonard Meyer. 1963. *The Rhythmic Structure of Music*. Chicago: University of Chicago Press.

Empson, William. 1966. *Seven Types of Ambiguity*. New York: New Directions.

Gagné, David. 1988. *Performance Medium as a Compositional Determinant: A Study of Selected Works in Three Genres by Mozart*. Ph.D. dissertation, City University of New York.

Hepokoski, James and Warren Darcy. 2006. *Elements of Sonata Theory: Norms, Types, and Deformations in the Late-Eighteenth-Century Sonata*. New York: Oxford University Press.

Jonas, Oswald. 1967. "Improvisation in Mozarts Klavierwerken." *Mozart-Jahrbuch* (Salzburg: Internationale Stuftung Mozarteum): 176–81.

Keller, Hans. 1986. *The Great Haydn Quartets: Their Interpretation*. New York: George Braziller.

Kirnberger, Johann Philipp. 1982. *The Art of Strict Musical Composition [Die Kunst des reinen Satzes in der Music, 1774]*, ed. and trans. David Beach and Jürgen Thym. New Haven: Yale University Press.

Komar, Arthur. 1968. *Theory of Suspensions*. Princeton: Princeton University Press.

Kruger, Theodore Howard. 1960. *"Der freie Satz" by Heinrich Schenker: A Complete Translation and Re-editing*. Ph.D. dissertation, University of Iowa.

Lerdahl, Fred and Ray Jackendoff. 1983. *A Generative Theory of Tonal Music*. Cambridge, MA: MIT Press.

Lester, Joel. 1999. *Bach's Works for Solo Violin: Style, Structure, Performance*. New York: Oxford University Press.

Levarie, Sigmund and Ernst Levy. 1983. *Musical Morphology: A Discourse and a Dictionary*. Kent, OH: Kent State University Press.

Mitchell, William. 1973. "Beethoven's *La Malinconia* from the String Quartet, Opus 18, No. 6: Techniques and Structure." *Music Forum* 3, ed. William Mitchell and Felix Salzer, 269–80. New York: Columbia University Press.

Novack, Saul. 1964. "Review: Recent Approaches to the Study of Harmony." *Perspectives of New Music* 2, no. 2: 150–58.

Oster, Ernst. 1977. "Register and the Large-Scale Connection." *Journal of Music Theory* 5, no. 1 (1961): 54–71. Reprinted in *Readings in Schenker Analysis and Other Approaches*, ed. Maury Yeston, 54–71. New Haven: Yale University Press.

Oster, Ernst. 1983. "The *Fantaisie-Impromptu*: A Tribute to Beethoven." In *Aspects of Schenkerian Theory*, ed. David Beach, 189–208. New Haven: Yale University Press.

Pastille, William. 1990. "The Development of the *Ursatz* in Schenker's Published Works." In *Trends in Schenkerian Research*, ed. Allan Cadwallader, 71–85. New York: Schirmer.

Quantz, Johann Joachim. 2001. *On Playing the Flute [Versuch einer Anweisung die Flöte traversiere zu spielen, 1752]*, trans. Edward Reilly. Boston: Northeastern University Press.

Rink, John. 1999. " 'Structural Momentum' and Closure in Chopin's Nocturne Op. 9, No. 2." In *Schenker Studies 2*, ed. Carl Schachter and Hedi Siegel, 109–26. Cambridge: Cambridge University Press.

Rothgeb, John. 1971. "Design as a Key to Structure in Tonal Music." *Journal of Music Theory* 15/1–2: 230–53.

Rothstein, William. 1991. "On Implied Tones." *Music Analysis* 10, no. 3: 289–328.

Rothstein, William. 1989. *Phrase Rhythm in Tonal Music*. New York: Schirmer Books.

Salzer, Felix. 1962. *Structural Hearing: Tonal Coherence in Music*. New York: Dover.

Salzer, Felix and Carl Schachter. 1969. *Counterpoint in Composition: The Study of Voice Leading*. New York: McGraw-Hill.

Schachter, Carl. 1999a. "Analysis by Key: Another Look at Modulation." *Music Analysis* 6, no. 3 (1987): 289–318. Reprinted in *Unfoldings: Essays in Schenkerian Theory and Analysis*, ed. Joseph N. Straus, 134–60. New York: Oxford University Press.

Schachter, Carl. 1999b. "Either/Or." In *Schenker Studies*, ed. Hedi Siegel, 165–80. Cambridge: Cambridge University Press, 1990. Reprinted in *Unfoldings: Essays in Schenkerian Theory and Analysis*, ed. Joseph N. Straus, 121–33. New York: Oxford University Press.

Schachter, Carl. 1999c. "Motive and Text in Four Schubert Songs." In Aspects of Schenkerian Theory, ed. David Beach, 61–76. New Haven: Yale University Press, 1983. Reprinted in *Unfoldings: Essays in Schenkerian Theory and Analysis*, ed. Joseph N. Straus, 209-20. New York: Oxford University Press, 1999.

Schachter, Carl. 1999d. "The Triad as Place and Action." *Music Theory Spectrum* 17, no. 2 (1995): 149–69. Reprinted in *Unfoldings: Essays in Schenkerian Theory and Analysis*, ed. Joseph N. Straus, 161–83. New York: Oxford University Press, 1999.

Schachter, Carl. 1999e. "Chopin's Fantasy, Op. 49: The Two-Key Scheme." In *Chopin Studies*, ed. Jim Samson, 221–53. Cambridge: Cambridge University Press, 1988. Reprinted in *Unfoldings: Essays in Schenkerian Theory and Analysis*, ed. Joseph N. Straus, 260–88. New York: Oxford University Press, 1999.

Schachter, Carl. 1987. "The *Gavotte en Rondeaux* from J. S. Bach's Partita in E Major for Unaccompanied Violin." *Israel Studies in Musicology* 4: 7–26.

Schenker, Heinrich. 1987. *Counterpoint,* trans. John Rothgeb and Jürgen Thym. New York: Schirmer Books.

Schenker, Heinrich. 1969. *Five Graphic Music Analyses.* New York: Dover.

Schenker, Heinrich. 1979. *Free Composition,* trans. and ed. Ernst Oster. New York: Longman.

Schenker, Heinrich. 1997a. "Chopin: Etude in G♭ major, Op. 10, No. 5." In *The Masterwork in Music: A Yearbook,* Vol. 1 (1926), ed. William Drabkin, 90–98. Cambridge: Cambridge University Press.

Schenker, Heinrich. 1997b. "Beethoven's Third Symphony: Its True Content Described for the First Time." *The Masterwork in Music: A Yearbook,* Vol. 3 (1930), ed. William Drabkin, trans. Ian Bent, Alfred Clayton, and Derrick Puffett, 10–68. Cambridge: Cambridge University Press.

Schenker, Heinrich. 1954. *Harmony,* ed. Oswald Jonas, trans. Elisabeth Mann Borgese. Chicago: University of Chicago Press.

Schenker, Heinrich. 1996. *The Masterwork in Music, A Yearbook,* Vol. 2 (1926), ed. William Drabkin, trans. Ian Bent, William Drabkin, John Rothgeb, and Hedi Siegel. Cambridge: Cambridge University Press.

Schenker, Heinrich. 2004. *Der Tonwille: Pamphlets in Witness of the Immutable Laws of Music,* Volume I: Issues 1–5 (1921–1923), ed. William Drabkin. New York: Oxford University Press.

Smith, Peter. 1994. "Liquidation, Augmentation, and Brahms's Recapitulatory Overlaps." *19th-Century Music* 17, no. 3 (1994): 237–61.

Straus, Joseph. 1987. "The Problem of Prolongation in Post-Tonal Music." *Journal of Music Theory* 31/1: 1–22.

Tovey, Donald Francis. 1949. "Some Aspects of Beethoven's Art Forms." In *The Main Stream of Music and Other Essays,* 271–97. New York: Oxford University Press.

Tovey, Donald Francis. 1931. *A Companion to Beethoven's Pianoforte Sonatas.* London: Associated Board.

Yates, Frances. 1991. *Giordano Bruno and the Hermetic Tradition.* Chicago: University of Chicago Press.

Zuckerkandl, Victor. 1971. *The Sense of Music.* Princeton: Princeton University Press.

Index